The Development of Postwar Canadian Trade Policy
The Failure of the Anglo-European Option

B.W. Muirhead traces the development of Canadian trade policy and trade patterns from the Second World War to the election of the Diefenbaker government in 1957. Scholars have emphasized the importance of this period in determining Canadian trade patterns, but have disagreed about the options Canada had and the decisions Canadian governments made. Muirhead demonstrates that Canada's options were so severely constrained by the postwar context that there were in effect no choices to make. He thus makes a strong case against the theory that Canada "sold out" to the United States.

Muirhead agrees that any government must work to maximize national income and independent choice. He shows that Canada actively pursued a policy of multilateralism and non-discrimination as epitomized by the General Agreement on Tariffs and Trade. In addition, the government tried unsuccessfully to resurrect commercial ties with the United Kingdom, its largest pre-war overseas market. Muirhead finds that in both these efforts Canada was thwarted by postwar realities that hindered its exploitation of markets in Britain and Western Europe. The United States remained the only market able and willing to absorb the billions of dollars of Canadian exports on which Canada's prosperity depended. Canadian policy was multilateral by preference, bilateral by necessity, and manifestly continental by default.

B.W. MUIRHEAD is an associate professor in the Department of History, Lakehead University.

The Development of Postwar Canadian Trade Policy

The Failure of the Anglo-European Option

B.W. MUIRHEAD

McGill-Queen's University Press
Montreal & Kingston • London • Buffalo

Legal deposit fourth quarter 1992
Bibliothèque nationale du Québec

Printed in Canada on acid-free paper

This book has been published with the help of a
grant from the Social Science Federation of Canada,
using funds provided by the Social Sciences and
Humanities Research Council of Canada. Additional
funding has also been provided by Lakehead
University.

Canadian Cataloguing in Publication Data

Muirhead, Bruce
　　The development of postwar Canadian trade
　　policy: the failure of the Anglo-European option
　　Includes index.
　　ISBN 0-7735-0922-4
　　1. Canada – Economic policy – 1945–1971.
　　2. Canada – Politics and government – 1948–1957.
　　3. Canada – Economic conditions – 1945–1971. I. Title.
　　HF1479.M84 1992　　　　338.971　　　　C92-090517-X

This book was typeset by Typo Litho composition inc.
in 10/12 Palatino.

Contents

Tables and Figures

Preface

This book started off some years ago as a part of my doctoral studies at York University. Being well steeped in the rhetoric of the "sell-out" thesis and prepared to do my bit in advancing the arguments of those who supported it, I plunged into studies of the development of Canada's foreign economic policy from 1945 to 1957 confidently expecting that the documentation then available in the National Archives of Canada, at the Bank of Canada, at various archives in the United States, and, later, at the Public Record Office would fully support the position that had become a touchstone of Canadian political economy. However, as I looked at the letters, telegrams, and memoranda of sundry involved politicians and officials, a different story began to emerge. I did not find a group of comprador policy-makers scheming how best to integrate Canada into the United States, or so closely linked, politically and economically, to the continental idea that they perceived Canadian prosperity to be dependent on intimate ties with the US. Rather, the picture emerged of concerned men, who were for the most part all too aware of the dangers of dependency, seeking to diversify Canada's economic linkages abroad. This book is thus the story of the failure of Canadian policy at one level – Ottawa was simply not able to make its wishes count in the global commercial context. With the failure of its preferred multilateral option, Canada did not have the luxury of choice in the postwar world but made the best it could of an unveiable situation through such international mechanisms as the GATT.

This book has benefited enormously from advice and encouragement given by those who oversaw the preparation of my doctoral dissertation, which forms the basis for a good portion of this book. First and foremost, I owe a large debt of gratitude to Jack Granatstein, former supervisor and now colleague, who read far more versions than any one person should have had to. As well, I gratefully acknowledge the critical advice received from Ian Drummond, who read the first three chapters and, through that, helped to make the last three more intelligible. My thanks also to the reader for McGill-Queen's, John English, and the anonymous reader for the Social Sciences Federation of Canada, both of whom went through the manuscript thoroughly. Their criticisms and advice, as well as those of Robert Bothwell, the external reader for the dissertation, improved the flow of the text and also helped to clear up ambiguities and shortfalls. There are a number of other people who read portions of the manuscript and I have also benefited from their advice. Among these are my colleagues at Lakehead, Stephen McBride, Patricia Jasen, Bill Morrison, and Ernie Epp.

Everyone at the institutions at which the research was carried out was very helpful in assisting me in the pursuit of documentation. Archivists at the National Archives of Canada, especially Gabrielle Blais, were most helpful in providing me with records that I wanted to see. Jane Witty, archivist at the Bank of Canada, went far beyond the call of duty in speeding my research along. Similarly, Sally Marks at the United States National Archives opened up avenues of research for me that would otherwise have remained closed. Finally, my thanks to the able staff at the Public Record Office in London, and those at the Harry S. Truman and Dwight D. Eisenhower Presidential Libraries.

I would also like to thank the editors at McGill-Queen's who helped to get this book through, in particular, Peter Blaney, as well as Joan McGilvray and Philip Cercone. All the deficiencies and shortcomings of this book are, however, my own.

My thanks also to the Social Sciences and Humanities Research Council of Canada, which partly funded the research for the book. Parts of this book have been previously published in slightly different form. My thanks to the *Journal of Canadian Studies, American Review of Canadian Studies, Journal of Imperial and Commonwealth History, Journal of the Canadian Historical Association, Canadian Historical Review,* and the *British Journal of Canadian Studies* for allowing the research to be included here.

Last, but certainly not least, I owe a huge debt to my wife, Sandra, for the help, encouragement, and advice I received from her. She heard this story far more times than was humane. This book is for her.

Abbreviations

ABC	America-Britain-Canada
BP	British preferential
CFEP	Committee on Foreign Economic Policy
CPs	contracting parties
ECA	European Cooperation Administration
EEC	European Economic Community
EPA	European Payments Area
EPU	European Payments Union
ERP	European Recovery Program
GATT	General Agreement on Tariffs and Trade
IBRD	International Bank for Reconstruction and Development
ICETP	Interdepartmental Committee on External Trade Policy
IMF	International Monetary Fund
ITO	International Trade Organization
mfn	most favoured nation
NATO	North Atlantic Treaty Organization
NTB	non-tariff barriers
OEEC	Organization for European Economic Cooperation
QR	quantitative restriction
RSA	Rest of the Sterling Area
UKCCC	United Kingdom–Canada Continuing Committee

Introduction: Bilateralism, Trilateralism, and Multilateralism, 1930–45

In general terms, this book is about the evolution of postwar Canadian trade policy, which was in large part the pursuit of multilateralism and non-discrimination and found its stride amid the ashes and ruins of World War II. If Canadians in the prewar era had been satisfied with, as R.D. Cuff and J.L. Granatstein have described it, a "bilateral imbalance within a balanced North Atlantic triangle," they no longer were.[1] In 1945 theirs were enlarged horizons, more befitting a major "middle power," and they intended to take full advantage of the new opportunities that beckoned. Any discussion of the development of Canadian trade policy between 1945 and 1957, however, inevitably leads to the "sell-out" thesis espoused by critics of the Mackenzie King and St Laurent governments. This book deals with that issue in the field of foreign trade.

In the eighteen years from 1939 to 1957, noted the conservative-nationalist historian Donald Creighton, "Canada made a number of crucial decisions about its direction. It chose one fork of the road to the future." That fork was not to his liking, as the Liberal governments of the period remade Canada in their own continentalist image: the influence of the United States on the Canadian economy "had grown more steadily dominant; but they made no conscious move to question or resist this growing domination."[2] Left-revisionist critics such as Melissa Clark-Jones, James Laxer, and Kari Levitt offer similar interpretations of postwar economic development, decrying the tremendous concentration of Canadian trade with the United States since World War II. As Laxer writes, "the

Liberal Party was the home of anti-nationalism. It was the home of all those in the country who were willing to see the work of [Prime Minister] Macdonald's National Policy undone and who sought accommodation with American power. C.D. Howe ... personified the new era of north-south economic ties."[3] The Liberals were also pilloried for their obsession with multilateralism. As Clark-Jones suggests, interest in multilateralism and non-discrimination, so prominent in the postwar era, was an American initiative, designed to realize American objectives and of only marginal importance to smaller US "satellites" such as Canada, a sentiment to which Creighton also subscribed.[4]

The intention of the conservative-nationalists and left-revisionists is to demonstrate the bankruptcy of the post-1945 policy of a succession of Liberal administrations. They conclude that the King and St Laurent governments, in encouraging economic development along continentalist lines, made Canada a hinterland supplier of raw materials for an expanding American empire in return for commercial security. The lure of easy markets proved too enticing and a Canadian perspective was lost because of this misguided choice.

However, the critics' analysis simply does not apply to the decade following World War II. They present the *results* of post-1945 economic development without any examination of the underlying *causes*. Their conclusion, that Canadian governments actively "sold out" Canada to the United States, is incorrect because it is derived from incorrect assumptions about Ottawa's ability to make choices in the post-war era and about the willingness of other countries to trade with Canada. In fact, Canada's options were starkly circumscribed. While Canadian policy was multilateral and non-discriminatory by preference, a reaction to the autarchy of the 1930s, this meant little when the country was faced with inconvertible European currencies and widespread tariff and non-tariff barriers to trade among erstwhile trading partners.

Ottawa worked hard to convince European countries, especially the United Kingdom, Canada's major prewar overseas market, of the benefits which would be gained from a system of freer trade and payments, but with little success. Inconvertibility and discrimination remained facts of life until at least the mid-1950s. The development of a continental economy in North America was the direct result of these realities. Nationalist critics of both the left and right have exaggerated the extent to which that development reflected the preferences of Canadian politicians and civil servants. Both recognized the perils inherent in continentalism but came reluctantly to the realization that they were powerless to resist those forces. In the critical period after World War II, when world commerce was in a state of flux, the United States represented the only available option for Canadian traders.

Trade with both Western Europe and the United Kingdom declined throughout the decade following the end of hostilities. How and why did that situation arise, given the tremendous interest that Ottawa had demonstrated in securing unencumbered access to those markets? And why did overseas governments adopt such uncooperative attitudes when dealing with Canadian trade, despite the fact that Canada, in the words of one British official, "leaned over backward" to assist?[5] Ultimately, pervasive dollar problems, economic and political crises throughout the postwar period, and the maintenance of soft and inconvertible currencies worked directly against the development of Canadian trade with the United Kingdom and Western Europe. But so too did the region's history. Moreover, in the case of the United Kingdom, it is argued here that London adopted an almost-punitive policy *vis à vis* Canada. As the British retreated from Empire and into Commonwealth, they scrambled to preserve what they could of their power, status, and prestige. In large part, that meant keeping the sterling area part of the Commonwealth together, for reasons of heritage and also for the potential it represented for Britain in terms of increasing trade and exports. Therein lay the rub. Canada was the only Commonwealth country which did not belong to the sterling area. Many in Ottawa felt that refusal to join drove London to excesses in Anglo-Canadian relations. Graham Towers, the governor of the Bank of Canada, reflected one spectrum of official opinion when he asserted, in late 1949, that the United Kingdom had always anticipated that Canada would join, which would then allow the British "to drain strength from us to help them."[6] Whitehall's disappointment became increasingly obvious over time. However, a brief excursion back to the 1930s is necessary to provide some context for what was to follow.

THE DIRTY THIRTIES AND BILATERALISM

The 1930s had been a bad decade for Canada. When the New York Stock Exchange collapsed on "Black Tuesday," the spill-over effect in Montreal and Toronto was immediate: more than 850,000 shares were dumped on that one day. As depression roared down on an unsuspecting country, export markets for Canadian wheat, forest products, and minerals dried up as factories closed and tariffs crept upwards. One of the most unpleasant shocks to Ottawa was the implementation of the Hawley-Smoot tariff by the United States, which drove average rates of duty against Canadian exports to a historic high of nearly 60 per cent. In retaliation, the Liberal government of Prime Minister William Lyon Mackenzie King raised Canadian tariffs against imports from the United States, and the situation darkened further. Thousands of jobs were lost as trade declined. When a new cabinet was announced to the nation on 9 August 1930 in the aftermath of the July general election, it was a Conservative one, headed by R.B. Bennett.

The new prime minister had promised voters that he had the solution; Liberal tariff policy had been timid and ineffective – unlike King, the Conservative leader had told election crowds he would "make [tariffs] fight for you." He would "use them to blast a way into markets that have been closed."[7] Most important, he intended to convince the British that they should place a tariff on a number of foreign goods and no duty, or a lower preferential rate, on Empire goods. He first made that proposal during the Imperial Conference of 1930, offering delegations a ten per cent preference in the Canadian market in exchange for a like preference in theirs.

The immediate British reaction was to label the proposal "humbug"; Ottawa did not intend to lower preferential and general tariffs, but merely to raise the latter by ten per cent if London granted a preference to Canadian goods. That was impossible, Chancellor of the Exchequer Philip Snowden, a doctrinaire free-trader, told Bennett, since Canada had imposed very heavy tariffs of between 23 and 40 per cent against English woollen and worsted goods, to say nothing of also recently raising them against a number of other UK exports. But, more to the point, when the Canadian prime minister asked that London accept the principle of imperial preference, the reply was a firm no. However, before the end of the 1930 Conference Britain and the dominions agreed to a general resolution, prepared by Bennett, that none of them would change preferential margins for three years or until the next Imperial Conference.[8] Real consideration of tarifs was deferred until an economic conference could be convened in Ottawa on Bennett's invitation.

The proposed Ottawa Economic Conference was an article of faith with the prime minister; as he told the House of Commons shortly before the Empire gathering in August 1932, he held "the firm belief ... that in such a conference lies the best assurance of the development of every part of the British Empire and of my own country as well."[9] Unfortunately for Bennett, this was not so; as Ian Drummond has pointed out, the room for manoeuvre was very limited. The dominions and India could not reduce tariffs on British manufactures because they were attempting to industrialize behind protective walls without which industrialization would not have been possible. Similarly, Britain could not impose onerous duties on raw materials because that would increase the cost of the end product, making British manufactured exports less competitive on world markets. Only for a narrow range "of construction goods and consumer goods – timber, meat, butter, fruit, cheese, tobacco, coffee, canned fish – did the scheme have anything to give."[10]

As a result, little of substance took place in Ottawa, although in the resulting Ottawa Agreements the British did impose higher tariffs on a number of non-Empire imports of interest to the dominions. In return, the British received an undertaking from Australia, Canada, and New Zealand to protect only "plausible industries" and not impose prohibitive duties on other UK manufactured goods.[11] While exports of Canadian raw materials to the United Kingdom rose, a product of the new preferential arrangements and gathering British recovery, the results were not nearly as spectacular as Bennett had hoped. That "left Bennett's last strategem shattered."[12] As the Depression deepened, so too did his mood of despair. No new or old markets flung wide their doors to Canada's exports, and the autarchic and "beggar-thy-neighbour" principles that characterized international behaviour worsened.

As Bennett contemplated the failure of his initiative, the United States, under the vigorous leadership of a new president, Franklin Roosevelt, took the lead in the proceedings of the International Monetary and Economic Conference held in London during June and July 1933. The primary purpose of the conference was to restore commercial and financial confidence among the nations of the world; the Americans envisaged a global marketplace where tariff and non-tariff barriers to commerce would not wreak havoc on trade.

The American ambition, however, seemed to have less to do with a concern for global freer trade than with finding markets abroad for US products, especially after the Ottawa Agreements. Americans were well aware that the United Kingdom's share of manufactured exports greatly exceeded theirs, a fact that they wished to change. The United States self-interest was patent and, as Ian Drummond and Norman Hillmer point out, "not for the first time, and not for the last, one side was assessing the other in terms that might more appropriately be applied to itself."[13]

Many of the ideas suggested by the United States at the World Economic Conference anticipated American support for multilateral and non-discriminatory policies after World War II. Unfortunately for the success of the meeting, many other countries, especially the United Kingdom, were not nearly as keen on these policies, for sound reasons. Many were labouring under massive deficits and high unemployment, while the Americans had an enormous trade surplus. In the context of the 1930s, the United States could not force Britain and others to comply with its demands; it would take a world war that destroyed Western Europe while simultaneously catapulting the United States to the pinnacle of global economic and political power to "persuade" other nations to comply with American policy.

However, Canada was very interested in the US plan, given its dependence on external markets and the disappointing results of the meeting of the empire in 1932. Accordingly, Ottawa lined up with its North American neighbour; as the Canadian minister in Washington, W.D. Herridge, told Under Secretary of State William Phillips, the British were too "defeatist" in their outlook. The prime minister, Herridge said with perhaps a touch of overstatement, "could see it more clearly from [the] point of view of North America and ... [the] injection of Bennett into [the] picture would fortify [the] President in his policies."[14]

Unhappily for Ottawa and Washington, the World Economic Conference did not grapple with the American proposal. Economic "survivalism" was much more compatible with the collective mood of conference participants. In September 1933 British Prime Minister Ramsay MacDonald spoke with Ray Atherton, the commercial counsellor at the US Embassy in London, about the physical inability of European nations "to lead the world towards economic reconstruction."[15] And when US proposals on monetary policy became known, the conference broke up. Simply, Roosevelt refused to commit the United States to a policy of internal stabilization of the dollar. By November the tariff truce, agreed to the previous June at the World Economic Conference, had fallen apart as many of its sixty signatories went their own way and tariffs continued upwards with their own ineluctable logic; the *Economist* called it "the intensification of economic nationalism."[16] There would be no widespread international cooperation on financial and commercial matters during the 1930s.

As a result of the collapse of the 1932 and 1933 conferences, the negotiation of a Canadian-American agreement took on added urgency, at least in Bennett's eyes. Washington had been receptive to an agreement in April 1933, aware, as was Ottawa, that total Canadian-American trade had fallen dramatically from a 1928 figure of about $1.3 billion to only $390 million by 1933. A large part of that decline was the deleterious result of prohibitive tariffs, largely on the American side with Hawley-Smoot. However, little progress took place over the next few years; by January 1935, with a federal election looming in the near future, Bennett was desperate that a treaty be signed, given the favourable effect on public opinion "in the direction of the Prime Minister and his Government" that such a development promised.[17]

Serious negotiations did not begin until July and by August the opportunity had slipped away. Before the negotiations could be concluded, Mackenzie King had been elected prime minister in the October campaign. So concerned was King to achieve an agreement that he personally visited the residence of Norman Armour, the US minister in Ottawa, even though, as Armour noted to the State Department, "he had taken office only the night before and ... it was a national holiday (Canadian Thanksgiving)."[18]

Following a later appeal to President Roosevelt, the difficult negotiations were concluded a few weeks after the Liberal victory. Under the agreement Canada received reductions on primary exports and some secondary products, while the duty-free status of a number of other goods was continued. In return, Ottawa granted the United States its intermediate tariff as a minimum with rates below that on about 80 items. As Granatstein has noted, it "was a major advance – the first trade agreement [ratified by Parliament] between Canada and the United States since 1854."[19]

No sooner were those negotiations finalized than the process began once more, this time with the United Kingdom. The objective was to expand on the trade agreements resulting from the Ottawa Economic Conference. The United States was interested in the proposed agreement and, as they had done since the inauguration of the Roosevelt administration in 1933, took the opportunity to provide both London and Ottawa with pointed reminders about their perceptions of the regressive effect of imperial preferences and bilateralism in general.[20] Indeed, so concerned was Washington that the administration held discussions with the British over the late winter and spring of 1936 to express US apprehension over London's application of "narrow national and international political considerations" to trade negotiations.[21] With Canada, a more sympathetic supporter of the US multilateral program, secretary of state Cordell Hull claimed that the United States was "engaged in too much of a 'lone fight' against trade barriers"[22] and requested Canadian help. Holding out a carrot, he told King that the US administration was hopeful of enlarging upon the 1935 Canadian-American trade accord in the near future. The unspoken *quid pro quo* was Ottawa's support of US policy in the on-going negotiations with Britain.

The King government was interested in the US proposals, both for economic reasons and because it saw the United States as a useful counterweight to British influence. But Canada also remained interested in an agreement with Britain, and to that end a Canadian trade delegation laboured in London for most of the summer of 1936. They were successful and the agreement was ratified in February 1937.

The Americans were not pleased with the accord as it conflicted with Hull's brand of economic liberalization. At the very least Hull wanted a reaffirmation of Canadian support for US multilateral proposals, which Canada gave. Even so, he felt the Anglo-Canadian Agreement would make "more difficult and possibly embarrass [State Department] efforts to secure an extension and enlargement of the Trade Agreements Act from the present Congress."[23] Again, the thorny issue of imperial preference had complicated relations with the United States. Canada, as a member of the Commonwealth and a signatory to trade agreements with both Britain and the United States, was caught in the middle of Anglo-American negotiating strategies.[24]

The difficulties of this proposition were demonstrated with a vengeance over the next two years as Ottawa was caught in UK-US difficulties and then, in 1938, in US-Canada trade negotiations. A potential Anglo-American agreement was hung up over the impossibility of reducing duties on certain American exports of forest and agricultural products to Britain because of London's agreements with various dominions to maintain margins of preference on those products and with others, such as the Baltic states, with whom agreements had been signed. Washington approached Canada, asking if Ottawa could not waive "part of its margin on certain commodities." Again holding out the carrot, the United States promised to extend more favourable treatment in a renegotiation of the 1935 agreement.[25]

However much the King government might have wanted to respond favourably, Britain was committed to *several* dominions to maintain margins of preference for most commodities on which the Americans were demanding action.[26] For that reason, the Americans were told, a Canadian undertaking would not help. Canada was also unwilling to sacrifice any preferential agreement with Britain on the altar of an Anglo-American agreement. This response did not endear Canada to its neighbour and, to complicate matters further in terms of Canada's relationship with the United States, the British, as a result of Ottawa's position on preferences, suggested that the Ottawa Agreements were blocking negotiations between the United States and the United Kingdom. As London explained, it "could not go back on the principles of preference" negotiated in 1932. Finally, as Ottawa had been apprised by Washington, the United States felt that the renewal of the 1937 Anglo-Canadian accord was a very serious impediment to trade liberalization generally: it would be "unfortunate if these conversations should result in commitments to the dominions which would make it impossible for the British Government, later on, to entertain our requests in respect of particular products of interest to us which are now covered by the Ottawa Agreements."[27] Even though the 1937 agreement actually reduced the amount and importance of imperial preference in the Canadian market and did not increase it the United Kingdom, the sticking point with the Americans was that preferences were not completely stamped out. The United States was coming to regard Canada as the obstacle to what they looked on as a vitally important step toward economic disarmament. While all sides eventually muddled through the various discussions, such misunderstandings were indicative of the very real problems that Canada faced in dealing with the United States and United Kingdom. And, while the 1938 us-Canada agreement was a good one, the result did not obviate the difficulties of the process.[28]

As the decade drew to a close, Canada found itself with increased trade with both the United States and the United Kingdom. But negotiating with London and Washington had been difficult, emotionally draining, and time consuming as Ottawa attempted to protect Canada's interests. Increasingly, the Canadian government was attracted to the American plan, promoted so vigorously by Hull, which called for multilateral trade negotiations between a number of countries; in the minds of Canadian ministers and bureaucrats such a program offered the best assurance that the risks of negotiating would be diffused while the potential benefits would be increased. But implementation would have to wait as peacetime practice gave way to wartime imperatives which, ironically, created the necessary will to experiment with new methods of international economic organization.

THE WAR YEARS

World War II brought with it a whole new array of problems for Canada. Not the least of these was the inconvertibility of British currency, implemented in early September 1939. At one fell stroke Ottawa's shaky balance of payments equilibrium was thrown into chaos. Britain, with the United States, was an essential pillar of Canada's North Atlantic triangle, in which a regular trade surplus with the United Kingdom helped pay for a Canadian deficit with the United States. With a "soft" pound came the imposition of exchange controls throughout the British-dominated sterling area, comprised of British dominions and colonies as well as certain other associated countries. The sterling area agreed to pool its resources for the benefit of the whole, allowing the United Kingdom to purchase goods and services on credit by accumulating sterling balances, thus postponing the day of reckoning. Before the war, sterling balances amounted to £540 million, of which £330 million were in the Empire/Commonwealth. By 1945 they had swollen to a massive £3.7 billion, of which £3 billion were in the sterling area. The currency could still be transferred freely between the countries of the area but could be made convertible outside its boundaries only in severely circumscribed and government-approved ways.[29] Private trade was also curtailed in many sectors as Whitehall took over the task of securing the necessary supplies for the war effort. This practice was extended into the postwar period, and even as late as 1949, 91 per cent of imports were subject to government control.[30]

Inconvertibility had ominous implications for Canada, which was the only Commonwealth country to remain outside the sterling area. Instead, reflecting its economic self-interest, Canada was part of the informal dollar grouping whose currency remained hard and convertible. Nor was Ottawa interested in amassing sterling in the form of balances which it could not use in the foreseeable future. Deputy Minister of Finance Clifford Clark summarized the government's attitude best when he told Grant Dexter of the *Winnipeg Free Press* in the first months of the war that he "would as leave ... be hit with a brick as a British pound these days."[31]

However, with the continuing UK demand for Canadian goods, the country had no alternative but to accept inconvertible pounds which piled up in Ottawa, the Department of Finance having agreed to accumulate sterling to absorb Britain's trade deficit with Canada.[32] Wartime demand also meant that Canada purchased more from the United States. As Cuff and Granatstein have written, "the irony was that the more Canada helped the United Kingdom, the further she was plunged into exchange difficulties with the United States."[33] Once the fighting began in earnest following the phoney war, Canada's commitment changed also, from one of "limited liability" to total mobilization. Economic relations with the United States deteriorated further, and Canada's reserves of American dollars fell to dangerously low levels. During the first six months of 1940, while Canadian exports to the United States had risen $55 million to $221 million, imports had more than doubled, to almost $400 million. The new under-secretary of state for External Affairs, Norman Robertson, had emphasized that development to King in early 1941: "Our merchandise exports to the United States are keeping up quite satisfactorily, but they do not come close to paying for the great expansion of imports from the United States required by our war industries."[34]

In the face of such an exchange crisis, the prime minister travelled south to Roosevelt's home at Hyde Park, New York, in April 1941. There the two leaders agreed on the Hyde Park Declaration, which promised a more effective integration of the Canadian and American economies. As a result, dollar problems cleared up as US contracts were let in Canada. But while exchange problems were now a thing of the past, and remained so for the duration of the war, there were other perplexing issues on the horizon which threatened to cause Ottawa equal difficulty.

As in the past, there were problems of protecting the Canadian interest when the British and Americans set out to coordinate strategy. For example, Robertson was very upset over Anglo-American negotiations with respect to Article VII of the Lend-Lease Agreement, which required that recipients of lend-lease aid adopt a policy of non-discrimination after the war. In the British case, this had implications for imperial preference. As he told Pierrepont Moffat, the US minister in Ottawa, he objected "to [the United States] assumption that this was purely an Anglo-American problem." In many cases, preferences were contractually secured to Canada and other dominions and could not be unilaterally abrogated by the British, something that Washington ignored in its efforts to shatter the Commonwealth's system of preferences.[35] While Ottawa generally supported American multilateral policy (although, unwilling to give up preferences for no consideration), the US attitude was a little too cavalier for the government to accept.

However, the Canadians found it gratifying to be invited to participate in planning the shape of the postwar commercial world. The Americans continued to preach the multilateral doctrine and many other belligerents had accepted that position, at least on paper, as the *quid pro quo* for lend-lease assistance. While Canada was not a direct recipient of US aid, it subscribed to the American vision as reflecting Canada's vital interests. To that end, beginning in 1942 it participated with the United Kingdom, the United States, and other like-minded nations in a series of international conferences that were concerned with postwar economic, financial, and commercial cooperation. These eventually bore fruit at Bretton Woods, New Hampshire, with the creation of the International Monetary Fund and the International Bank for Reconstruction and Development and, later, at Geneva, Switzerland, with the General Agreement on Tariffs and Trade.

But Ottawa also undertook several bilateral initiatives with the United Kingdom designed to ensure that Britain would not be "in hock" to Canada after the war. A $700 million loan and a $1 billion gift, in 1941 and 1942 respectively, went part way toward addressing the imbalance in Anglo-Canadian trade, while the Mutual Aid Agreement, implemented in 1943, rationalized the aid process to Britain. The British were grateful for the relative "leniency" of Canadian assistance as compared with that of the United States. During a visit to Ottawa in August 1944, John Maynard Keynes, then in the employ of the UK Treasury, told Minister of Finance J.L. Ilsley that "unquestionably Canada [had] given the United Kingdom a much better deal than anyone else [had]."[36] That was true, partly because a commercially secure Britain was in the Canadian interest but also because there was genuine regard for the role played in the war by the United Kingdom. But the assumption was that the United Kingdom would be "on side" in multilateral terms after a brief postwar transitional period. In large measure, it was felt in Ottawa that Canadian prosperity depended on this alliance.

However, by 1944 there were some indications that London was moving away from multilateralism. In the meeting between Keynes and Ilsley the British laid out a very bleak scenario: imports exceeded exports by some £1 billion in 1944; civilian consumption had fallen from a base of 100 in 1939 to 79 by 1944 whereas, in the United States, it had *increased* from 100 to 115 over the same period. Finally, and perhaps most ominously, the United Kingdom had liquidated overseas assets worth approximately £3 billion and had run up onerous bills in the sterling area, as table 1 illustrates. Moreover, some members of the British cabinet, who were not without popular support, told their prime minister, Winston Churchill, that they would not stand for any "multilateral nonsense." Countries that wanted to export to Britain after the war would have to take British goods in return; Britain intended to "'luxuriate in the position of a debtor country.'"[37] All of that, some Canadians thought, seemed to imitate "the policies worked out for Germany [in the 1930s] by Dr. Schacht."[38] Obviously, coping in the transitional period would be difficult.

This was where matters stood with Britain as German resistance crumbled in May 1945. Canada had become immeasurably wealthier during nearly six years of war – industry now employed more Canadians than ever before, agriculture was hard-pressed to keep up

Table 1
Britain, foreign assets, 1938 and 1944 (£ millions)

Long-term investments	£4,582
Minus long-term liabilities	400
Minus short-term liabilities	270
Net Assets, 1938	3,912
LOSSES, 1938–44	
Repatriation of long-term investments	£1,090
New long-term liabilities	253
New short-term liabilities	1,930
Minus new short-term investments	270
Total Losses	2,998
NET ASSETS, 1944	914

Source: W.S. Woytinsky and E.S. Woytinsky, *World Commerce and Governments*, (New York: The Twentieth Century Fund, 1955), 212.

with demand, and unemployment was non-existent. The country was prosperous as never before. However, the stark fact remained that Canadian prosperity continued to rest on the fragile base of international trade; the war had not changed that fact. Recognition of this impelled the government to commit itself to a policy of multilateralism and non-discrimination and pursue it single-mindedly during numerous wartime meetings among Allied powers. However, efforts to advance this policy failed, largely because European reconstruction interfered with trade liberalization and shut out Canadian exports. With the failure of the multilateral effort during the critical half-decade from 1945 to 1950, that left the United States as the only market able and willing to absorb large quantities of Canada's exports and thus help to ensure domestic prosperity. Canadian policy was multilateral by preference, bilateral by necessity, and manifestly continental by default.

1 The Decline of Anglo-Canadian Trade, 1945–50

"After the war we must protect our best market to the extent of helping the UK rebuild its economy," Minister of Munitions and Supply C.D. Howe told Prime Minister King in mid-1944.[1] Faced with the potential disruption of North Atlantic trade due to the continuing economic problems of the United Kingdom, the King government had reason to be concerned over the general thrust of British policy. Ottawa was most anxious that Britain return, with some Canadian assistance, to a convertible and non-discriminatory regime. British prospects, however, were not encouraging.

Even the thought that the Britain might not agree with these policies caused tremendous concern in Ottawa, and the government actively planned for future contingencies. Without the vital UK export markets, Canada would be unable to pay for imports from the United States and would end up "ground between the upper and nether millstones."[2] What was needed, according to Governor of the Bank of Canada Graham Towers, was a major salvage operation to avert the trend toward a complete postwar breakdown in international trade relationships. It was toward this end that in February 1945 the Canadian government suggested the possibility of offering a substantial loan to the United Kingdom to help see Britain through its anticipated transitional period difficulties.

The British preferred to deal with Washington first, hoping to negotiate a $3 billion grant and a $5 billion loan. They were unsuccessful: the most the United States would offer after discussions lasting a gruelling three months was a $3.75 billion loan on relatively stiff terms. The war was over, London was only one of many suppliants, and Britain also posed a definite challenge as a potential trade rival. Following that disappointing experience, a UK delegation came to Ottawa in search of Canadian credit in February 1946. In general, the Ottawa mandarinate disliked the hard line taken by Washington. Indeed, Towers was so distressed over UK prospects after the American negotiations that he urged Prime Minister King to be particularly generous. As the governor pointed out, the United Kingdom "was relatively weak" and Ottawa's interest lay "in strengthening the United Kingdom ... within the limits of our power to do so."[3] He supported the idea of an interest-free loan, although such an offer ran contrary to the terms of the all-important Anglo-American agreement.

Canada was generous, offering, without much hesitation, $1.25 billion, the sum asked for by British negotiators. In a further act of generosity, Canada cancelled Britain's indebtedness under the wartime British Commonwealth Air Training Plan, an amount totalling more than $400 million. In a related though separate negotiation, a four-year Anglo-Canadian wheat deal was finalized in June 1946, offering wheat to the United Kingdom for the first two years at a cost lower than the world price. This was an attempt by the federal Liberals, especially James Gardiner, Saskatchewan's cabinet representative and minister of Agriculture, to iron out the peaks and troughs of farm incomes, a political imperative after Saskatchewan returned only two Liberals to Ottawa in the June 1945 election. (The wheat deal came back to haunt the government as prices paid per bushel climbed steadily through the half-decade following 1945, reaching the lofty heights of $3.16 by Christmas 1947, as compared with the $2.00 that the British were paying for Canada's crop. The eventual amount of further – and unanticipated – assistance extended in this way was more than $365 million.)

Aid to the United Kingdom was practical bilateral politics, given Canada's dependence on the British market for a number of products. It was an article of faith in Ottawa that exports spelled domestic prosperity and therefore that any interference with the market which in the 1920s had taken on average 35 per cent of total Canadian exports would have far-reaching implications. But it was also an attempt by Ottawa to "to do its part" in helping to ease Britain back into the convertible and non-discriminatory trading world that was the perfervid object of so much of Canadian policy. Lord Keynes, the central figure in the UK Treasury during World War II, said as much to Chancellor of the Exchequer Sir John Anderson, pointing out that Canada's assistance was linked to "its well-known concern for liberal trading policies and that Britain should not 'disappoint them if we can help it.'"[4] Although there was certainly an element of self-interest in the Canadian position, it is also true that the country did substantially more, relative to its size and resources, than any other in helping the United Kingdom's postwar recovery. In the process, Ottawa extended itself to the limit.

A SHORTAGE OF DOLLARS: CANADA AND BRITAIN, 1947

Following the granting of loans to Britain, Canada's trade with Britain improved. Total Canadian exports increased by 20 per cent in 1946 and a good proportion of that increase went to the United Kingdom. Under these circumstances Ottawa was reasonably optimistic that the postwar world would meet its expectations. One result of that ill-founded confidence was the restoration of parity between the Canadian and American dollars. This represented "an expression of faith in Canadian industry" and most business people favoured it, believing that parity "would restrain domestic inflation at little cost to Canadian exports."[5] However, partly as a result of this decision, imports from the United States increased very rapidly as Canadian consumers and businesses began to stock up after wartime deprivation, leading to ever-larger deficits in Canada's trade with the United States. This trend was further aggravated by increased British exports to sterling area countries, up from about 45 per cent of total UK exports in 1946 to 48 per cent by 1950. These had increased for a number of reasons, but the end result left Canada importing certain commodities from the United States which had traditionally come from Britain. To make matters worse, many of the British goods that did find their way to Canada were priced out of the market. For example, English china and pottery, shirts and haberdashery, and automobiles all met with sales resistance because of cost.[6]

As a result of those and other developments, Canada's US dollar deficit rose dramatically. And in early 1947, at the height of the buying binge, Britain began to experience serious financial troubles of her own, sustaining the first of several postwar dollar crises that threw the entire balance of Anglo-Canadian trade into complete disarray. This was reflected in the very rapid rate at which London was using the Canadian credit. By the end of March 1947, the chancellor of the Exchequer, Hugh Dalton, was so concerned over the rate at which both the Canadian and American loans were being drawn on that he formally warned the cabinet that it was "racing

through [the] dollar credits at reckless and ever-accelerating speed."[7]
In effect, the British were living partly off the largesse of Canadian
and American taxpayers, and Canada, at least, could not sustain
that contribution to England while at the same time incurring a
growing deficit in her trade with the United States. If 1946 had been
the "annus mirabilis" for the United Kingdom, as Dalton later
claimed, then 1947 was "annus horrendus."[8] Ottawa would certainly
have echoed that sentiment as its balance of payments with the
United States worsened.

Throughout the spring of 1947, the UK and Canadian dollar situations continued to deteriorate. Ottawa asked London to refrain
temporarily from further drawings on the Canadian credit. This did
not please the British, who considered such a request to be an in-
fringement of the agreement. If the credit were restricted, unless
Ottawa made further concessions London would have to consider
curtailing such dollar imports as poultry, bacon, eggs, and cheese
which, like wheat, were subject to long-term contractual arrangements. In the end, the United Kingdom was allowed to continue to
draw on the credit, but the King government demanded a *quid pro
quo* known as the 50/50 deal: London would have to match its drawings on the loan with an equal amount of convertible currency. While
the British were reluctant to agree, there were few alternatives. However, the UK government made it known that the token import
scheme first arranged in May 1945, in which the British had allowed
token imports of those commodities traditionally supplied by Canada before the war, was in jeopardy. The policy was an attempt to
ensure Canadian producers of at least a presence in the UK market
during the transition period, "to encourage them for a better future,"
and had been much welcomed for that reason.[9]

Canadians found such threats of reductions in imports of Canadian products distasteful and unhelpful. Deputy Minister of Finance
Clifford Clark instructed Robert Bryce of the Department of Finance
to prepare a memo that presented Canada's case against the undue
use of import restrictions, reiterating the obvious to London. Canada
had:

1 given a loan much larger relatively than that of the US,
2 kept our price levels down,
3 given export credits exceeding our favourable balances at a time when
  we are losing US dollars,
4 shown our willingness to increase imports from UK, etc.[10]

However, given their own problems and the imminence of non-resident sterling convertibility, a necessity under the terms of the Anglo-American loan agreement, the British paid little heed to Canada's demands for reassurance.

There was a ray of light on the horizon, however, one that Canada and Britain could only hope would grow brighter. On 5 June 1947 the US secretary of State, General George C. Marshall, announced in a speech to graduating Harvard students that the United States would begin the process of rehabilitating Western Europe by partly funding the Continent's dollar shortage. If Ottawa could convince Washington to pay for certain "offshore purchases," such as Canadian wheat for Britain, both Commonwealth countries would benefit. But the Marshall Plan, or the European Recovery Program (ERP) as it was formally called, could not be put into action until Congress approved it. That did not happen for some months, during which time Anglo-Canadian political and economic relations continued to suffer and crisis management became the order of the day.

London introduced non-resident sterling convertibility on 15 July 1947, as required by the terms of the Anglo-American loan agreement. This fateful move lasted slightly longer than one month and resulted in the loss of millions of borrowed dollars – $700 million in July alone. Of all the currencies of the European belligerents, sterling alone was now freely convertible and other countries simply cashed in their accumulated (and abundant) soft pounds for hard (and very scarce) dollars to buy much-needed North American goods. Dalton pointed out the obvious when he announced the suspension of convertibility on 21 August, noting that "the burden of the desperate dollar shortage of so many other countries was simply shifted to our shoulders."[11] The British government emerged from the crisis, as Sir Alec Cairncross points out, "with little credit"; the cabinet "was content with drift," while the Bank of England had offered very suspect advice.[12]

In the aftermath of the convertibility disaster the British claimed to be unable to continue the 50/50 arrangement. Their situation was now simply too acute to permit payment in US dollars. And if Canada needed American exchange, so the British claimed, then it was obvious that she was doing "relatively little ... to conserve United States dollars at a time when all countries were denying themselves things they wanted because of the dollar shortage."[13] In other words, Ottawa should embark on its own program of restricting imports from the United States, as Britain was doing. Needless to say, Canada disagreed with this view of its exchange problems.

The reality was that Canada was not experiencing a dollar crisis because she was impoverished; rather, exchange difficulties were

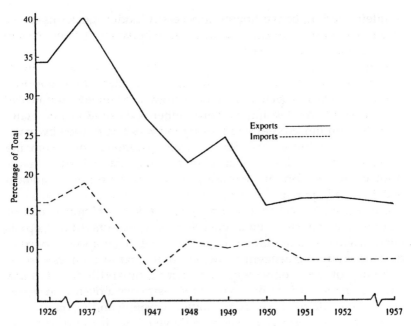

Figure 1
Canada's trade with Britain, 1926–57

the result of a number of factors. In large part they were a reflection of a high level of Canadian prosperity which manifested itself in the purchase of American products. As well, Canada's exchange problems were a reflection of the difficult international financial position of the United Kingdom and the fact that Ottawa had provided a disproportionate share of the money needed for British and West European recovery. Be that as it may, the disagreement over the exchange positions of both countries did nothing to contribute to a greater understanding of each other's problems.

With the return of inconvertibility Canada's worst fears were realized as restrictions on commodities imported from the dollar area were imposed. For Ottawa, the crux of that problem was clear: more than 40 per cent of Canada's exports were in four products – wheat, newsprint, woodpulp and lumber – much of which had traditionally gone to Britain.[14] Put bluntly, it was feared that much of what could not be sold in the United Kingdom could not be sold at all. Further, some Canadian goods, such as eggs and bacon, were produced almost entirely for export to Britain. The *New Statesman* pointed out a fact that Canadians recognized all too well: even if Ottawa could re-direct part of its trade, "it would be quite unable by such means to offset the loss of the British market."[15] Ever on guard against a further loss of custom, the government in Ottawa applied increasing pressure on London to reverse the decline in Anglo-Canadian trade statistics.

As those statistics worsened, so too did Canada's dollar position; as sales to Britain declined, imports from the United States rose. With the growing deficit, on 17 November 1947, the Canadian government announced a program of import and travel restrictions directed against the United States. It also sought a loan from the Export-Import Bank, an agency of the US government, Ottawa wanted $500 million over ten years but the best the bank would do was $300 million over five.

With such a bleak scenario confronting it, in late October 1947, in strictest secrecy, the Liberal government approached the Department of State to determine the possibility of negotiating a comprehensive trade agreement. It was either that or, an American summary of an informal exploratory meeting concluded, Canada "would be forced into discriminatory restrictive policies involving greater self-sufficiency, bilateral trade bargaining and an orientation toward Europe with corresponding danger of friction with the United States, if not economic warfare."[16] Inevitably, such a policy would be politically disastrous and economically crippling. That was where matters stood as the Canadian restrictions went into force.

The secret negotiations continued until April 1948, by which time other developments had superseded them in importance. Marshall assistance was on the horizon and would help clear up the remains of Canada's dollar problem as the country became an off-shore supplier to Europe. As well, Canada, Britain, and the United States were now discussing the possibility of a North Atlantic security pact, which would be ratified one year later as the North Atlantic Treaty Organization (NATO). As early as March 1948, the Canadians were busy convincing the other two delegations to include some reference to the alliance as an economic, social, and moral force in the world. The result was Article 2, the so-called Canadian article, which, while never amounting to anything concrete, promised intra-NATO economic collaboration instead of a bilateral North American deal. Finally, and perhaps of most short-term importance, Mackenzie King had soured on the trade agreement for a variety of reasons. Nor was the secretary of state for External Affairs, Louis St Laurent, who would be prime minister himself in eight months, any more interested. As R.D. Cuff and J.L. Granatstein have noted, "as a French Canadian, and particularly as one facing a general election in 1949, [he] could not afford to leave himself open to the charge that he had sold Canada to the Americans by scuttling Imperial preferences and ties."[17] The negociations were therefore quietly broken off.

While all this lay in the future, in late 1947 the forces that prompted a Canadian search for alternatives had poisoned the atmosphere between Canada and the United Kingdom. It was in that context that they undertook to negotiate the latter's 1948 import program in discussions that a Ministry of Food memorandum called "the most important which are in sight." In the ministry's estimation, "nothing less than the future pattern of Canadian agriculture and Canada's future economic position in the British Commonwealth may be determined by these discussions."[18] If they failed, not much hope could be held out for the Anglo-Canadian relationship.

Sir Percivale Liesching, the permanent secretary of the Ministry of Food, led the British food mission to Ottawa in November 1947. His mandate was "to extract every possible advantage from Canada."[19] That included, so a strategy memo noted, breaking long-term contracts. As Prime Minister Attlee was told by a senior aide, "if we do not [now] make the cuts necessary to protect our reserves, we run a very real risk of having cuts of a wholly different order of magnitude forced upon us in the not very distant future."[20]

At the top of the UK "hit list" were the bacon and egg contracts. While the United Kingdom recognized the hardship this would create for Canadian egg and hog farmers, the latter of whom had geared their production to suit British consumer tastes, there was, in London's opinion, no other course. As well, the United Kingdom anticipated cuts of £4 million in timber from Canada, a reduction that would necessitate "very delicate negotiations" as Britain absorbed approximately 40 per cent of the output of British Columbia's largest industry.[21] In the case of wheat, the contract would be honoured as long as the world price did not fall below the minimum set by the four-year deal. However, wheat was a special case and London was only too well aware of that fact, especially given the concern expressed by some ministers, notably the minister of Food, John Strachey, over the necessity (political and otherwise) of ending bread rationing.[22] To achieve this he badgered his cabinet colleagues to allocate more scarce dollars to purchase additional quantities of wheat at a price substantially higher than that being paid Canadian producers. Similarly, other contracts also had to be maintained, especially steel and non-ferrous metals which were vital for continued UK recovery. From the British perspective, the problem with metals was that those commodities would find ready buyers in the United States who would pay in hard currency. In pre-negotiation strategy sessions in London, the bottom line was that when dealing with unpleasant issues such as a revision of the 50/50 agreement, Canada accumulating sterling, or abrogation of long-term contracts the British mission would have to be careful that it did not "drive the Canadians at once into breaking off contracts which we wished to continue."[23]

When the actual negotiations began in late November, the position of the United Kingdom came as a horrible shock to the Canadians, who had discounted rumours of a UK "hard line" as mere bargaining strategy. The British were playing for large stakes in late 1947 and a reflection of that was their intention, as they told the Canadians, to "[keep] some contracts, [reject] others, and [spend] money on base metals, particularly copper, urgently needed in the UK." Gardiner, "found it impossible ... to take seriously Liesching's statement." In his opinion it was a case of renegotiating all, or none, of the agreements; he would not be party to negotiations that "doublecrossed" and made "suckers of" Canadian farmers. [24]

There was no cabinet agreement on this issue, however, with Gardiner and Minister of Finance Douglas Abbott staking out competing positions. Moreover, the prime minister, recently returned from London where he had listened to a chilling account given by Britain's foreign secretary, Ernest Bevin, of the deepening conflict between East and West, was adamant that the British delegation not return home empty-handed, for political, if not economic, reasons.[25] And Liesching, always the consummate negotiator, exploited the leverage he had to good advantage. For example, in conversation with Towers he pointed out the obvious problem related to continuing secure markets for Canadian farm products if Ottawa adopted the hard Gardiner line. The governor conceded that the United States was probably not a substitute market.[26] In the sanctity of the cabinet room, ministers agreed; the United Kingdom remained indispensable as a destination for the country's exports. Nothing, it was thought, could change that imperative. As Liesching had intimated to Towers, and as St Laurent observed in cabinet, the fact remained that "the price structure of Canada [could not] stand complete or extensive diversion of food exports to the US," the only possible hard currency market.

In the end, through increasingly bitter negotiations, a compromise was worked out. The political implications of failure to arrive at an acceptable conclusion were too sobering to contemplate. Both in Canada and in Britain, to say nothing of the United States, the outcry would be tremendous. With the Cold War deepening, such a sign of economic disunity between two very close allies would be dangerous. Even so, the agreement eventually accepted by the British created divisions within the Canadian government. The decision to meet the British more than half way was Prime Minister King's alone, Abbott's previous attitude notwithstanding and, according to the UK's high commissioner in Canada, Sir Alexander Clutterbuck, "ran against the entire body of financial opinion from [the minister of Finance] downwards."[27]

The arrangement would run only until the end of March 1948, when all of its components would be re-evaluated. The token import scheme remained in place, the British would be allowed to draw $45 million over the three months, and a formula was devised to meet the sterling area deficit with Canada. Finally, and most important from the UK perspective, the wheat contract was maintained; that was the clinching factor, "the cardinal point of the whole business," Sir Stafford Cripps, chancellor of the Exchequer, claimed.[28] With wheat selling in Chicago in December 1947 for $3.16 per bushel, the Canadian price for 1948 of $2.00 per bushel looked far too good to pass up. Once again, Canada had extended itself to the limit to reach agreement with Britain.

While the negotiations were successful in that an agreement was reached, they were also very traumatic for both sides and did nothing to improve relations between the two countries. The under-secretary of state for External Affairs, Lester Pearson, vehemently denounced the whole process, especially the extension of the credit. In his opinion "we had no right to be giving Britain any credit at all now. If we were strictly logical, we should completely cancel the remaining portions of the British credit." Canada had negotiated a short-term loan from the Export-Import Bank to address its immediate dollar problem and Pearson, at least, saw a fundamental inconsistency in that: the Canadian government could not afford to borrow on a short-term basis to extend long-term credit to the British. As well, after all the recriminations and anger that characterized the process, the talks had produced only "an interim, makeshift policy." Pearson concluded by noting that the 1947 food negotiations "had been the most difficult he had ever known."[29] Part of the distasteful atmosphere was certainly a result of Britain's economic condition in 1947, but it was also partly as a result of changing British perceptions over the role that the sterling area and Europe would play in UK recovery. In short, the area and the Continent were to be emphasized as Britain pulled back from convertibility and non-discrimination.[30]

Bad feelings continued to plague Anglo-Canadian relations. No sooner had the UK delegation returned home than letters began crossing the Atlantic "interpreting" the recently signed food agreement. The British felt that they were not in any way committed to providing dollars to Canada after 31 March, just as the latter was not bound to supply dollars to Britain. As well, if hard currency was not forthcoming after that date, the British calculation was that the contracts ended: "no arrangements were made as regards the period thereafter." The Canadian interpretation differed substantially: London had entered into contractual obligations to accept certain products at certain prices for the *whole* of 1948. As Pearson told High Commissioner Clutterbuck, "the inability of the United Kingdom to finance purchases under the contracts in question does not itself cancel the obligation which the United Kingdom Government have accepted."[31]

There was also controversy over whether the British could draw a maximum of $15 million per month from the credit, or whether they were entitled to a block sum of up to $45 million to be taken whenever they wanted. Naturally, London favoured the flexible rate of drawing, feeling that the restrictions on UK drawings suggested by Ottawa "made nonsense of the settlement." While the Canadian government did not object to a certain amount of flexibility, at the rate of UK drawings in late January 1948 the $45 million credit would last only until the end of February. And then, Towers asked Clutterbuck, what would be done in March? The British were not reassuring with their answer – "when the money runs out, we talk."[32]

London was also becoming increasingly concerned over the operation of the token import scheme, which had been reaffirmed during the December negotiations. The Foreign Office especially was adamantly opposed to it. As members of that department wrote, when the United Kingdom could barely pay for necessary imports from hard currency countries, the drain on its reserves "for quite unnecessary imports" would probably be too much to sustain. Moreover, since Canada was sending token imports to Britain, the United Kingdom could hardly oppose US demands for similar treatment that would soak up more hard dollars for luxury goods. And maintaining US assistance was a great concern for a Labour government which did not want to alienate "the 'big business' support of ERP in the USA whose influence counts for so much."[33] Therefore, rather than meet American demands, a more preferable policy would be to upset Ottawa.

These developments were not encouraging. In an effort to relieve the pressure cooker of Anglo-Canadian relations and make some plans for the black hole after 31 March 1948, Cripps took the step of suggesting that Ottawa and London involve the United States in their problem; after all, it was clear that the solution lay in Washington. Cripps hoped that the result of an Anglo-Canadian plea to the United States would be some sort of commitment that Washington would extend the financing of UK purchases in Canada backward to 1 April when (and if) the ERP finally went into effect. If such an American guarantee was forthcoming, then London would be prepared to take some risks in the matter of UK-Canada trade. If, however, ERP assistance did not materialize, either in time or in sufficient measure, then very disagreeable issues would have to be faced very soon in relation to financial arrangements between Britain and Canada.

While the Canadians denigrated a joint approach, fearing that it would be seen as the Commonwealth "ganging up" on the United States, the Canadian ambassador in Washington, Hume Wrong, presented the Anglo-Canadian case for ERP aid in early February. The meeting was "depressing." In short, the Americans would make no promises about the availability of Marshall aid or how it would be distributed.[34] When told of the US response to the Canadian representation, senior officials at the UK treasury were "pretty shaken."[35] They had counted on a sympathetic American attitude and a firm commitment that the United States would pick up the cost of dollar purchases as of 1 April, regardless of when the ERP finally passed Congress.

In the circumstances, the British initiated a campaign to retain access to Canadian credit after 31 March, asking for a further $15 million for April. While the first reaction in Ottawa was to refuse, from his vantage point in London High Commissioner Norman Robertson counselled otherwise. It seemed to him that the situation on which the Americans had based their February decision to make no promises had been altered later in the month. The Communist takeover in Czechoslovakia had "produced a much higher temperature in the United States ... which is likely to ensure a more rapid passage of the ERP legislation than would have seemed likely even a fortnight ago."[36] For Canada to appear unwilling to advance a further credit would seem small-minded and perhaps jeopardize Ottawa's chances of substantial offshore purchases. By late March, the Canadian government offered more.

And, much to Ottawa's delight, Robertson's analysis was correct; the Marshall Plan was passed into law on 3 April 1948. One of its first acts was to assume responsibility for certain British purchases from Canada. On 5 May 1948 the European Cooperation Administration (ECA), the administrative arm of the ERP, authorized $35.5 million to the United Kingdom to buy Canadian bacon, wheat, and flour. In the ensuing ten months, $670 million of ECA money was spent in Canada. As a result the country's exchange position quickly cleared up, although the United Kingdom's financial situation did not improve markedly.

It was partly for that reason that Chancellor Cripps made plans to visit Ottawa in September. In preparation for his visit, Sir Henry Wilson-Smith, a senior official at the Treasury, went to Ottawa in early August and Sir James Helmore of the Board of Trade followed late in the month to discuss Anglo-Canadian problems and try to soothe ruffled Canadian sensibilities, which needed soothing. As various memoranda produced in the depths of Whitehall pointed out, Canadians felt a certain amount of resentment and irritation toward London, caused by the fact that:

(1) we do not have sufficient regard for the Canadian difficulties, particularly their own acute dollar shortage; that we have been anxious to go on drawing dollars on credit and have been giving no effective return in exports for the extensive Canadian sales to us: and more especially, that we have tended to consider our drawings on the Canadian credit as a matter of right and not as an act of generosity from Canada which can be withheld at her discretion.

(2) Canada has geared her agricultural economy to suit the United Kingdom market at our request, but that we are constantly changing in our demands (and incidentally paying less high prices than we are willing to pay other suppliers).

(3) we are not sending them an adequate share of our exports ... to help meet the gap.

(4) More generally, the atmosphere of mutual confidence and pooling of information is lacking and that, after long silences, there is a tendency to summon Canadians for urgent consultations when a crisis arises.[37]

As well, Sir Andrew Jones, of the UK Food Mission in Ottawa, hypothesized that Canadians were beginning to think that "they made a mistake when they decided to base their agricultural economy on the continuance of long-term agreements with the United Kingdom."[38] Further, by mid-1948 Ottawa did not believe that the United Kingdom was interested in re-establishing multilateral and non-discriminatory trade in the near future. As High Commissioner Clutterbuck told Cripps, UK actions over the past year had destroyed that confidence and had "raised grave doubts both as to our objectives and our methods."[39]

With both Wilson-Smith and Helmore, the Canadians hammered away at what they thought to be the central issues, and which the British had already identified: why was the United Kingdom not investing more in Canada? Why was the United Kingdom not sending more of its exports to Canada? Why was the United Kingdom not addressing the important issue of its high-cost economy which, they suggested, was driving Canada into increased dependence on the United States? It also seemed clear to Ottawa that the British preferred whenever possible not to deal with Canada. For example, the volume of foodstuffs that the United Kingdom intended to purchase from Canada during 1949 was so small that it seemed pointless to enter into any contracts at all. Finally, restrictions London had imposed on the lucrative Canadian trade with the British West Indies were causing much "heart-burning and ill-feeling."[40] Canadians described the British position as totally inflexible and self-interested to the point where some senior officials wondered whether a policy of particular toughness did not stem from British bitterness over Canadian membership in the dollar area.[41]

While Canadians were put partly at ease by Cripps in September, tensions remained high. The separate interests of Ottawa and London could not be reconciled, given conditions in late 1948. In part, that was the reason for the establishment of the United Kingdom – Canada Continuing Committee (UKCCC), a forum where very senior officials from both countries would meet on a regular basis to discuss mutual economic and political problems. Both sides hoped it would bring about a closer, or at least a less traumatic, relationship. Given the high profile Cripps' visit to Ottawa and the establishment of the UKCCC, High Commissioner Clutterbuck was optimistic that the "rot" in Anglo-Canadian relations had finally been stopped.[42] And 1949 did prove to be a crucial year for the commercial relationship, although not in the way that Clutterbuck had suggested. Rather than improving, the association was seriously impaired.

ANOTHER DOLLAR CRISIS: BRITAIN IN 1949

By 1949 the worst of the United Kingdom's economic problems seemed to be over. Generally, the British situation was not unpleasant and Cripps was sanguine about the country's domestic prospects: housing starts were up, the tremendous investment in social services was proceeding apace, and supplies of consumer goods were increasing. The most notable aspect of the United Kingdom's recovery during 1948 had been the tremendous increase in productivity. As the chancellor proudly noted, "although the industrial population increased by only two percent, industrial production as a whole rose by over ten per cent and is now, on rough calculation, over fifteen per cent above pre-war."[43]

However, the situation remained more problematic in terms of Britain's trade relations with dollar countries such as Canada. Canadian exports to the United Kingdom were still stringently restricted by London. There was also some speculation in early 1949, as a downturn in the US economy spilled over to affect Britain, that these restrictions were to be tightened further as part of Britain's continuing struggle to balance its dollar account.[44]

Both the United Kingdom and Canada recognized the magnitude of the task that confronted them in finding a solution to the problem of ever-decreasing trade volumes, especially after March 1949 when the ERP discontinued funding of UK wheat purchases from Canada.[45] However, the British were unsure that they could do more. In a memorandum given to Howe, which differed in tone, if not in substance, from the September 1948 meetings, Cripps spelled out in bleak language the future that lay ahead for Anglo-Canadian trade. The United Kingdom was committed to the United States to secure "viability" by the end of the Marshall period. This it could do only by adjustment of its trade with North America. It was against that background that the problem of Anglo-Canadian economic relations had to be viewed. The British remained wedded to the notion that policy developed with respect to Canada had to be carefully related to their much bigger problem with the United States. Further, they were not at all sure that they would be able to survive in a non-discriminatory and fully convertible world without large infusions of American dollars, even by June 1952 when the ERP came to an official end. In the memo, the chancellor pointed out that the British were "already buying all we could afford from our own dollar earnings and all that we can persuade the Americans to allow us to buy in Canada with the dollars with which they provide us under ERP."[46]

Given the shortage of dollars, it remained official UK policy to import from soft currency markets whenever possible. At a January 1949 meeting of the UKCCC, the British told the Canadians what to expect in the future. For example, they claimed to be especially interested in a long-term French program that envisaged a large increase in the production of wheat for export. The target was one million tons and, while the British acknowledged that this figure was optimistic, they were quite prepared to import 500,000 tons of French wheat if it was available when the Canadian wheat contract expired.[47] Cabinet had also considered substantial purchases of wheat and other commodities from the Soviet Union.[48] In both cases, unless prices "were very much out of line, the United Kingdom would, for balance of payments reasons, prefer to take French [or Soviet] wheat rather than supplies from dollar sources."[49] Purchases of the magnitude considered could, of course, have direct and immediate implications for the sale of Canadian wheat to Britain, making it necessary to lower wheat imports from Canada to reflect the changed circumstances.

As well, surpluses in apples, fish, bacon, and other commodities that had traditionally gone to the United Kingdom were now unwelcome there for exchange reasons. In 1949, only seven per cent of Britain's bacon imports were to come from Canada and, the *London Times* speculated with some assurance, this percentage would be reduced to zero in 1950.[50] Poland and Denmark were now the favoured sources of supply. Similarly, Canada had historically exported much of its fishery production to Britain. In 1947 fish exports to the sterling area accounted for 23 per cent of the Canadian catch, down from 41 per cent in 1938. In 1949, however, it was estimated that the sterling area would take even less, a mere $8 million worth of fish products, less than ten per cent of the total. Instead, the United Kingdom purchased 90,000 cases of canned salmon and 65,000 cases of crabmeat from the Soviets. The British market for Canadian beans, honey and berries had also been completely eliminated by official fiat. As was the case with wheat, the United Kingdom was now directing those purchases to other soft currency countries or to countries behind the Iron Curtain, which was particularly irksome. Indeed, as Secretary of State for External Affairs Lester Pearson observed, if continued such a policy "would raise questions which go to the root of Canada's external economic policies."[51]

The ease and willingness with which London entered into these exclusive bilateral and barter deals was disturbing after all that Ottawa had done. As Prime Minister King had earlier asked, "How can we continue to pour out dollars from Canada to keep Britain on her bilateral feet?" [52] The deals also placed a very real burden on Britain's economy in the form of imported materials that were more costly than the comparable product from Canada. And while Canadian ministers recognized that the United Kingdom had few dollars with which to buy anything from Canada but essential products (which perhaps made dollar purchases of canned salmon and crabmeat seem slightly out of place), there was an element of unrequited expectation in their denunciation of British policy – after all, as King had said, his country had done much for Britain. Seen in that context, his rhetorical question was more of a *cri de coeur*.

By 1949, Ottawa feared that the story graphically told in table 2 would permanently lock the United Kingdom into a system of escalating costs and higher priced goods that would make British ex-

Table 2
Comparison of price levels for selected products, Australia, Canada, and Finland

Commodity	Unit	1938	Average c.i.f. price		February 1949 £	Percentage increase 1949 over 1938
			1947	1948		
WHEAT						
Canada	cwt	.39	.97	1.01	1.21	208
Australia	cwt	.39	–	1.53	1.54	299
WOODPULP						
Canada	cwt	13.55	36.31	40.84	39.20	189
Finland	cwt	8.91	32.45	43.10	43.12	384
NEWSPRINT						
Canada	cwt	.45	1.43	1.50	1.50	231
Finland	cwt	.53	1.57	2.24	2.67	329

Source: Economist, 26 March 1949, p. 572.

ports to the dollar area even less competitive. As the influential British weekly the Economist rightly pointed out, neither the British government nor British businessmen seemed to recognize the fact that "no compulsion can be put on the Canadian buyer to purchase British goods which are ... too dear."[53] If not "corrected," the consequence of such arrangements would be to forever divide the world into two isolated trading regimes comprised of soft and hard currency countries. Canada had fought against that possibility since 1945, in part because it had been an article of faith among policymakers in Ottawa that serious difficulties would arise if that unhappy situation developed.

That was the issue Canada raised at the first meeting of the UKCCC in January 1949. The delegation's main objective was to persuade UK exporters to send more goods to Canada, a theme that had been propounded by Ottawa. Clark had called it the "direction of exports" argument. As matters stood, the British were systematically exploiting markets in soft currency countries for goods that would find a ready reception in Canada, such as certain grades of steel and tin. While the United Kingdom regularly lectured Ottawa on the necessity of buying more British goods, British policy did not match British rhetoric. In discussing this issue with his friend Bruce Hutchison of the Winnipeg Free Press, John Deutsch of the Department of Finance and a member of the UKCCC delegation bitterly observed that London seemed to be more interested in securing its own short-term future through bilateral and barter trading arrangements with soft currency countries than in entering into any meaningful dialogue with North America designed to return Britain to a system of freer trade and payments.[54] The British kept saying that they would try to send more goods, "but they simply [could not] so long as they [were] guaranteeing to deliver those goods to their own sterling partners ... There [were] only so many goods and they [were] committed to the various barter deals." If such frustrations were not addressed, then Canada would have no other choice but to intensify its economic links with the United States at the expense of Britain; instead of being a bridge, "Canada would tend to become a stumbling block between the American and European worlds."[55]

Certainly Deutsch had a point, which London recognized, but the very lucrative and secure markets in the sterling area shone too brightly for British exporters to pass up. With huge and unsecured sterling balances credited to the accounts of some Rest of the Sterling Area (RSA) countries such as India and Pakistan, British exporters had ready-made markets, made all the more enticing when coupled with the ambitious development plans of these newly independent countries. Further, they tended to be traditional British markets and, at a time when commodities for export were in short supply, UK exporters favoured these familiar and protected soft currency markets over the more competitive ones in hard currency countries. As a result, British exporters had no incentive either to cut prices or improve delivery dates in order to exploit dollar markets.

The entire British import-export situation was sufficiently alarming that Howe led a very senior Canadian delegation of cabinet ministers and officials to the United Kingdom to impress upon the British a sense of "the anxiety which existed in Canada at the disappearance of markets in the United Kingdom for various Canadian products."[56] He also pressed the United Kingdom to send more goods to Canada. As well, Towers and Deputy-Governor Donald Gordon informed Clutterbuck, of the "growing agitation on this score," noting that if the United Kingdom persisted, "pressures might be set up which might shift the whole outlook of the country towards the United States as the only remaining economic life-line."[57] In response to both representations, however, the British listed their own not inconsiderable problems, especially their deteriorating dollar position.

By the second quarter of 1949 the British dollar deficit had almost doubled, to £157 million. While the Howe delegation had been received by the British with encouraging remarks, in private memoranda the chancellor and other senior cabinet ministers described the Canadian attitude as "unconstructive" under the changing circumstances. The general feeling was that Canada was intent "only on getting concessions in order to satisfy particular Canadian interests, while pressing on us the merits of multilateral, non-discriminatory trade and convertibility and of buying in the cheapest market regardless of exchange difficulties."[58] That was the Canadian position and, while it may have been as self-interested as Cripps had suggested, Canada was also very disappointed that the billions of dollars invested in British recovery had not resulted in more direct benefit to Canadian exporters.

As Britain's dollar position became more pressing, in mid-June London outlined the situation to the new Canadian prime minister, Louis St Laurent, and his minister of Finance, Douglas Abbott. The gold and dollar deficit was increasing at an alarming rate while British reserves had fallen from $1.9 billion to $1.6 billion. The main culprit, so the chancellor maintained, was the effect of the 1949 US recession on sterling area economies. As a result, the United Kingdom was placed in an increasingly serious position *vis à vis* the United States. Ironically, however, Britain's payments position with Canada remained quite sound. Despite the Anglo-American situation, there had been no significant increase in the sterling area's total deficit with Canada, although London chose to ignore this fact. This development was largely the result of two factors. The first was an aggressive marketing campaign undertaken by the Canadian government with assistance from British manufacturers. The second was that UK purchases from Canada were already at a low level and most of the expenditure of dollars in Canada was for essential goods which the British could afford.

But while Cripps was aware of both the Canadian situation and the fact that British exports to Canada had remained at relatively constant levels, his view of the situation remained unchanged: as noted above, the Anglo-Canadian condition was seen as part of a deteriorating Anglo–North American situation, made worse by a continuing lack of dollar exchange. With Britain's dollar position worsening daily "very prompt and decisive action was necessary."[59] The United Kingdom response was to call for a meeting of Commonwealth finance ministers.

Canada, however, was uncertain that it would attend. There were a myriad of considerations to take into account, not the least of which was the country's relationship with the United States. If a delegation did travel to London, it was imperative that it not be interpreted in Washington as a "ganging up" by the Commonwealth on the United States; too much depended on American goodwill. And if the meeting was to concentrate on the aftershocks of the US recession, then perhaps a sterling area, as opposed to Commonwealth, conference was in order, like the one held in the fall of 1947. The Canadian government did not want Washington to draw a parallel between a 1949 meeting and the talks held in Ottawa in 1932 where the British Empire had gathered to raise tariffs against non-Empire goods. If that connection were made, the United States could easily make economic life unbearable for Canada and the sterling area. Certainly Prime Minister St Laurent was aware of that problem; as he told Clutterbuck, such a meeting could "awaken anti-British feeling [in Washington] which [was] never far below the surface."[60]

As ministers were occupied with the June 1949 election campaign (which the Liberals won), Norman Robertson, the newly appointed secretary to cabinet and the most powerful mandarin in Ottawa, carried Canada's worries about the United States to London. He had attended the 1932 Ottawa meeting and was all too well aware of the "disturbing similarity between the approach this time and the one followed in 1932–33." Robertson told British Prime Minister Clement Attlee that the Commonwealth approach was fundamentally wrong-headed. London, he pointed out, "should be made to learn from past mistakes and refuge should not be taken in recriminations against the United States."[61] Nor, it seemed, were the British at all willing "to accept or ... to understand the Canadian position." [62] In their defence, they were dealing with an extremely difficult financial crisis of major proportions, almost certainly the reason why few of his arguments made any impression.

However, his advocacy of an Anglo-American meeting to discuss the dollar crisis did yield fruit: talks were arranged to take place in early July. While the Americans were initially uninterested in Canadian participation, they were prevailed on to permit it. The us ambassador in London, Lewis Douglas, counselled his superiors in the Department of State that Ottawa should sit in on the talks, noting prophetically that "unless we are able to prevent the development of an unfortunate United Kingdom policy, Canada will be compelled to decide whether to go with the uk or the United States – a question which, however resolved, would have adverse effects everywhere." That was a long-term consideration to be taken into account, but there was another, more immediate, reason for Canadian attendance at the July meeting. As Douglas pointed out, Canada, "by sitting in would find it easier to attend the meeting of Commonwealth finance ministers called for July 11 and there to play more effectively the part of *amicus curiae.*"[63]

Ottawa sent a high-level delegation made up of Abbott, Robertson, Deputy Minister of Trade and Commerce Max Mackenzie, and Louis Rasminsky of the Bank of Canada to meet with us Secretary of the Treasury John Snyder and the British. The most interesting point to emerge from the tripartite discussions was the UK outline of a program to sharply reduce hard currency imports to save about $450 million in 1949–50. From the Canadian perspective, an overly large proportion of the cuts appeared to relate to Canadian exports to the United Kingdom, particularly base metals, wood products, and foodstuffs.[64] Abbott was also handed a list of eight things that Canada could do to help ease the short-term position of the United Kingdom, items that could be discussed at an upcoming UKCCC meeting.

The America-Britain-Canada (ABC) discussions did not resolve any of the underlying tensions. As for the communiqué, Sir Roger Makins of the Foreign Office told Secretary of State for Foreign Affairs Ernest Bevin that "we had a little bit of a struggle over [it]."[65] The *Economist* was more caustic, noting that "the only thing to do was put into it everything that anyone had said."[66] In other words, the document was useless as a policy statement. It was fine to note that the objectives of ABC economic policy remained convertibility and non-discrimination, but the real issues were skirted as the participants attempted to paper over cracks created by disagreement. Moreover, such unacknowledged dissension could have implications for the recently ratified NATO Treaty. However much they might publicly trumpet their tripartite success, problems would have to be squarely faced in the days ahead. And that would be difficult for, on the basis of the recently completed discussions, Snyder was doubtful that a *modus vivendi* could be reached between London and Washington. He cabled home that it was difficult to see how any fruitful results could be obtained so long as the British refused to take certain fundamental steps that would make the UK economy more flexible. As for Cripps, Snyder found him discouraging; "while [he] purport[ed] to be striving toward multilateral trade and non-discrimination it [was] apparent that [he] consider[ed] attainment of those objectives to be subservient to requirements of maintaining stability and thus protecting rigidities ... of sterling area as a whole."[67] There was also a sneaking suspicion that the British again wanted US help, which prompted Snyder, so Secretary of State Dean Acheson noted in his memoirs, to get "out of the country as fast as possible ... He flew back [to Washington] like a modern Paul Revere crying 'The British are coming!'"[68]

Snyder reiterated these critical views in his rather gloomy report to the president. The British position remained one of curtailing imports from both Canada and the United States and redoubling efforts to find alternative sources of supply in soft currency areas. Indeed, William Hallman, a *Time* correspondent who had accompanied Snyder on his European trip, reported that Cripps had confided to a Fleet Street friend of Hallman's that "British or Anti-Communist continental Socialism – working together in a sterling area could save the world from any possible dangerous setback if the United States had an economic crisis."[69] If he actually thought this, the chancellor certainly had an inflated opinion of the place of the United Kingdom in the postwar constellation; without the constant infusion of Canadian and US dollars, the British situation would have been worse.

Two days after the July 1949 tripartite talks ended, the Canadians and British met again, this time under the aegis of the UKCCC. Robertson, Clark, Rasminsky, and Mackenzie attended for Canada while Wilson-Smith of the UK Treasury, Liesching, now permanent undersecretary of the Commonwealth Relations Office, and Sir Frank Lee of the Ministry of Food represented Britain. The participants addressed many of the points outlined in the British paper given to Abbott during the ABC discussions. Of most interest to Robertson and his colleagues was a British request to increase weekly drawings on the remainder of the Canadian loan in order to help the United Kingdom through its dollar crisis. Clark flatly stated that this was not possible. Indeed, the Canadians found the British proposal astonishing, given the UK policy that had unfolded over the previous few days. Clark quite correctly told Wilson-Smith that he "did not see how an increase in that rate could be justified."[70] Even ignoring the effect of reductions in Canadian exports to the United Kingdom that London intended to make as a result of its dollar situation, it was questionable that the present rate of drawings could be financed without jeopardizing Canadian reserves. Clark made one more telling point: Canada would undertake to do what it could for Britain, but there was a strong relationship between that "and the action which the UK might take to reduce costs and generally to provide evidence that there was some hope of the country returning to multilateral trading." After all, that was one of the reasons the loan had originally been offered.

Following hard on the heels of the UKCCC meeting, the Canadians attended the Commonwealth finance ministers' meeting that Attlee had called in June. The bulk of the discussion dealt with the dollar crisis and how the United Kingdom proposed to deal with it. Among the measures considered, the British demanded that Ottawa accept inconvertible sterling for some proportion of area purchases made in Canada and adopt a tariff policy involving thoroughgoing discrimination against the United States.[71] Further, taking general aim at the hard currency bloc, Harold Wilson, the president of the Board

of Trade, outlined what he thought was important in terms of rec-
tifying the sterling-dollar imbalance. Part of that involved surplus
countries such as the United States and, to a lesser extent, Canada
freeing their markets to deficit countries like Britain. Further, it was
incumbent upon the former to pay stable prices for imports, especially for colonial raw material exports that were subject to wild
fluctuations in price.[72] Cripps also addressed the conference, attempting to persuade RSA governments to reduce dollar expenditures 25 per cent by switching imports from dollar to sterling
sources.[73] He pointed out that with reserves of only £385 million
the area had no alternative; its future was at stake.

While Abbott vigorously objected to the proposed dollar import
cut, his arguments were ignored. But he had a deeper worry: how
would the United States react to the sterling area program? As Douglas had remarked to Acheson, any increase in the level of UK-US
disagreement created a spider web with Canada caught in the
strands.[74] More immediately, however, it might be difficult to re-
open ABC discussions on the basis of the plans then being discussed
in London. A meeting to deal with tripartite relations had been
planned for September in Washington and anything that could jeopardize its success was almost too horrible for the Canadians to contemplate. In the mood prevailing in mid-1949 the Washington
conference was seen as perhaps the last opportunity for some sort
of agreement that could benefit Canada to be struck between the
United States and the United Kingdom. But if the sterling area, led
by Britain, persisted in loudly blaming the United States for its economic woes, there was a distinct possibility that Washington would
either refuse to proceed with the discussions or make the British
pay handsomely for their remarks, which could affect Canada as
well.

As Anglo-American economic relations hit bottom, Ottawa continued to counsel patience and understanding on both sides, although to little effect. The Americans were fed up with British carping and criticism, while the United Kingdom was bereft of new ideas
on how to deal with the dollar crisis. As the *Economist* noted in late
July, "All that ministers could advocate was a tightening of trade
restrictions."[75] Although the results of the finance ministers' meeting and the increasingly problematic nature of the UK-US association
were not well received by the St Laurent government, they at least
had the effect of spurring the Canadians on in preparing for the
critical September talks.

The tripartite talks, the British dollar crisis, and the effect of both
on the Canadian economy were overwhelming favourites as topics

of conversation and interest in Ottawa. Committees were struck and the resources of the Departments of Finance, Trade and Commerce, and External Affairs, as well as the Bank of Canada were devoted to preparing position papers. Ottawa also responded favourably to an American invitation to join in preparations while keeping the British fully informed. The ultimate objective was to use whatever influence Canada had in Washington and Westminister to reconcile American and British opinion as much as possible in the process of determining the agenda. Certainly it was a delicate tightrope to walk.

The activity in North America in preparation for the ABC conference was in marked contrast to the lack of the same in England. With the absence from London of several senior officials and ministers, especially Cripps who was in Switzerland recovering from exhaustion, A.E. Ritchie of Canada House reported to External Affairs that the British would be lucky to produce anything constructive.[76] There was widespread pessimism that the situation would not improve before the officials' party left for Washington in late August. Nor did it: once in the American capital, British officials remained uncertain and directionless. Wrong cabled Ottawa that UK civil servants gave the impression of "talking to a rather tired brief." Indeed, one official acknowledged that he and his colleagues felt "completely ineffective" because of uncertainty in Britain's policy.[77] Robert Hall, director of the economic section, UK Treasury and a participant in the tripartite talks, was also critical of the situation in Britain. Generally, developments were not encouraging; as he confided to his diary in late August 1949, "it is absurd that a Government of professed planners should not only have no one who understands planning, but also no one who understands monetary policy and the theory of international trade. I do not say that it is essential that these should be left to theorists, but at least there ought to be more than one person who is capable of appreciating the theoretical considerations. The Bank [of England] seems to me to be quite unaware of all the work that was done about its own behaviour in the 19th century."[78] It was not a promising start to discussions that many British policy-makers felt would determine the future of the Anglo-American "special" relationship.

The mood of the United Kingdom's ministerial delegation that arrived in early September was not very different. Ambassador Douglas had advised Acheson that the British would be "rather desperate ... smarting from the public criticism with which they had been so generously lashed by the press in the United States."[79] Certainly he had a point; in meetings prior to their departure, the UK ministers felt that the Americans would be totally uncompromising in their demands for increased access to the British market. It could be expected that British ministers would be sensitive, suspicious, and probably unreceptive; as Clark dejectedly told a contact in the US embassy, there would be no rabbits pulled out of any hats.[80] With Britain obviously "unrepentent," the Canadian government expected the worst to happen, with the United States, tired of being whipped by the UK press and British politicians, demanding that its delegation obtain visible concessions.

But there were some rabbits in evidence. Much to the surprise of the Canadians, reasonableness reigned everywhere. Even in the area of ECA-financed wheat sales to Britain by Canada, the United States was amenable. While obtaining approval might be difficult, given the mood of the Congress, the ECA undertook to provide $175 million to pay for British wheat purchases from Canada, a practice that had been discontinued in March 1949. The ECA had then been concerned that wheat would be declared surplus in the United States. The Canadian delegation, with its constant pressure on both the British and the Americans to seek a *modus vivendi*, could rightfully take some of the credit for the satisfactory way in which the conference developed. But the United Kingdom also helped generate goodwill by announcing its intention to devalue the pound from US$4.03 to US$2.80, thus removing a major irritant in Anglo–North American relations. Canada also devalued its dollar by about nine per cent. Finally, all sides pledged themselves to increase the flow of trade.

The press release reflected the new attitude, which was quite favourable to the United Kingdom. Despite British and Canadian fears, no onerous concessions had been extracted by the United States. The *Economist* rightly noted that the "conclusions are in every way as satisfactory as the British delegation had any right to expect."[81] Official London also recognized its good fortune: in a meeting of Commonwealth and UK government bureaucrats, Sir Edward Plowden, head of the United Kingdom's economic planning staff, reported quite favourably on all aspects of the ABC meeting. He noted that UK ministers and officials had gone to Washington in a very pessimistic frame of mind and had been quite prepared to find US authorities uncooperative and critical of UK financial policies. As events had transpired, however, "the atmosphere could hardly have been better." In Plowden's mind at least that "augured well for the future of UK-US relations in the economic and political fields."[82] The UK ambassador in Washington, Sir Oliver Franks, echoed that sentiment in his report to the prime minister.[83]

Unfortunately, the relatively successful conclusion of the tripartite talks did not solve Canada's economic problems. The $175 million ECA allocation to the United Kingdom for Canadian wheat was a welcome relief to both sides, yet serious and disruptive issues remained. The most pressing was that exports to Britain remained at a low level, raising the question of how Canada was to pay for its American purchases, which continued to climb ever higher. This was real cause for worry. As Canadians remembered very well, reduction in Canadian sales to Britain and increased imports from the United States had created havoc with the country's finances in 1947, which had necessitated the implementation of draconian measures, a traumatic experience that Ottawa did not want to undergo again. The fervent hope in the Canadian capital was that the regenerated ABC atmosphere would provide a boost for Anglo-Canadian trade.

But that was most unlikely. As the critics pointed out, the old nemesis of the RSA, with its ample sterling balances, remained. The British would not re-direct sales to North America merely because their products were now cheaper in that market. If the same product could be sold at an unchanged sterling price in the sterling area, then it was probable that it would still find its way there. For British traders contemplating a switch, there was also the cost of penetrating the dollar market "with its risks and difficulties." Further, as the *Economist* prophetically pointed out, attitudinal change among British exporters was most unlikely.[84] Past diversionary schemes had failed as had the present program, "Operation Columbus," announced amid much publicity in early 1949. Voluntarism simply did not work in that context. Britain's businessmen continued to sell "in Empire markets where established connections of long standing, ample war-created sterling balances, a heavy demand and a not-too-critical acceptance of British merchandise made for a comfortable and lucrative export trade."[85]

Nor, because of import quotas and dollar restrictions, did Canada's exports to soft currency countries increase during the months following devaluation. The American consul-general in Montreal highlighted that fact in a report to the Department of State, remarking that the British tendency to restrict imports from Canada was approaching "disastrous proportions."[86] That was a sentiment echoed by some in the UK civil service.[87] The implications of such a policy were obvious. In paper submitted by the Canadian delegation at a UKCCC meeting in Ottawa in September, officials warned of the probable consequences of import restrictions against Canadian goods. They pointed out that

those who are most willing to "Buy British" are in most cases those who know that they must buy if they are to sell, those who are directly or indirectly employed ... in the export industries such as agriculture, forestry, mining and fishing. The United Kingdom market is important to each of these industries every year. The desire to promote the sale of United Kingdom goods in Canada would obviously be diminished for individuals here who depend themselves upon sales to the United Kingdom should they be faced with diminishing export prospects.[88]

Ottawa hoped that the United Kingdom would modify its import program from Canada, which was "based solely on the United Kingdom's minimum essential needs [to meet] relatively few, relatively small Canadian problems."[89] Canadian officials suggested a course of action that would keep Canada at least in the British bacon and cheese markets by specifying the tonnage of both to be purchased at "bargain prices." Similarly, Canada hoped that Britain could see her way clear to ease her draconian import program with respect to such commodities as newsprint and lumber. Additional expenditures by London for this enlarged program would be in the $20–30 million range, a relatively insignificant amount that would buy substantial Canadian goodwill. While this plan had been put forward by Mackenzie on a personal and informal basis with no official authorization, he was sure his minister would champion it in cabinet if the British accepted. As it was, he was attempting "to keep the doors of negotiation open."[90]

But Britain remained firm; again pleading very real dollar problems, the government refused to reconsider its program in the ways proposed by the Canadian delegation. However, if further Canadian assistance was forthcoming to finance its newsprint, lumber, bacon, and cheese purchases, then London would be more than willing to enter the Canadian market on a larger scale.

Relations between Britain and Canada, which had been troubled throughout most of 1949, the success of the September tripartite talks notwithstanding, were not improved by such demands. The United Kingdom had already reduced its purchases from Canada to a minimum. It had cut eggs, paper, and pit-props, slashed lumber "almost to the bone," and UK "bacon purchases were now so small as not to matter."[91] To Finance Minister Abbott it appeared that London was being purposely difficult. As he pointed out to Cripps, the sterling area's dollar deficit with Canada was completely covered: the resources available from sterling area earnings in Canada, ERP funded offshore purchases, and the drawings on the Canadian loan would "exceed by a very substantial margin the deficit arising with Canada from a minimum Import Programme such as we have in mind."[92] According to Canadian figures the combination of the three sources would allow the United Kingdom to purchase goods from Canada valued at more than $650 million. Even with this volume of expenditure, the United Kingdom would be left with sufficient dollars to augment her reserves for increased purchases from other sources. In effect, if Canada was to provide additional financial assistance to Britain, it would only go to support the United Kingdom's position in other areas or to reduce the British dollar deficit with other countries. The UK demand so aroused the Canadian government that there was some speculation in London that Ottawa might suspend further drawings on the Canadian credit, on which the British were then drawing at a rate of $10 million per month.[93]

Abbott also refused to consider the proposal made by Cripps that Canada should accumulate blocked sterling. To have done so would have effectively meant a further extension of credit to Britain, something that had already been explicitly refused. In a canvas of a few senior officials, the Canadian refusal was wholeheartedly supported. For example, Dana Wilgress, the Canadian high commissioner in London, observed that to do so would amount to nothing less than "a mortgage on Canada's future."[94] Deustch agreed; accepting sterling so long as the United Kingdom made so little progress in dealing with its fundamental problems would put Canada on "a slippery slope in our dealings with that country, to say the least."[95] Abbott himself realized that the accumulation of sterling which Canada could not use at that time or in the forseeable future was not "in accord with the fundamental realities of our economic relationships."[96] More and more it appeared, as Governor Towers had warned, that London was determined to follow a "sterling versus dollar approach at the same time hoping that [it could] persuade [Canada] into the sterling area group."[97] Finally, Abbott, rejecting Cripps' request, had no intention of meeting with his British counterpart – a mild rebuff "might be salubrious at this stage."[98]

Ottawa found London's attitude profoundly disturbing. To Deputy Minister Clark, it was "utterly tragic."[99] To Howe, it appeared that the two countries "were heading for fresh trouble in [their] trade relations" over the insignificant amount of $20–30 million.[100] British policy was being developed as if the September talks had never taken place. The rigidity of the UK position in this instance was in stark contrast to the new spirit supposedly manifest in all three capitals following the talks. Apparently, the new-found sense of partnership, highly touted after Washington, was to operate only when it suited the British. High Commissioner Clutterbuck did not disagree with the Canadian analysis and, in concert with a number of senior officials from the Foreign Office, the Treasury, and the Bank of England, entreated his government to show some flexibility in its dollar import program from Canada. The British cabinet, obsessed with its limited dollar balances and annoyed in turn by the Canadian attitude, declined. That sentiment, as Makins wrote, was reinforced by "a body of opinion in the British Cabinet which was intensely critical of and indeed hostile to Canada and the present Canadian government."[101] Certainly as 1949 came to an end Canadians had little to cheer about over the economic relationship with Britain.

Developments were not any more encouraging in the new year. In January 1950, the Commonwealth gathered at Colombo, Ceylon, in a meeting that, from Ottawa's perspective, only served to reinforce the generally pessimistic interpretation of Anglo-Canadian trade possibilities. According to the delegations attending, the short-term prospects of the sterling area were not good. Even though the British had recovered 60 per cent of their pre-crisis reserves by the end of 1949 (and 100 per cent by April 1950), the RSA was not faring as well. At Colombo, the forecast figure of the total gold and dollar deficit was revised upward, on the basis of reports submitted to the United Kingdom by RSA countries, from $861 million to $996 million. On the import side, the sterling area had made energetic, and in most cases successful, attempts to cut down on imports by the 25 per cent asked for at the previous summer's Commonwealth meeting in London. Certainly there was little comfort here for Canadians interested in the UK market. And even more damaging, the Department of Finance was forecasting sales at an even lower rate in 1952–53 than in 1951–52.

Increasingly, Britain was becoming unreliable as a destination for Canadian exports. For example, the *Economist* offered the opinion that the hope of Canadian agriculture returning to the British market had been "virtually killed" by the 1949 experience.[102] A similar situation existed with respect to newsprint. Since 1946 Canadian producers had been selling less each year to the United Kingdom. It was a moot point whether the British would buy even the tonnage contracted for in 1950 because of dollar problems and other priorities. As the *Economist* correctly pointed out, "Canadians have every reason to feel that they have been badly treated."[103]

Howe, heretofore a firm supporter of trade with Britain, was also souring on the relationship, given Canada's troubles in that market. In comments on a memorandum of Pearson's he indicated that he felt that Canada had been too "soft" on Britain and too biased against trade with the United States. There were some in cabinet, such as Pearson, who were "a little too frightened of the American bogey and, therefore, just a little too anxious to do everything to help the

British." In the postwar period too much of Canada's efforts in the trade field had been concentrated on the United Kingdom; in Howe's opinions, "we should be vulnerable indeed with all our eggs in the UK basket." He was not adverse to cultivating RSA and Western European markets and advocated increased effort in that direction. However, he ended where he began, with the US market, to his mind the *only* one that could ensure Canadian prosperity.[104]

Howe was the senior minister in St Laurent's government. At the cabinet table he sat on the prime minister's right.[105] His views on the matter were sure to be taken seriously by a government that wanted a smoothly functioning economy and domestic tranquility. The certainties of the US market contrasted sharply with the uncertainty in the United Kingdom. As the minister pointed out to his cabinet colleagues, British estimates of future dollar imports showed that London hoped to cut its purchases in 1951–52 by as much as one-third from 1948–49 levels.[106] This was language that the Canadian cabinet understood. The attractive alternative to an unreliable Britain was the United States.

In the winter of 1949–50, the problem of continuing prosperity had also become an issue in the House of Commons. As members returned from a winter break to begin a new session of Parliament on 16 February 1950, the marked increase in unemployment and the attendant downturn in economic activity was a source of concern.[107] It thus seemed doubly important not to take chances by tinkering with trade flows upon which so much of the country's prosperity depended.

Still, despite Howe's tough words about the British, the Canadian government remained concerned about the UK's role in Canada's economic future. This future, it was felt, lay in secondary manufacturing. Nearly 80 per cent of Canada's sales to the United States were made up of wood and pulp and paper, base metals, certain farm products, and fish. As the world's largest industrial power, the United States was not interested in purchasing large volumes of Canadian manufactured goods. Indeed, as the Bank of Nova Scotia *Monthly Report* had noted in 1949, the US market "for Canadian manufactured goods [was] not providing any real substitute for such markets in the Dominions and Empire."[108] Further, the expansion of sectors such as pulp and paper and smelting would not be able to absorb the workers and the productive capacity that would become idle as a result of the loss of overseas markets for metal products and machinery. As well, while the United States currently provided a ready market for certain Canadian exports, there was no certainty that this trend would continue. There was also almost no chance of diverting any of Canada's agricultural surpluses in such commodities as wheat or hogs to US centres.

For those reasons, overseas markets remained important to Canada. The Cabinet Committee on Economic Policy had explored the matter in November 1949 and concluded that, if not the United Kingdom, then where? A memorandum prepared in the Economic Research and Development Branch of Trade and Commerce for the committee forecast that, with an adverse economic situation in the United States, "1950 does not promise to be a year in which Canada can hope to shift to the American market export surpluses that are no longer saleable overseas."[109] While this had been accomplished in 1947 and 1948 and the redirection of Canadian exports had greatly eased the adjustment to the loss of overseas markets, conditions had changed for the worse in the United States. It appeared that Canada would face difficult trade problems in the year ahead. Again the perception was that the country still needed a stable British market; Canada had a very small margin of safety in its international accounts as a whole.

It was this fact that induced Ottawa to continue its efforts to assist the restoration of British multilateralism and convertibility. Canada was not yet willing to abandon all hope of ever re-establishing the old North Atlantic triangle, though the prospects of doing so seemed bleak. The continued failure of Canada's overseas customers to earn necessary dollars through trade and investment rather than through loans was forcing Ottawa's hand in this matter. But Anglo-Canadian trade problems were increasingly pushed into the background as the United Nations, led by the United States, went into Korea in force in the summer of 1950. The resulting boom in raw materials processing, weapons manufacture, and steel and aluminum production helped Canada settle more and more comfortably into a continental role.

2 The Failure of the Multilateral Option: The General Agreement on Tariffs and Trade, 1945–51

In the immediate postwar period, the Canadian government considered a number of trade policy options in its search for economic stability. These included British preference, bilateralism, and multilateralism. In the words of Robert Bothwell and John English, this situation represented a maze in which there was no "right" choice, but only varying shades of gray.[1] Each policy had its advantages, but also its limitations. British preference, which was of potential benefit to Canada, had caused trouble with the United States during the 1930s and had the potential to undermine the Anglo-American and Canadian-American relationships in the 1940s. And the US attitude was of critical importance when dealing with the matter of Canada's trade: memories of Hawley-Smoot remained fresh in the minds of politicans and bureacrats. The second policy approach, bilateralism, had been largely discredited during the 1930s when its practice had damaged the country. However, Ottawa had not been above making bilateral agreements when they suited Canadian purposes. The fact remained, however, that the international context had changed significantly and what was good for the 1930s goose was not necessarily so for the 1940s gander. Of the three options, multilateral and non-discriminatory trade was most appealing in Ottawa, given Canada's dependence on foreign trade for its domestic prosperity. Of not inconsiderable weight in the determination of that result was the fact that Washington had again taken up the multilateral torch, but this time it burned much brighter because of the economic desolation that characterized much of the rest of the world.

As a result, Ottawa welcomed the conference held in Bretton Woods, New Hampshire, in 1944, where the International Bank for Reconstruction and Development (IBRD) and the International Monetary Fund (IMF) had been established. The IMF was to be the financial component of the multilateral system and was designed to regulate exchange rates and prevent the competitive devaluations that politicians and officials of the 1940s thought had characterized the national policies of the 1930s.[2] Later, it was confidently expected, establishment of an International Trade Organization (ITO) would create procedures to enable contracting parties (CPs) to undertake multilateral *and* non-discriminatory tariff reductions and, in conjunction with the IMF, allow disputes among participants to be worked out without resort to damaging trade wars or other, even less acceptable, forms of international behaviour.

Certainly the ITO was expected to be one of the key building blocks in Ottawa's postwar economic policy. It was to be structured to extend to all participating governments the tariff reductions negotiated by any two members through the most-favoured nation clause. The self-defeating autarchy of the previous decade was to become a thing of the past. In the first flush of Allied victory, a brave new world was being planned, in Ottawa at least, that would restore multilateralism, non-discrimination, convertibility and, ultimately, freer trade.

During the postwar period Canadian support for such international organizations was at its peak. As the government stated in its White Paper on Employment and Income of April 1945, it had pressed and was "continuing to press ... for a wide collaboration in the reciprocal reduction and removal of trade barriers." It also attached "special importance ... to the reconstitution of multilateral trade on a firm basis, arrangements under which the proceeds of our exports may be spent wherever we desire to obtain our imports."[3] In ministers' minds, multilateralism promised to be the best insurance against the buffetings of international trade.

THE INTERNATIONAL TRADE
ORGANIZATION AND THE GATT:
GENEVA AND HAVANA, 1947–48

The idea of an international trade organization had its origins during the war. Certain elements in the United States, the State Department and the executive in particular, supported its establishement. Despite its relative self-sufficiency, the United States had been hurt by the autarchy of the 1930s and was concerned to prevent any recurrence of the "beggar-thy-neighbour" philosophy that had characterized the decade. Washington also saw the GATT as an opportunity to put an end to Britain's imperial preference, a system which it had long viewed as "economic aggression," and expand its own trade boundaries accordingly.[4] The United States intended to use whatever force, moral or otherwise, was needed to encourage less committed allies to see the postwar world through American glasses. To that end it had demanded as a condition of Lend-Lease that signatories to the agreement subscribe to Article VII, which called on aid recipients to reduce discriminatory trade barriers and "free" international commerce. Although not a direct participant in Lend-Lease, Ottawa was glad to participate in the movement toward an international organization, for the promotion of multilateral trade was at the top of its agenda too.

Discussions among interested parties had continued throughout the war years and in December 1945 the US government had published *Proposals for Expansion of World Trade and Employment* as an appendix to the Anglo-American Loan Agreement. This document contained the State Department's conception of the postwar commercial world. According to the *Proposals*, the United States intended that all margins of preference were to be open to negotiation and that London should accept a no-new-preference rule. British agreement to this condition was in large part a reflection of its desperate need for US help in the transition period. And perhaps, as Joyce and Gabriel Kolko suggest, British acceptance was in part a belief that "America's deep commitment to its own trade controls, preferences [with Cuba and the Philippines] and agricultural program would, on the basis of reciprocity, permit England numerous means for later defending itself."[5]

As a result of the professed US commitment to the establishment of a multilateral and non-discriminatory system, the United Kingdom, Canada, and other important trading countries joined with Washington in planning the International Conference on Trade and Employment to design an international trade organization. The United Nations Economic and Social Council sponsored the discussions and also nominated a preparatory committee of eighteen countries (of whom seventeen attended) to prepare a draft convention for the trade organization. This group was to make the necessary arrangements for convening a full conference on trade and employment, at which a charter would be finalized.

In October and November 1946, Canadian representatives met with those of sixteen other nations in London in the first session of the preparatory committee to discuss a US elaboration of its *Proposals*, the *Suggested Charter for an International Trade Organization*. Among the more important of the principles at stake in the negotiations were the eventual elimination of preferential tariff systems, the elimination of discriminatory quantitative restrictions, and the strict control of export subsidies.

A drafting committee, set to rework the *Suggested Charter* in accordance with the decisions reached at London, met at Lake Success, New York, and completed its mandate by late February 1947. On 10 April in Geneva, twenty-three contracting parties convened the second session of the preparatory committee on trade and employment which continued to work on the charter. This task was of vital importance to the Canadian government and the very capable chairman of the Canadian delegation, Dana Wilgress, accurately reflected Canada's interest in multilateralism and non-discrimination, suggesting that the contracting parties should "seek to accommodate the differing situations and the legitimate aspirations and needs of the various nations of the world, [but] must not ... resort to expedients and indulge in incompatibilities which would destroy our general objective."[6] For Wilgress, the prospect of an emasculated charter was almost worse than the prospect of no charter at all. He put his considerable energy, and that of his delegation, to work in securing Canadian policy objectives. When required, the Canada delegation acted as a mediator between the United States and the United Kingdom and was an important influence generally during Conference deliberations. Indeed, much to the delegation's surprise, it was referred to by other CPs as one of the "Big 3."[7]

The result of those deliberations was a draft charter which the contracting parties agreed would be put before the World Conference on Trade and Employment to be held in Havana, Cuba. The *Final Act*, adopted at the conclusion of the second session in Geneva, was a reflection of the lofty aspirations that motivated the contracting parties. The most important of its provisions was Article I, the heart and soul of the ITO/GATT, that committed the CPs to extend "immediately and unconditionally" to every member "any [trade] advantage, favour, privilege or immunity granted by any contracting party." Article I also contained a reference to a no-new-preference provision in the United Kingdom and bound London, among others, to a promise of no extension of imperial preference. Article XI provided for the general elimination of quantitative restrictions (QRs) while Article XIII prohibited the *discriminatory* application of QRs. As it noted, "no ... restriction shall be applied by any contracting party on the importation of any product" from another CP, unless it was applied to all contracting parties.[8]

However, there were also escape clauses in the *Final Act*. For example, while Article I banned the enlargement of preferential arrangements, it did not eliminate those already established. With respect to the elimination of QRs, Article XI did not extend to export prohibitions or restrictions temporarily applied to relieve critical shortages of foodstuffs or other essential products. In addition, Article XII allowed CPs to restrict, in a *discriminatory* fashion, merchandise imported from hard currency countries to "forestall the imminent threat of, or to stop, a serious decline in its monetary reserves." Similarly, Articles XIV and XIX permitted exceptions to the rule of non-discrimination, the latter as the result of any emergency. Finally, Article XXVIII provided for the modification of tariff schedules after 1 January 1951. In short, the GATT was a "good faith" agreement from which its CPs could deviate without fear of substantive retaliation, especially in the case of a large and important member.

As well, the GATT was unlike other international agreements in that it was not an "international organization" in the usual sense of the word. This reflected, predominantly, potential problems associated with US ratification: in order to avoid having to submit the agreement to Congress, it had to be framed as a "trade agreement" within the meaning of US trade agreements legislation. Other limitations were imposed on GATT's legal structure as well. Governments agreed "to accept legal obligations of the General Agreement 'provisionally,' and further, except for tariff concessions and the most-favoured-nation guarantee ... [agreed] to bind themselves only 'to the fullest extent not inconsistent with existing legislation.'"[9] The interpretation of this phrase would become very contentious later.

Concurrent with the formulation of the document on the GATT, the contracting parties also began to negotiate the first round of multilateral tariff reductions sponsored by it, pending the implementation of the ITO. Canada was actively involved. Negotiations were conducted bilaterally, on a product by product basis under the "principal supplier" rule, the results of which were extended to all other CPs through the most-favoured nation rule. For its part, Canada negotiated good agreements with the United Kingdom and United States, its two main trading partners, and also came to an understanding with the United Kingdom over future practice with respect to imperial preference. Anglo-American negotiations, however, threatened to run aground as the result of a fundamental conflict over imperial preference and an acceptable agreement was obtained only after much bargaining.

In the case of Canada and the United States, negotiations went relatively well. The United States continued the duty-free status of all important Canadian exports bound as a result of the 1938 trade treaty. [10] Further, a concession was obtained on virtually every item of which Canada was the principal supplier. In many cases, as with lumber, shingles, wheat, and flour, Washington reduced tariffs by 50 per cent, the lowest the president was permitted to go under the Trade Agreements Act, the legislation which empowered the executive to enter into trade agreements with foreign countries. [11] By the end of negotiations, Canadian officials estimated that concessions extended by the United States would bring the general level of American import duties to the lowest point since the Underwood Tariff, which had been in force from October 1913 to May 1921. Under that tariff, exports from Canada to the United States had increased by more than 200 per cent. It was worth noting, a Canadian memorandum pointed out, "that the value of [our] exports to the United States did not again reach the levels of 1920–21 until the recent war years." [12]

Canada and the United Kingdom also reached agreement on a number of points, although their ability to secure mutual tariff concessions was limited by existing preferential arrangements. However, many preferential rates of duty were reduced, and rates of duty were also bound against increase over a much wider field than before. As well, Ottawa suggested that Canada and the Commonwealth should review existing agreements with the object of freeing each government from the contractual obligations to maintain stated margins of preference contained in those agreements – that is, to eliminate the difference between the most-favoured-nation rate and the British preferential rate. As Prime Minister King told Britain's Clement Attlee, "the difficulties associated with the rigid obligation to maintain specified margins of preference to one another would in the circumstances of the wider multilateral approach clearly outweigh the bargaining advantages in future negotiations." [13] Maximum flexibility was obviously the objective in the Canadian capital.

In pursuit of that aim and to bring the 1937 Anglo-Canadian trade agreement into harmony with the agreements made at Geneva, Canada and Britain exchanged notes on 30 October 1947. They would continue to extend to each other the benefits of imperial preference, except where those rates of duty had been modified by the GATT negotiations. As well, each recognized the right of the other to reduce or eliminate preferences. Finally, the two governments agreed to accord to each other's exports "treatment not less favourable than that accorded to like goods ... of any other country." [14] Nevertheless, the continuing British application of a wide range of non-tariff barriers against hard currency Canada, kept in place because of the United Kingdom's very straitened economic condition, served to negate the benefits to Canada of both imperial preference and any tariff reductions negotiated. Nor did things improve, at least in the short term. British economic weakness was made all too evident when the premature introduction of non-resident sterling convertibility in July 1947 resulted in the loss of $ 700 million in one month alone. In large part, this was the reason for the hostility that permeated the Anglo-American negotiations.

The bitterness between these two important contracting parties nearly ended the session and, indeed, the entire postwar experiment in regulating international trade. The crisis arose in late August with American disappointment at the lack of progress in their negotiations with the British. In a meeting with Sir Stafford Cripps, the president of the Board of Trade, William Clayton, the assistant secretary of State, said that US public opinion "would judge the success of these negotiations by the success achieved in 'cracking the Empire preference system.'"[15] As matters stood, the Americans were not even denting it. The British in turn relied on British public opinion to justify their policy: to be seen as destroying the principle of imperial preference would be to lose the confidence of the electorate. They also saw no reason to consider reductions in imperial preference while the United States maintained similar preferences with Cuba and the Philippines. Moreover, while the negotiations were underway, Congress began considering a 50 per cent tariff on imported wool, which greatly concerned both the Australians and the British, as well as all those stauch multilaterlists among various other delegations. Given what was seen as American duplicity, the sterling area stood firm against US pressure. There the matter remained for more than a month as counter-offer followed counter-offer.

Clair Wilcox of the American delegation met with the Commonwealth delegation on 15 September in a renewed effort to break the logjam. As he explained, the US Administration was trying to reverse economic policy which had been followed in th United States for more than 150 years. It was to be doubted, Wilcox suggested, "whether the American people and ... Congress will acquiesce in what may amount temporarily to a unilateral reduction of the US tariff, to numerous escape clauses in the ITO charter, to the provision of another 15 or 20 billion dollars of aid for Europe, when they can see no immediate gains for the US." Still, Washington was willing to make an attempt and submitted a revised offer that would eliminate some preferences over a period of thirteen years. If the Commonwealth could not approach the elimination of preferences on that basis, then Wilcox questioned "whether it is intended that we should ever approach it."[16] And if that should be the case, he noted, then it was most unlikely that the Marshall Plan, introduced by Secretary of State George Marshall the previous June, would successfully negotiate Congressional hurdles.

The Canadian delegation largely agreed with the United States, feeling that on a tactical level Britain had "played its cards badly."[17] Certainly the British knew the stakes for which they had been negotiating since 1941; to fold now would be to risk the wrath of Washington as the Americans needed some movement, however slight, to demonstrate to Congress that by reducing US duties they had secured some modification of imperial preference. Nor was it impossible to accommodate the Americans on a tactical level. Symbolic gestures would certainly have bought some time in Washington. Indeed, Ottawa's imposition of quantitative restrictions against some US exports in November 1947, a result of the deterioration of Canada's economic condition, was met with relative equanimity in the United States, at least in part because of the perception of Canada as having been helpful to the United States in previous discussions.

Wilgress said as much, suggesting that with a bit more British tact and understanding of the US position, the impasse would have dissolved with less acrimony. Indeed, he considered that a good deal of what had happened was because the negotiations had been left almost entirely to the Board of Trade which, in his opinion, was not competent to deal with them: an anti-American bias was more noticeable in that department than in any other, a fact that did not help the situation. All in all, he felt, "it would have been wise for the United Kingdom to have entrusted the leadership of the Delegation at Geneva to a high official of the Foreign Office."[18]

The breakdown in Anglo-American negotiations threatened to end the entire multilateral trade program. In a meeting with the secretary of state for External Affairs, Louis St Laurent, two members of the Department of Finance, its deputy minister Clifford Clark and John Deutsch, unhappily contemplated relatively unpalatable options. While a direct approach to high State Department officials in Washington to persuade them to "go easy" on the British was ruled out, it was agreed that Canada's high commissioner in the United Kingdom, Norman Robertson, travelling to New York on board the same ship as Clayton, should be instructed to "do what he can to soften Clayton's mood in order to forestall a possible recommendation from him for an immediate cessation in United States–United Kingdom negotiations." As well, the group discussed the implications of "intimating" to the British that Canada would probably have to obtain release from the the remaining obligations of the 1937 UK trade agreement if negotiations in Geneva did not succeed; clearly, they believed that some difficult decisions would have to be made in that case, feeling that Canada could not remain suspended between a straitened the United Kingdom and the United States. That was a worst-case scenario, however, and Clark and Deutsch undertook to prepare a memorandum on the consequences of such a termination.[19]

From Geneva, Wilgress supported the abrogation policy and took it a good deal further. To such a confirmed "multilateralist," a good case could be made in favour of immediately denouncing the 1937 accord. Most important, Canada would then have a freedom from bound margins that would greatly help in reaching a more satisfactory agreement with the Benelux countries (Belgium, the Netherlands and Luxemburg), the United States, and France. As well, such a dramatic gesture would, Wilgress noted with some understatement, "take these negotiations out of the rut in which they have been proceeding and would give us enormous prestige as being leaders along the road to placing multilateral trade on a firm foundations."[20] Wilgress' draconian suggestion and the Clark/Deutsch memo were never acted on as the United Kingdom and the United States sorted out their disagreements at the eleventh hour.[21] Despite its immense power, the United States could not afford to force the point with Britain and imperial preference remained in place. Even so, it increasingly appeared to many among Canadian bureaucratic and political ranks that Western Europe and Britain would take a long time to recover from the effects of World War II.[22]

But when the dust had settled at Geneva, the results were beyond anyone's expectations, especially given the intense disagreement which had characterized the session. The conference chairman, Max Suetens of Belgium, summed up the general feeling when he noted that the signing of the accord "marked the completion of the most comprehensive and far-reaching organization ever undertaken in the history of world trade."[23] In the end, the United States had not distorted the GATT by forcing its position on other contracting parties, while the British had also been accommodating. Tariffs had fallen like skittles and, while Western Europe and the United Kingdom still maintained tough import restrictions against dollar goods, it was felt in Ottawa that multilateralism had been given a good start. Prime Minister King, echoing Sueten's comments, was positively joyous over the results; Geneva was "epoch-making." He confided to his diary that "What [negotiators] McKinnon and Deutsch [had] achieved with their staffs is truly amazing. It presents a programme that it will take all of next session and which is one that we could sweep the country on were we to encounter too much opposition to it." As the supreme compliment to the delegation, the prime minister ended by noting that "It made me almost wish that I had said nothing about not leading the [Liberal] Party through another general election."[24] In the House of Commons he was equally fulsome; the negotiations embodied "the widest measure of agreement on trading practices and for tariff reductions that the nations of the world have ever witnessed ... For Canada, the importance of the general agreement can scarcely be exaggerated. The freeing of world trade on a broad multilateral basis is of fundamental importance for our entire national welfare."[25]

To complement the fine results of the Geneva session, the Americans appeared to be committed to aiding European economic recovery, given Secretary of State George Marshall's pronouncement in June 1947 that it was the intention of the Truman administration to partly fund Europe's dollar shortage. While the ERP remained in the realm of declared policy only and had yet to run the gamut of Congressional hostility, it was a not unimportant ingredient that was being stirred into the European mix. Certainly Western Europe responded positively to the American initiative, desperate as it was for US dollars with which to purchase much-needed hard currency goods.

By late 1947, Canada was also becoming very interested in the possibility of the ERP, despite King's rather self-satisfied diary musings, as the country plunged into a dollar crisis of its own: after years of war-induced denial, Canadians were stocking up on US goods, leading to a balance of payments crisis. Indeed, by November the situation had deteriorated to the point where the minister of Finance, Douglas Abbott, introduced emergency legislation into Parliament that would curtail imports of certain products from the United States. In addition, partly in response to the country's deteriorating economic condition and also because of the idea that Europe was "finished" in economic terms, the prime minister had sanctioned top secret discussions with Washington to investigate the possibility of the establishment of a North American customs union. It seemed to some at least that Canada's options were becoming increasingly circumscribed and the country's commercial relationships increasingly problematic.

Those concerns were brought out very clearly by developments at Havana, Cuba, where work on the ITO charter continued. From November 1947 until late March 1948, delegates laboured over the task of finishing and ratifying an ITO document. But even while they discussed the most pressing issues of non-discrimination and the abolition of QRs, national interest was becoming a more important factor. In the course of hundreds of interminable meetings, amendments were incorporated into the charter "chiefly by small nations interested in protecting nascent industries from British and American competition."[26]

It became increasingly difficult for the "internationalists" among the group to reconcile divergent interests and points of view. For example, the wording of the critical section dealing with tariffs, preferences, quantitative restrictions, and exchange controls almost provoked the British to withdraw from the negotiations, which would have ended the proceedings entirely. Their chief complaint, perhaps reinforced by the difficulties at Geneva and echoed throughout the next decade, was that the ITO/GATT arrangement was a badly crafted and unbalanced document that did not adequately reflect the needs of countries in a deficit situation. All the emphasis was placed on countries which faced balance of payments difficulties removing their import restrictions and abandoning discriminatory practices, but there was virtually no reference to the obligations of creditor countries. Nor would the Americans agree to recognize any. This fundamental conflict in philosophy continued to plague the operation of the GATT for many years.[27]

At one point the British delegation left Cuba in protest against what it considered to be unjust treatment. It returned, according to Herbert Moran, chief of the economics division at external affairs, only because the British cabinet decided that representation at Havana was the better course to follow: it would "have a bad political effect to smash the trade charter after all the work done on it."[28] Moran could have also said that an equally compelling reason was the desperate UK need for Marshall dollars: to have withdrawn from the conference would have placed London's access to ERP assistance in jeopardy when (and if) it materialized.

The British attitude was only the most graphic indication of the great difficulties facing the CPs as Western Europe struggled to regain some semblance of economic balance. By early 1948, the charter was "marked off by reservations on the part of this and that nation."[29] Indeed, the *Economist* noted that at one point it contained "five articles and 55 escape clauses."[30] In an exceedingly pessimistic interpretation of the negotiations, Michael Heilperin, the economic advisor to the International Chamber of Commerce, wrote that his most striking impression was "the strength of economic nationalism throughout the world." The very concept of a world economy was alien to the collective mind-set. In short, it was "the duty of national delegations to be guided by the national interest of their respective country's policy."[31] That was not surprising, but it still came as an unpleasant intrusion of reality after the paeans sung to international cooperation only a few months earlier. Bilateral agreements were now commonplace with all European governments negotiating them. As Continental recovery proceeded apace, it appeared, at least from the Canadian perspective, that autarchy was being "reinvented."

It also seemed in Ottawa that the ITO charter had lost much of its directive power since there was little in it to compel reluctant members to obey. On the subject of GATT generally and the Havana meeting in particular, Deutsch was in agreement with the prevailing North American pessimism. He felt that the "whole conception of ... Havana [was] going sour." He had never been much impressed by it and, as a general attempt to free world trade "and make good the ideals of the Atlantic charter and the lend-lease agreements ... the Havana charter [was] a wash-out."[32]

But despite all the problems, on 24 March 1948 a charter for ITO was initialled by fifty-three contracting parties at Havana. The act of signing did not imply any obligation of acceptance, however, and the great majority of the nations attending would not take formal action until American intentions were known. In a very direct way, Congress would decide the fate of the ITO for all. Until then, the GATT would provide an interim mechanism through which the contracting parties could negotiate tariff reductions. After the ITO had been approved, the GATT would be absorbed into it. As was made very clear at Havana, the GATT was intended to *anticipate* the ITO but not to take its place. A publication by the Interim Commission for the Trade Organization, *The Attack on Trade Barriers*, noted that "it could not be accepted with equanimity that the International Trade Organization should not be brought into being ... and that governments should rest content with the restricted facilities of the Agreement." The latter missed "no short putts, but [sank] no long ones."[33]

Ottawa remained hopeful that the ITO would be approved, even after the relatively disappointing experience at Havana. Canadians had been involved in all the discussions and conferences that had taken place regarding the ITO since the war ended, providing valuable suggestions and also acting as a multilateral conscience when one was needed. Indeed some, like Wilgress, had chaired important committees and handled often irreconcilable demands with aplomb. (Wilgress had done this to the point of angering Ottawa with his singularly internationalist approach to the task.[34]) Wilgress believed that the ITO embodied principles on which Canada should stand firm. As he had pointed out to Under-secretary of State for External Affairs Lester Pearson in late September 1947, Canada would be immeasurably worse off if the trade organization was compromised. It "would commit us irrevocably to the system of bilateral trade. It would be impossible for us to put the clock back because of the vested interests which would grow up under the system of import restrictions and bilateral deals."[35]

At both Geneva and Havana the Canadian delegation fought tenaciously to secure the general recognition that tariff and non-tariff barriers were inimical to sound national economic growth. In the two succeeding sessions at Annecy, France, and Torquay, England, the Canadians struggled equally hard against more formidable odds to encourage the freer flow of trade. Unfortunately, the intervening years had seen a further hardening of attitudes and, as European recovery proceeded, a reluctance in London, Paris, and other capitals to reduce the incidence of non-tariff barriers (NTBs) to trade and enter more fully into a non-discriminatory regime that would benefit Canadian exporters.

THE ANNECY NEGOTIATIONS, 1949

As had been the case during the tariff round at Geneva in 1947, the GATT negotiations in France occurred at a time when international economic conditions had taken a turn for the worse. The US economy had entered a recession, while the sterling area's dollar deficit and the draconian measures needed to balance its books militated against a liberalizing attitude. European governments faced similar pressures and pursued a similarly cautious tariff policy. In the United States, sentiment in Congress was hardening against the ITO: while it was not rejected out of hand, neither did American legislators endorse it. In effect, the ITO was held in a state of suspended animation pending definite presidential and congressional action. In addition, the Trade Agreements Act, the legislation that permitted the president to enter into trade agreements with foreign countries, was allowed to lapse while the negotiations were in progress (it was not renewed until 1951), which was interpreted by the conference in France to mean that the United States had become less interested in international trade cooperation. And Congress was believed to have "shown its colours" the previous year when it had inserted a "peril point" clause in the Trade Agreements Act. As the Kolkos point out, the clause prevented tariff reductions on any products as soon as American industry "felt the pinch of foreign competition."[36]

Finally, several countries wishing to take part in the GATT arrived at Annecy having already increased tariffs or with proposals to increase them.

The result of these uncertainties was to throw the GATT meetings into a state of confusion. Representatives were especially at odds over how to deal with a passive United States; was Washington withdrawing from the leadership of the multilateral and non-discriminatory movement or was it not? That uncertainty was detrimental to the operation of the GATT for, as Eric Wyndham-White, the head of the secretariat of the interim commission for the ITO, pointed out, "it was almost pathological the way in which other countries took their lead from the United States."[37]

In 1949 American policy was indistinct and confused. Until Washington formally announced its intentions, other countries would not act. In concrete terms, this meant that few of the standing committees to make the GATT work could be struck, a situation which greatly affected the success of the Canadian campaign to secure recognition that some sort of intersessional machinery should be established to deal with GATT issues on a regular basis. Ottawa felt that, while the ITO remained unratified, the GATT should be made "to operate efficiently in the meantime; in other words, no defaulting on the provisions of GATT should be permitted simply because of the uncertainty surrounding ITO." Unfortunately, there was no unanimity on this question and, despite a certain sympathy with the Canadian position, the United States could not offer overt support because of Congressional suspicion.

This "faltering of purpose" at Annecy was not what Canadian policymakers had expected when planning their approach to the session. It was hardly an auspicious beginning to the second round of tariff negotiations under the GATT. Canadians were certainly aware of what seemed to be an increasingly tentative commitment to non-discrimination and multilateralism in Washington, as they were of Western Europe's postwar record in that regard. As a reflection of that anxiety, Ottawa insisted that the NATO treaty, signed in May 1949, include a reference that would bind its signatories to multilateral and non-discriminatory principles. Despite some reservations by the Americans, Article II, the so-called Canadian article, was accepted. However, it was never implemented.[38]

But even given such Canadian efforts, the climate prevailing in early 1949 was not conducive to multilateralism. Indeed, the prognosis at Annecy was sobering and, while the discussions did make some progress in freeing world trade, the Canadian delegation was only too well aware that the GATT framework offered a medium

Table 3
Value of imports of major OEEC countries from Canada ($ millions)

Importing Country	First half 1949	First half 1950	Difference	Percentage Change
Belgium	21.8	18.3	−3.6	−17
Denmark	2.4	0.3	−2.1	−88
France	24.4	13.4	−11.0	−45
Germany	7.1	4.1	−3.0	−42
Italy	6.7	2.5	−4.2	−63
Britain	389.7	245.0	−144.7	−37
Total	449.1	283.6	−168.6	−38

Source: J.J. Polak, "Contributions of the September 1949 Devaluations to the Solution of Europe's Dollar Problem," IMF Staff Papers, vol. 2, September 1951.

through which Canada could try to persuade and bargain but never dictate. Motives among the contracting parties themselves were suspect, while the negotiations themselves "did very little to lift the tone of the conference"; the efforts of conference officials "to expedite the work was largely neutralized by the ... prolonged debates which preceded the adoption of compromise measures." Indicative of that attitude was "a resurgence of ... protectionist spirit."[39] That became the prevailing theme of Annecy.

Rather than international trade being freed from the shackles that bound it, the opposite seemed to be happening: more and more countries were seeking refuge behind restrictions as "convenient" balance of payments problems grew more pressing. A typical reaction to that development was the observation that "the only portions of the Agreement in full force are the escape clauses."[40] As well, the majority of import regulations and QRs imposed by European countries were not in accordance with either the letter or the spirit of GATT. As a result, American officials increased their estimate of the per centage of quantitative restrictions that were protectionist from 33 to 80 per cent.[41] Instead of moving toward freer trade on an expanding multilateral basis, the North Atlantic economy appeared to be headed toward increased restriction and an intensified division of the international economy into exclusive trading areas. Quite clearly, as table 3 illustrates, straight tariff reductions were obviously of little consequence. Western European imports from Canada had actually *declined* following Geneva and Annecy. And while European devaluations certainly played a role in that result, so too did quantitative restrictions, exchange controls, and import quotas.

Renewed clashes between some of the contracting parties also threatened the very fabric of the agreement. The United States wanted to "throw the book" at the British for their intensification of restrictive measures in July 1949, a result of Britain's dollar problem. It took all the skill that Canada's delegation possessed to convince its southern neighbour of the senselessness of the proposed course. Support from GATT members would be needed to make the charge stick and, under the circumstances, it was doubtful that other contracting parties, many of whom were suffering similar experiences, would consider that the United Kingdom had substantially intensified its restrictions against dollar goods. As one Canadian delegate noted, "the utility of a consultation ... seemed in itself uncertain."[42] Certainly the British had no desire to consult with anyone over the issue at that time. In its role as mediator, Canada arranged an informal consultation between the two delegations which resulted in an agreement not to pursue the issue. Still, the entire process had not been encouraging: an American memorandum labelled the British crisis and proposed course of action "a stiff jolt to this program" and the State Department in particular remained adamantly opposed to Whitehall's handling of the deteriorating condition.[43] The net result of the Annecy intrigue was to greatly contribute to "a rising anti-British sentiment in [US] Government circles, ... [even among] people who [were] generally friendly."[44] For their part, the British made plain their displeasure by denouncing the United States and making not so veiled threats about withdrawing from the organization.

Perhaps reflecting the ill feelings generated among some of the CPs, the tariff exercise itself yielded meagre results, at least from the Canadian perspective. Concessions obtained by Canada from all sides were small – about $35 million out of a total trade of some $2 billion. The Canadian delegation might well have agreed with the characterization of the results of the session by a Conservative backbencher as "only a drop in the proverbial ocean."[45]

But even given the lacklustre results and the fact that Ottawa and Washington did not negotiate, Annecy continued the trend developing between Canada and the United States as the latter reduced tariffs on some items of interest to Canadian exporters. The rate on hollow steel bars was reduced by 50 per cent, while that on birch plywood declined from 25 to 20 per cent, and on alder plywood, from 50 to 25 per cent. As well, US tariffs on certain types of paper, paperboard, and meat extracts went down. For its part, the United

Kingdom took some action on preferences, reducing margins of preference on a number of commodities, sometimes to zero, as in the case of aluminum. That, of course, had the potential to work against Canadian exports. However, import restrictions in place in Britain and Western Europe prevented equal application of the negotiated reductions to dollar countries. As a result, the Toronto *Globe and Mail* pointed out that "the relatively few US tariff concessions obtained indirectly may look more solid and useful to the Canadian exporter."[46]

For many countries, Canada among them, the negotiations were more valuable for their symbolic commitment to non-discrimination and multilateralism than they were for the actual results. With little else to emphasize, Wilgress pointed out to an Associated Press reporter that, regardless of the disagreements and increasing restrictions on trade, the discussions indicated the intent of the contracting parties to at least discuss the issue of trade barriers in a multilateral forum. As well, he noted, the CPs still pledged themselves to the achievement of those conditions necessary to restore world trade.

The fact remained, however, that in the final analysis the situation was bleak. The *Economist* editorialized of the closing ceremonies that "never since the proposed International Trade Organization began to take form in 1945 have the prospects for the immediate application of the ideals of free and multilateral trade for which it stands appeared as dim as they do today."[47] Internationalism appeared to some to be a concept whose time had come and gone: like the hydra, national interest was difficult to corral. And, despite the symbolic value of the GATT, Wilgress agreed, feeling that there would soon be a large-scale application of the escape clause in the agreement. Indeed, it was not overly pessimistic to predict "that before long nearly half of the contracting parties will be substantially intensifying [discrinminatory] import restrictions."[48] Barriers to international trade would be raised to safeguard the financial and balance of payments positions of members.

The summer of 1949 had turned out to be a particularly difficult season in terms of trade liberalization, what with dollar shortages and the intensification of tariff restrictions. Americans were indeed having second thoughts about the ITO. Legislators and businessmen were increasingly sceptical of it – by 1949 the GATT was more compatible with the collective mood. With the ITO, the US would have subscribed *permanently* to a far-reaching set of international trade rules that included escape clauses allowing the rest of the world to discriminate against the United States for a variety of reasons. Because the GATT was a much less "effective" organization, relying more on moral force and suasion, senators and representatives had at least indirect control over it. As well, American participation would require, at the least, their triennial approval through the Trade Agreements Act. Finally, the *Economist* offered the opinion that by 1949 Washington attached more importance to other institutions as instruments of world trade recovery since it appeared that the ITO initiative had largely slipped through American hands.[49] Congress never had the opportunity to pass judgement on the ITO. Because of its certain defeat, the Truman Administration withdrew the charter before it was put to a vote and by late 1950 the ITO was dead.

The sentiment of postwar cooperation in trade seemed to have dissipated as nations set about the task of rebuilding their economies. Indeed, the increasing importance of protectionist motivation in the development of import restrictions was the primary issue facing the GATT. It represented a challenge to one of its fundamental principles, that QRs on imports should not be used as a protective device. With Canada and, to a lesser extent, the United States opposed to such developments, and the United Kingdom and Western Europe favouring them for obvious reasons, the GATT was increasingly riven by dissension, a development most clearly brought out by negotiations held during 1950–51 at Torquay, England.

CANADA AT TORQUAY

The Torquay negotiations, held between November 1950 and April 1951, were the third round of multilateral tariff discussions among the participating countries of the GATT and the first following the untimely demise of the ITO. That created complications for most delegations as they struggled to make the GATT fit into a context for which it was not, strictly speaking, intended. While most accepted the changed circumstances with good grace, Britain, almost alone of the important trading nations, expressed a certain hesitation. War in Korea had broken out in June 1950 and the Western world, led by the United States, took action against the perceived threat from international communism. This created problems for some European economies, such as the British, leading to inflationary pressures and, ultimately, another UK dollar crisis as rearmament took on a new meaning. Partly as a result, the negotiations undertaken among the ABC triad were fraught with difficulty. Indeed, in a severe set-back, no agreement had been reached between Britain and the United States by the end of the Torquay conference.

Failure to reach agreement had much to do with the domestic condition of the British. By 1951 they were immersed in the difficulties of their third, and worst, dollar crisis since the war, this one partly caused by Korea-inspired rearmament, and London expressed a marked reluctance to consider further reductions in the structure of imperial preference. There was also much speculation that, with a majority of only three in the House of Commons, the Labour government was not going to jeopardize its position and provide fodder for the Conservative opposition during an upcoming election. It had no intention of sacrificing imperial preference on the alter of multilateralism: as the *London Times* pointed out, Prime Minister Attlee had no wish to be stuck defending his government against "new charges of selling out the Empire."[50]

However, Labour Party problems did not deter the United States from launching an attack on UK policy, as it had done on every possible occasion since 1932. But the more the Americans pushed, the more the British resisted. The president of the Board of Trade, Harold Wilson, travelled to Torquay several times to urge that no margins of preference be given up. As a result, Deutsch felt that at Torquay Britain was "more rigid ... than at Geneva" on the subject of imperial preference. [51] He was correct, but by 1951 the United Kingdom was convinced that it had been precipitous in agreeing to the no-new-preference rule in the first place. Britain was no closer to multilateralism and non-discrimination than it had been for several years prior to Torquay, a very disappointing fact of economic life. More than ever, it relied on the sterling area and the preferences that held the area together. One reflection of this was the increase in British exports to the area, from 45 per cent of total British exports to about 48 per cent between 1946 and 1950. Rather than limiting the use of preferences, the United Kingdom now wanted to extend them. Moreover, the no-new-preference rule had generated a good deal of opposition to the GATT in the United Kingdom. To many it represented "a practically unilateral concession on [Britain's] part entirely different both quantitatively and qualitatively from anything which was provided for in the document [at Geneva] by way of concessions on the part of others."[52]

The UK delegation therefore refused even reasonable offers that affected the *principle* of imperial preference. For example, Canada had agreed to release the United Kingdom and other Commonwealth countries from any obligations that would have prevented those countries from meeting American requests. However, the US delegation complained, "even in the case of items (such as canned salmon) on which the preference *was bound only to Canada*, and on which Canada had granted releases, the UK refused to make any offer."[53] The perception on the US side was that the British would settle for nothing less than "the grant by the United States of all or nearly all ... [of the] controversial offers, which made up the bulk of the requests the United Kingdom had made on the United States." They wanted concessions on such items as woolen and cotton textiles, leather, and china and earthenware, with "other good offers thrown in," without offering anything substantial in return.[54] The UK strategy was to gain an agreement with the United States that reflected the postwar imbalance in trade between the two and, as London had earlier made clear, one that was consistent with the broad objectives of the September 1949 tripartite talks. However valid and just British demands were, such an unbalanced agreement was impossible, something the Americans had already indicated: Congress would never approve it and the administration would be left defending a politically impossible situation.

Instead, the US delegation urged the British to consider joint action – the United States would lower its tariffs against certain sterling area goods while the United Kingdom would undertake to phase out imperial preferences. But that, for the latter, was politically impossible. When the British refused to budge, continuing to demand an unbalanced agreement as late as March 1951, the US ambassador in London was instructed to communicate to the Attlee government that such tactics would not bear fruit. It was emphasized that if the British were not more forthcoming on the general issue of Commonwealth preference it was a distinct possibility that no agreement would be reached, regardless of the damage such a result might inflict on the GATT.[55] By the end of March, both sides had gone as far as they could and, despite a last-minute appeal by UK negotiator Sir Stephen Holmes, Anglo-American negotiations were terminated. The attitude had "been bad and bitter from the outset"; there would be no agreement.[56]

Canada was also experiencing difficulties with the United Kingdom. For example, the British had requested that all Commonwealth delegations meet in London to coordinate strategy for the upcoming GATT conference. As London had noted, it was impossible for Commonwealth negotiators at Torquay to secure maximum advantage from their individual bargaining power unless they all knew from the start what the others had to offer. To the British, the pre-Torquay meeting would play an essential role in the success of what were implied to be *Commonwealth* negotiations. Ottawa disagreed and, while a Canadian delegation eventually attended, cabinet initially insisted that on no account was External Affairs to send Canada's offers to the United Kingdom in advance of the meeting. Still, as the British complained in a post-conference brief, even with prior consultation, the Canadians remained unsympathetic to UK objectives throughout the actual negotiations.

Once the meetings were underway, the United Kingdom put pressure directly on Ottawa through Sir Alexander Clutterbuck, its high commissioner, regarding Canada's willingness to negotiate on preferences. It seemed that the British were most concerned over the serious effect a reduction in Commonwealth preferences would have on sterling area solidarity and on an RSA commitment to see Britain through its latest dollar crisis. In a letter from Clutterbuck to Pearson, the British indicated an increasing anxiety "at the way in which certain of the tariff negotiations now in progress at Torquay are developing and particularly about their possible effect on the margins of preference enjoyed by some major items of UK goods normally exported to Canada."[57] In view of Canadian discussions with the United States and other interested third parties, the matter was, as the letter suggested, one of some urgency. In concrete terms, London was particularly concerned over preference reductions to earthenware goods, rayon yarns, machinery, and iron and steel manufactures.

The British manoeuvre did not evoke a sympathetic response and the minister of Finance, Douglas Abbott, refused to carry on parallel negotiations to those going on in England. Torquay, not Ottawa, was where the British should make their representations. While his government was concerned about the course of Anglo-Canadian negotiations, and about trade as a whole, it was not ready to compromise its position with respect to the United States or any other country that offered suitable compensation. The Canadian policy remained that the government had never regarded preferential arrangements "as entirely inflexible in nature, or as operating in a manner which constitutes an impediment to the achievement of that wider area of international cooperation which is always desirable."[58] Commonwealth preferences were not set in stone in Ottawa.

After three months, the Torquay negotiations had not produced any real results. From the Canadian point of view, they could only have been retrieved by a successful conclusion to the UK-US tariff negotiations. One negotiator, Finance's Simon Reisman, admitted that the Canadian delegation felt it would have done much better had it not even come to Torquay but conducted a separate Canada-US negotiation at a higher level. He felt it would not have been overly difficult "to work a big deal" with Washington "if we had access to the top people."[59] While the delegation was merely halfway through a six-month negotiating session under the aegis of the multilateral GATT, some within the group were prepared to shift their focus to a bilateral deal with their southern neighbour and resurrect the spirit of 1947.

Reisman was correct that it was difficult to negotiate within the agreement, and this applied equally to Canadian-American discussions. They had been fitful since early December 1950 when both sides had completed a preliminary review of their situations. By early February 1951 the Canadians were convinced that only a small, largely symbolic agreement was possible. If that happened, and given that the United Kingdom and the United States did not come to an acceptable conclusion, then "the whole Torquay business [would] fall flat."[60] As well, the Canadians could not begin discussions with the Benelux countries until the United States had responded to Canadian offers: most of the items of interest to those countries figured in the probable offers to the United States in the event that Washington accepted an agreement with Canada.

A North American agreement continued to be elusive. Indeed, by mid-March the situation had "taken a turn for the worse."[61] Two weeks before the conference ended, Reisman noted that "we are farther away from an accord with the United States" than early in February. It was a distinct possibility that agreement would be reached on only three of the eleven items that the Canadian delegation had regarded as the nucleus of a solid arrangement with Washington. It was not impossible that Canada would not achieve any success with the United States and, given the way events were unfolding, almost a certainty that no agreement would be reached with the Benelux countries. Finally, while Reisman was sanguine about the possibility of an agreement with France, Germany, and Italy, this would not be substantial. After six months of difficult negotiation, there would be little to show. As Torquay wound down, so too did the Canadians: the frustration and anxiety of working in a difficult environment caused morale problems and, as Reisman noted, "general low spirits."[62]

The United States, however, regarded the Canadian negotiation as vital, both in terms of North American relations and because of Canada's willingness to negotiate on preferences. With respect to the former, the acting American chief, Carl Corse, pointed out to W.T.M. Beale, the acting chief of commercial policy staff, in mid-March that a breakdown in negotiations with their northern neighbour would adversely affect Canadian enthusiasm for North American defence cooperation under the principles of the Hyde Park

Agreement reaffirmed in October 1950. And, Corse noted, an agreement would increase the degree of integration of the two North American economies. On the issue of preferences, Canada's commitment not to stand in the way of reductions by members of the sterling area of preferences it enjoyed in their markets was a tremendous incentive for other Commonwealth countries to conclude successful agreements with the United States.[63]

Corse urged that the issue of a Canadian-American agreement, largely on Canada's terms, be discussed at the highest levels in the Departments of State, Treasury, Defense, Agriculture, Commerce, and the Interior; no stone should be left unturned in convincing the relevant bureaucrats and politicians of the necessity of acceding to Canadian demands. In the end, the Americans returned with a list of negotiable items that included much of what the Canadians wanted. The final agreement contained some 400 items of interest to Canadian exporters, sales of which had totalled some $120 million in 1949.[64] The Canadian delegation had reason to be satisfied: it had held firm and won much of what it wanted.

As for the remainder of the negotiations, there was little that could be said. At Geneva in 1947 213 sets of bilateral negotiations had been completed, while at Annecy in 1949 147 had been concluded. Greater things had been expected of Torquay, given the large number of countries participating. It was hoped that 400 separate discussions would be initiated but, as it turned out, fewer than 200 were started and only 147 were completed, the same number as at Annecy.[65] A more ominous development was the increasing use of tariffs and NTBs as instruments for protection of domestic industries and agriculture. With respect to the former, sixteen CPs made use of Article XXVIII, which allowed members to modify or withdraw any tariff concession given at Geneva or Annecy. Among the countries resorting to its use were some of Canada's largest overseas markets such as Britain, the Benelux group, France, and Italy. In total, almost 300 concessions were withdrawn or modified. The *International Financial News Survey* noted that, because of this phenomenon, "the difficulties encountered in lowering rates of duty are probably greater today than at any time since the end of the war."[66]

If, as some had proposed, trees were to be planted in commemoration of the conference, then the *Economist* suggested a "'Gattery' of weeping willows would be appropriate."[67] The air of optimism that had prevailed in September 1950 as the contracting parties first gathered was largely dissipated. The divisions between countries and blocs were too significant to be overcome and international trade showed few signs of returning to any unrestricted patterns.

Deutsch, an important member of the Canadian delegation, echoed those sentiments. In his estimation, Torquay had been "a total bust, except for Canada and the US." But as a bureaucrat who had been heavily involved in the Ottawa-Washington free trade negotiations in 1947–48 and hoped that perhaps the GATT would accomplish what the continentalists in Canada had been unable to achieve, he saw that as a promising development. In his analysis, the multilateral world was "dead for the visible future and Torquay [was] its tombstone." [68] Other Canadian officials spoke privately of the "failure of Torquay," most feeling that it would lead to the end of the GATT.[69] As for the attitudes of the major contracting parties, Deutsch suggested that the United States was "bitter" about the failure of the tariff negotiations, while the British persisted in clinging "to their sterling cage and would impoverish themselves thereby." Certainly the prospect of a fourth round announced so optmistically in September for Toronto in 1953 was quietly forgotten as the various delegations packed up and left for home.

LOW TARIFFS VS HIGH TARIFFS AT TORQUAY

While trade negotiations were taking place at Torquay, the very difficult question of intra-European tariff disparities was also being worked out away from the central discussions. This issue was one that went back some months and had caused increasing acrimony among several members of the European dominated Organization for European Economic Cooperation (OEEC) which spilled over to affect the GATT. It was discussed at Torquay and the undercurrent of tension generated had an adverse impact on the conference. Active efforts on the part of low-tariff European countries to find some solution to the European tariff disparities problem went back to early 1950. The low-tariff group had little to bargain with, however, and found itself at a distinct disadvantage because "their domestic industries would have to accept the competition of industries protected by high tariffs, thus preventing them from competing abroad in foreign markets."[70] As table 4 illustrates, there was a large discrepancy in tariff rates.

Even under the auspices of the GATT, the bilateral conduct of negotiations had hampered countries with low rates in their attempts to obtain overall reductions in the high levels assessed by neighbouring countries. As the "Memorandum by the Delegations of the Benelux Countries on European Tariff Negotiations" had pointed out, "Even if a low tariff country obtained the reduction of a high

Table 4
Unweighted index of tariff levels of selected countries

Country	Unweighted Index of Tariff Level
Denmark	2.0
Benelux	9.1
Norway	9.3
United Kingdom	16.3
France	22.2
Italy	23.4
Germany	26.5

Source: W.S. Woytinsky and E.S. Woytinsky, World Commerce and Governments, (New York: The Twentieth Century Fund, 1955), 284.

duty from one of its neighbours, in exchange for the *binding* of its low duty, it would still be left facing the high rates of its other neighbours. What is more, it would by the binding of its low rate have lost part of its bargaining power. With no compensation, high tariff countries such as Italy, France and the United Kingdom were loath to negotiate with their low tariff partners."

Speaking for the low-tariff Benelux bloc, D.P. Spierenburg, the head of the Dutch delegation at Torquay, noted that although his country's ultimate aim was to obtain a free interchange of goods and services and do away with all restrictions on international trade, Holland might be forced to reimpose certain quantitative restrictions if the tariff problem was not addressed.

The Dutch had a point which, it was generally conceded, "went to the very root of the General Agreement." According to Wilgress, the great risk "was that there might be a move toward increasing low tariffs to compensate for high tariffs."[71] Given such a probability, the implications for the GATT were very grim – it had been developed to protect against just that sort of development. It was Wilgress' fear that if the problem was not solved, the agreement could very easily be wrecked. Indeed, the Dutch had succeeded through the OEEC in obtaining the adoption of certain provisions in the organization's liberalization code which could operate to relieve low-tariff countries of their trade liberalization commitments in the event that other European countries retained their high tariffs; as the memorandum flatly stated, the Benelux countries would not liberalize beyond the 60 per cent OEEC level. This was formalized in a resolution adopted by the organization in late October 1950.

The disparities in tariffs was an intruding feature in GATT discussions: unless action was taken, the Benelux countries insisted they would refuse to rebind the Geneva and Annecy tariff schedules and sign the Torquay Protocol. While Canada did not have any direct stake in the resolution of the problem, it was very concerned about the outcome, particularly if it led to increased protectionism. As an American analysis of Ottawa's position noted, Canadian action would be "determined almost entirely by its calculation as to the degree of risk which any course entails in the development of a European preferential bloc."[72] As a result, Canada greatly preferred the dispute to be arbitrated within the organization that was at least ostensibly dedicated to the achievement of a *multilateral and non-discriminatory* world, the GATT, as opposed to the *European* OEEC; any OEEC-sponsored resolution would place "greater emphasis ... on an exclusively European solution, perhaps in conflict with GATT principles."[73] The tariff disparities question was, however, not settled at Torquay and dragged on for a number of years, becoming an issue in the 1956 Geneva round. It was one more vitiating element in European relationships within the GATT that had a negative impact on trade relations in general.

THE CANADIAN REACTION TO TORQUAY

As a result of Torquay, there was a distinct coolness toward the GATT in Canada. Certainly interest such as that following the first tariff round in Geneva was non-existent. In a post-mortem meeting of the Interdepartmental Committee on External Trade Policy (ICETP) on 25 June 1951, attended by some American observers, a senior bureaucrat Hector McKinnon, offered three reasons for this change of attitude.[74] First, he pointed out that the failure of the US Congress to ratify the ITO charter in 1950 had been interpreted by Ottawa to be a sign that the United States was losing interest in multilateralism and non-discrimination, at least as established under the ITO's aegis. Similarly, congressional failure to to act on the Customs Simplification Bill, which had been agreed to in principle at the September 1949 tripartite talks, seemed to indicate a lack of American commitment to freeing international trade from the red tape that sometimes threatened it more than QRs and tariffs. Finally, the discouraging character of the amendments to the Trade Agreements Act suggested that the United States had moved "as far as it was likely to do toward trade liberalization and that there probably would be a reversal from now on of the trend in recent years."[75] All in all, it was a rather depressing picture. When the Americans asked for a statement from the ICETP that reaffirmed support for the economic objectives of the GATT, the consensus among the Canadians was that a repudiation was more likely than a reaffirmation. As ICETP Chairman Norman Robertson noted, "Circumstances did not seem to be promising."[76]

But, by its very nature, a repudiation of multilateralism and the GATT meant a growing acceptance of what Canadian policy makers such as Deutsch had long preached, namely increasing continentalization in economic matters. More and more, Canada was in step with its southern neighbour as Europe and the United Kingdom refused to reduce tariff and non-tariff barriers to trade. As Deutsch presciently pointed out to Bruce Hutchison of the *Free Press* in the aftermath of Torquay, "since the British [and Europeans would not] trade, the pressure to combine the trade of Canada and the US [would] increase."[77]

While Deutsch and McKinnon, among others, welcomed this development, many in the bureaucracy and cabinet remained uneasy. For example, Pearson had warned of the obvious risks to Canadian sovereignty posed by an intimate economic relationship with the United States. But to have refused an agreement would have surely bordered on the absurd. Canada had negotiated well with the United States within the confines of the multilateral GATT without conceding overly much. The country desperately needed markets for its expanding economy and could simply not afford to reject what amounted to an American overture. It was dependent upon exports and had to search out buyers where it could. With the potential of some traditional markets greatly reduced for various reasons, the United States represented security in a way that Britain and Western Europe did not.

From his vantage point in Paris as a member of the Canadian delegation to the OEEC, Louis Couillard of the Department of External Affairs articulated what some in government feared and knew to be true, "the road to the once sacred objective of non-discriminatory multilateral trade [was] being detoured more and more in view of the continuing disequilibria and the growing maze of artificial controls."[78] *That* was the reality and, much as it might have tried, the Canadian delegation at Torquay could not change that fact. Enshrining non-discriminatory principles in international documents remained a long-term objective.

CONCLUSION

Despite the hopes placed in the GATT during the first five years postwar, the institution was a marked disappointment to Canadian multilateralists. If the first round of tariff negotiations at Geneva had marked the high point of international cooperation, Torquay represented the ebb-tide. During this critical period for Canada, there was no re-establishment of equilibrium in international transactions, which had been shattered by the war. Indeed, the Second World War had reduced the pattern of world trade and capital movements "to a heap of rubble" that by 1950 showed few signs of regaining any firm structure.[79] As a result of the widespread use of NTBs and discrimination against dollar products, tariff reductions negotiated with the Continent remained relatively meaningless – they were not put into widespread use. And by 1951 Canadians were less inclined to be charitable in ascribing motives for European non-tariff barriers. Indeed, the imbalance in GATT trade benefits had become "highly irksome to commercial and political interests" in Canada"[80]

By 1951, much of the enthusiasm for GATT and ITO had dissipated. The ITO charter had never been submitted to a vote in the US Congress and, without United States support, the organization was dead. The GATT operated in its stead. "The whole pattern of what emerged as the General Agreement on Tariffs and Trade was determined by the relations between the President and the Congress and resulted in a form which found its justification in expediency rather than logic."[81] As well, while tariffs were declining, non-tariff barriers to trade were intensifying. They were especially inimical to Canadian exports and proved much more intransigent than tariffs. With the increased popularity of quantitative restrictions and exchange controls it mattered little, the *Economist* noted, "whether ... goods [were] liable to a duty of 50 or 500 per cent."[82] Moreover, the GATT itself remained in a state of unofficial limbo until the mid-1950s, awaiting American approval.

Canadian hopes for a multilateral and non-discriminatory world had been dashed by the reality of the postwar context. Not surprisingly, the rarefied atmosphere of Bretton Woods had been replaced by a more earth-bound attitude of national interest, an unhappy development that became most evident throughout the course of the three early tariff rounds held under the auspices of the GATT at Geneva (1947), Annecy, France (1949), and Torquay, England (1950–51). As Robert Hudec has pointed out, "GATT could really not escape the larger world political situation any more than its governments could."[83]

It was ironic that what was intended as a "multilateral and non-discriminatory" agreement drew Canada closer to the United States. However, even agreements with the United States were not as binding as Canadians hoped. There was always the peril point clause to deal with and, after Torquay ended Congress enacted another similar escape clause provision, which was incorporated into the Trade Agreements Extension Act of 1951 to protect US producers. If an aggrieved party could demonstrate that as a result of tariff reductions imports increased dramatically "either actual or relative, or to cause or threaten serious injury to the domestic industry producing like or directly competitive products," then that tariff concession had to be withdrawn.[84] Despite these problems, there were no real alternatives and, as the *Economist* pointed out, Canadians had come to see Canada-US trade as "nothing to be afraid of." [85] With the occurence of what could only be described as the failure of the multilateral option as far as Canada was concerned, a bilateral North American economic relationship was the only real option – and why tamper with prosperity?

3 "Hold That Line": Continued Dollar Discrimination, 1950–57

The years following 1950 proved to be critical in terms of the Anglo-Canadian trade relationship. The war in Korea, which began in June 1950, imposed a burden on all of Canada's allies, but particularly on the British. Re-arming caused a sharp burst of inflation and a world-wide shortage of certain raw materials, many of which were available only from the dollar area. This resulted in increased prices, which contributed materially to balance of payments and dollar crises in Britain during 1951. Determined to lessen the impact of these developments, the Labour government and, after October 1951, the Conservative government of Winston Churchill, intensified import restrictions against dollar goods.

Since 1945 that had been the approach adopted by the United Kingdom when confronted with dollar difficulties. Canadians firmly believed that such a policy, dealt "with symptoms rather than with the underlying causes of the problem." Restrictions "[did] not provide a solution ... [and had] undesirable effects on the structure of the economy which aggravate[d] the problem and [made] the achievement of a lasting solution more difficult."[1] As a result of its constant iterance of the dangers of protectionism and its moral certainty regarding the debilitating effects of restriction and discrimination, Ottawa was often regarded as a *bête noire* at meetings with the British. The British were no more interested in listening to Canadian lectures and moralizing on the necessity of multilateralism and non-discrimination during the early 1950s than they had been in the 1940s. But by this time the UK problems and their effect on

Canadian exports mattered less and less to Canada. With American rearmament and the continuing development of a continental economy, more of the country's goods were travelling south than ever before. And unlike the situation with Britain, forecasts promised more of the same. Many Canadians rejoiced in the publication of William Paley's seminal report, *Resources for Freedom*, that foresaw a 400 per cent increase in American imports of industrial raw materials, many of which would be obtained in Canada.[2]

By mid-decade, Canada was settling into a role as the northern supplier of various resources to US industry. And, to complement these exports, Canada's imports of US goods stabilized at approximately two-thirds of total purchases. A similar pattern was evident in terms of investment: billions of American dollars poured in which were much welcomed by Canadians who needed outside financial assistance. Ottawa also actively sought out UK capital but was largely unsuccessful as British investors preferred the sterling area where they could place money freely without having to navigate the tangled web of British exchange controls. The Canadian government could live with that, however, even given a rather alarming dependence on the United States; with the UK disinterest in Canada, there was no alternative.

GROWING CANADIAN FRUSTRATION

Anglo-Canadian trade relations continued to decline during 1950, despite some evidence of improvement in the British economy. By the second quarter, the sterling area's net gold and dollar surplus amounted to $180 million, an increase of $140 million over the first quarter and $812 million over the first quarter of 1949. The chancellor of the Exchequer, Sir Stafford Cripps, noted two factors that contributed to Britain's happier state. The first, and perhaps more important, involved improvements outside his control, such as the recovery of sterling area sales to dollar countries. In particular, he cited the continued high level of demand in the United States for raw materials at prices considerably higher than in 1949. As well, the increase in UK exports to Canada had helped to ease his country's situation. He attributed the second factor to the Labour government's "own policies and actions," including here developments such as the "positive encouragement" that had been given to exports to the dollar area in general and the retrenchment that had dominated sterling area policy in its dollar imports. While cuts on the order of $800 million per year would have satisfied the undertaking given at the Commonwealth finance ministers' meeting of July 1949, the eventual reduction in dollar imports was more than $1 billion. The devaluation that had been announced in September 1949 had also helped make British goods more competitive with those of the dollar area.

However, the chancellor also noted some less favourable aspects. The major part of the increase in British reserves was directly attributable to the assistance being given Britain under the ERP. Cripps cautioned the House that the amount of aid available from ERP in 1950–51 would be less than in 1949–50 and the entire program would end in 1952. He also noted that "the exceptional accretion of funds following devaluation cannot continue indefinitely." Dollar imports into the sterling area had been running well below the established limit, and some increase was inevitable. Finally, inflation was again becoming a problem for the United Kingdom, a development which threatened the benefits of the September 1949 devaluation.[3]

Cripps argued that the United Kingdom's dollar position, however much improved it might be, was not strong. Given the crises of 1947 and 1949, he was adamant that the country's gold and dollar reserves had to be increased and this meant continued dollar restriction. As a result, Cripps showed no signs of compromise on the subject of economic relations with Canada. Indeed, he promised more of the same unpalatable restrictionist diet that Ottawa found so distasteful.

As had been the case throughout the postwar period, the Canadian government was frustrated by what it saw as an uncooperative British attitude: a meeting of senior mandarins had concluded that it was unrealistic to assume "any significant increase in US dollar earnings from overseas," despite continued Canadian attempts to sell more in Britain and Western Europe. The important consideration was the unemployment that would be created if markets for manufactured goods and specialized agricultural products were lost. The deputy ministers of those departments most involved with export trade worried about this issue throughout late 1949. It was their considered opinion that "the outlook for 1950 was not promising." In the report of the Cabinet Committee on Economic Policy to cabinet, the committee observed that "our problems in meeting unemployment are likely to be more severely complicated by export and balance of payments difficulties than appeared likely in 1949. If we get into serious difficulties it will be in considerable part due to limitations on export markets which, in light of recent experience, will be very difficult to overcome directly."[4] As the committee recognized, the Canadian economy was geared to exports; it would be disastrous to lose existing markets where Canadian trade had been curtailed, let alone potential ones which the GATT promised for the future.

However, Canadians were losing in both markets. The problems associated with the sale of newsprint and agricultural products in overseas markets were symptomatic of Canadian difficulties over a wide range of goods. During the first six months of 1950, London refused to release any dollars to buy newsprint, prompting even the *Economist* to question British strategy. The decision not to buy in Canada, it said, demonstrated a marked lack of foresight: it took no account of "the past, the future, nor of Britain's good relations with Canada." Canadian suppliers for their part had "behaved generously" and now had every reason "to feel that they have been badly treated."[5]

A statistical analysis of market share prepared in 1949 by the Department of Finance showed that in the prewar period overseas markets, primarily the United Kingdom, had taken about 18 per cent of Canadian newsprint production. By 1946, this total had fallen to approximately 14 per cent and by 1949 it was down to eight. The result of this downward spiral was shaken confidence among producers in a continuing market in the UK.[6] By early 1950, the American market was saturated and the potential for increased newsprint exports to the United States was bleak. That market could not absorb the tonnages released by British and European reductions, which left Canada with large stocks of unsold newsprint and unused capacity in the mills. More troublesome were prospects for the future. If overseas markets were lost because of currency difficulties, it was unlikely that they would ever be regained, given the peculiarities of the newsprint industry. And if history had taught Canadian pulp producers anything it was that "American publishers ... [were] not dilatory in exploiting any over-supply to depress prices, to the serious detriment of the newsprint industry in Canada."[7]

By late 1950, however, given the changed circumstances resulting from by the Korean War, the United States was taking all the newsprint that Canada could produce and the doubts about publisher behaviour had disappeared. Indeed, when the British suddenly needed an extra 100,000 tons of Canadian newsprint in late 1950, there was some difficulty in obtaining it, even when they offered a firm three-year contract for 400,000 tons. Canada House refused to assist, despite the personal intervention of the president of the Board of Trade, Harold Wilson. Nor would the minister of Trade and Commerce, C.D. Howe, or his department get involved. The unilateral abrogation by Britain of long-term newsprint contracts with Canada in mid-1947 still rankled and Ottawa could now take "revenge" as Canadian mills "were sold out."[8] London was told that in light of recent experience, producers were not prepared "to sacrifice for the United Kingdom market."[9]

Agricultural products were even more problematic. A 1949 Trade and Commerce report had warned that the United Kingdom's long-term plans called for a sharp decrease in imports from Canada. By 1952, the United Kingdom hoped to be in a position to purchase from Canada only those commodities that were not obtainable in the sterling area. If that materialized, the "situation [would] call for drastic revision in Canada's foreign policy with respect to exports of agricultural commodities." The Department of Trade and Commerce had also assessed the potential of the US market as a destination for Canadian agricultural goods. Its conclusions were not encouraging: Canada could not expect "a satisfactory outlet for major exportable agricultural products into the United States." But more to the point, the United States was a major competitor with Canada for the ERP market and elsewhere. The memo noted that with the expectation of the second largest grain crop in US history competition between North Americans would increase. Nor was there any relief in sight for Canadian producers. Continued subsidies paid to American farmers would ensure that a "fairly high level of production would continue in the United States."[10]

Subsidies and the ERP guaranteed that American farmers would make inroads into what Canadians had thought of as their markets. For example, the United States had assured markets for approximately 12 million tons of bread grains per year for the next five years in Western Europe, about twice Canada's potential sales. Further, in the 1950–51 European Cooperation Administration (ECA) estimates of UK wheat imports from North America showed, the United States as providing Britain with $117 million worth as compared with $150 million from Canada. While the Canadian total was somewhat larger, based on past experience it should have been *much* larger. If the forecasts were correct, US food exports to Britain would rise from $45 million to $150 million by 1951 while Canadian food exports would drop from $378 million to $195 million.[11] Canada vigorously protested the ECA estimates but there was little it could do other than rely on American (and British) goodwill.

To that end, the United Kingdom was pressed to import from Canada, especially in light of the improvement in its balance of payments situation. The general British response, however, was to explain that the present favourable dollar position could only be regarded as temporary. Rather than relaxing import restrictions, they felt they must retain them because sterling area reserves were still too low. That policy was carried out with extreme thoroughness and dollar imports were pruned to the minimum. Such greatly reduced levels had implications for delivery times and quantities. As the deputy minister of Agriculture, J.G. Taggart, explained to a British UKCCC delegation in June 1950, since Canadian exports of bacon to Britain, for example, now amounted to only ten per cent of total bacon production, it would not be possible to make regular deliveries; most would come at the end of the season. But despite the comparatively small volumes of bacon and other "traditional" commodities such as cheese, apples, and honey being exported to the United Kingdom, both Taggart and Deputy Minister of Trade and Commerce M.W. Mackenzie emphasized the symbolic and political significance of the British market. Canada had always included Britain among her best customers and it was difficult to conceive of any other situation. Moreover, with the Conservative opposition hammering the government over the decline of Anglo-Canadian trade, it was important that "Canada should not be [totally] excluded [from UK markets]."[12]

The British attitude reflected the official policy of continuing retrenchment, despite vastly improved conditions. That, more than anything, contributed to a feeling of disillusionment on the Canadian side: despite its healthier reserves, London was unwilling to move even part way toward addressing Canadian concerns. Throughout 1950, Westminister took every opportunity to ensure that its view prevailed among the RSA with respect to trade with dollar countries. Most important, the area agreed in May, with certain reservations, to maintain trade at 75 per cent of the 1948 import level, as decided the previous July.

After the United Nations "police action" in Korea began, however, rearmament required increased spending by the West. The war also raised fears about Soviet intentions in Western Europe, prompting Canada to send a brigade and eleven full-strength air squadrons to the Continent as its contribution to NATO at considerable expense to federal coffers. Indeed, the defence budget increased to eleven per cent of net national income in 1951.[13] Similarly, the British strengthened their defence presence in Europe and also agreed to spend more dollars to stockpile raw materials and purchase military equipment to meet new commitments. As a result, prices of those commodities in demand rose dramatically, to the point where the new chancellor of the Exchequer, Hugh Gaitskell, noted that import costs would be up by at least £350 million in 1951. That sort of forecast terrified the British Cabinet, and the government attempted to secure an RSA promise that any modifications in the sterling area system would be held to a minimum. The Canadian high commissioner in the United Kingdom, Dana Wilgress, suggested to Ottawa that Gaitskell "clearly wanted the other [area] countries to agree to limit their dollar imports according to some generally accepted formula."[14]

The chancellor's limit was an allowance of ten per cent. He was unsure that UK exports would exceed £2.3 billion in 1951, compared with an import program of about £2.7 billion, an inflated figure that owed much to rearmament. The result would again be a large deficit, with invisible income like payments from overseas investments not large enough to offset the import estimate. A paper circulated by Gaitskell to Commonwealth delegations during a meeting of finance ministers in London in September 1950 asserted that, even with an increase in invisible income, "the conclusion is inescapable that we face the prospect of a rapid deterioration of our overall balance of payments and the re-emergence of a deficit in place of the current surplus."[15] At a minimum, the chancellor insisted that the area should increase its reserves two- or three-fold from the current $2.75 billion.

However, there was now a certain amount of RSA restlessness over British policy. While agreeing in the abstract that it was desirable to continue to build up the central reserve, several countries remained committed to ambitious development programs. In particular, India, Pakistan, and Ceylon were adamant about the need for material progress to raise the standard of living of their people. The southern dominions, Australia, New Zealand, and Southern Rhodesia, also disapproved of what they considered to be an overly harsh regimen and pressed for continued high investment in their countries. They felt that development should not be hampered "by undue rigidity in their dollar expenditures."[16] Gaitskill discovered that it was impossible "to obtain agreement to any formula limiting Commonwealth dollar expenditure."[17] While the reaction of the RSA to further British demands could not be construed as rebellion, it did represent dissatisfaction. For sensible reasons, the sterling area was unwilling to give up or postpone plans in favour of British rearmament; some chinks in area solidarity were beginning to appear.

However, whatever the RSA attitude, London intended to intensify restrictions against dollar imports, prompting the governor of the Bank of Canada, Graham Towers, to respond. Certainly, he noted, Canada recognized both the trials which the British had experienced in the five years since 1945 and those which loomed large in the immediate future: import costs were rising, Marshall Plan aid was being reduced, and the outflow of capital to the sterling area continued unabated. Those were all serious and perplexing issues. But the situation was not completely bleak. Towers noted that world trade had improved dramatically during 1950, eliminating the vast dollar deficits of mid-1949. The massive export surpluses of the United States were also at a more manageable level, as was the general trade position of the United States *vis-à-vis* the rest of the world.

Canada was now in a much better economic state than it had been during the later 1940s. Between 1945 and 1947, both its dollar deficit and overseas surplus had been very large. Since July 1949, however, the country's US dollar deficit was relatively small while its surplus with the rest of the world was slightly larger, leaving it "in [virtual] balance for the first year for which there are records." That was a change of the first magnitude. Imports from the UK had risen from $186 million in 1947 to more than $400 million by 1950. From the RSA, the increase had been from $157 million to $243 million. As a consequence, the US share of the Canadian market had dropped from 77 to 67 per cent. That was an encouraging development which policymakers in Ottawa, ever conscious of Canada's tremendous dependence on the US market, hoped would continue.

The heart of Towers's presentation lay in his criticism of the effect continued British restriction was having on the sterling area economy. It was inevitable that armaments-induced inflation, would be communicated to the RSA, which would make the area even less competitive with the outside world. In short, Towers concluded that the dollar risks of introducing a greater measure of non-discrimination were not as great as the British supposed. He was not advocating a full-scale changeover from restriction to wide-open trade, but rather asked if "there could not be a move in that direction?"[18]

The answer was no, for London remained totally preoccupied with the dollar problem and uninterested in addressing its *overall* balance of payments and external liability problems, although, as the Canadians pointed out, there was no one perfect time to liberalize. As Douglas Abbott later told Gaitshell, if steps were not taken "until it [was] clear that no risks [were] involved, they [would] certainly be long delayed."[19] To that, Gaitskell would probably have replied "Amen."

Canadian predictions of RSA problems were accurate, given the demands that were building up within the area. Inflationary pressures were intensifying, while the British concentration on rearmament and the concomitant reduction in exports to the RSA were leading to increases in sterling balances (up some £130 million in the first half of 1950) to the extent that they could have "serious implications for the economic stability of the UK."[20] Accumulated balances in sterling area countries would be used to purchase goods in either the United Kingdom or other area countries. Those additional demands on British products would increase the upward pressure on prices and contribute to further inflation. Canada remained convinced that relaxation of import restrictions would relieve British difficulties to some extent and that some liberalization was well within the capability of the United Kingdom. While it was estimated that the UK dollar deficit would be slightly more than $1 billion in 1951–52, as compared with $6 million in 1950, the RSA dollar surplus would be approximately $1.085 billion in 1951–52 as against $788 million in 1950. The *total* sterling area deficit for 1951–52 was forecast to be a paltry $33 million.

In view of these figures, it was Ottawa's position that United Kingdom and RSA importers should be allowed to "shop around" within the dollar area, as such a concession would greatly relieve inflationary pressure in the sterling area. Further, as Abbott explained, such a step "would be in our mutual interest ... it is particularly desirable that the impediments to the freer flow of goods between our countries be reduced to a minimum ... [and] it may well be that a growing number of the remaining restrictions [would be] rendered ineffective by the lack of supplies and that others will have restrictive effects that become increasingly undesirable."[21] However, the British were not in an experimental mood. With a very slim majority in the House of Commons, the Labour government was not prepared to undertake a major new initiative in the field of foreign trade policy. As well, there was a general perception that the UK economy was very tight, finely balanced, and lacking in resilience. By December 1950, the situation had deteriorated. It had been aggravated by a rise in the price of imports which had outpaced the increase in export prices: rubber and wool prices had trebled while the price of tin had doubled. As well, the index of prices of imports into Britain in February 1951 was already 25 per cent higher than the average of 1950, and 50 per cent higher than 1949.[22] This created a serious upward wage-price spiral that increased the difficulty of holding inflationary pressures in check.

Because of the problems being experienced in the UK economy, Anglo-Canadian trade suffered one reverse after another. The British *Economic Survey for 1951* cast doubt on increased trade, suggesting that the country's gold and dollar situation would inevitably deteriorate if RSA needs were to be met and rearmament to continue. As Gaitskell pointed out in a letter to Abbott, Britain's overall sol-

vency was at stake. This meant continuing to husband dollar resources because, in the chancellor's mind, the most important element in Britain's worsening balance of payments situation was its
deficit with the dollar area.

The UKCCC met again in May 1951 and the Canadian delegation
learned that the British would not reduce import restrictions. However, the United Kingdom did want more Canadian raw materials
to meet its defence commitments; Korea-inspired demand had created a whole new situation. Indeed, the under-secretary of the Treasury, R.W.B. Clarke, pointed out that obtaining an increase in raw
material production "was now as pressing a problem ... as had
previously been that of the dollar balance of payments."[23] British
plans called for a four per cent increase in industrial activity which
would be jeopardized if they did not receive deliveries of necessary
primary products. Otherwise, Clarke noted with a hint of blackmail,
there could be "no solution to the United Kingdom problem." Britain
wanted metals such as copper, nickel, zinc, and lead as well as timber
products and was prepared to spend $260 million on such purchases
and a further $520 million elsewhere.

But as Mackenzie and Taggart had explained in 1950, requests of
that nature were not as easily filled as they would have been in the
late 1940s. When London wanted to spend $63 million on forest
products in 1951–52, up from $12 million in 1950, the order was
declined: Canadian and US demand had exhausted almost all available supplies.[24] As well, the unhelpful British attitude to the 1946
UK-Canada wheat contract had, according to Lester Pearson, "reduced the Canadian Government's willingness to help Britain" secure supplies of scarce commodities.[25]

Increasingly, London discovered that it had placed itself out of
the Canadian market. British reluctance to take Canadian products
on a regular or even token basis had adversely affected exporters.
For example, with respect to token imports, a principle on which
exporters placed some importance, London unilaterally and arbi-
trarily reduced imports of Canadian manufactured goods from a 1951
total of $7.5 million to $5.6 million in 1952.[26] The market that had
taken about 38 per cent of Canada's total exports during 1937–39
had now been reduced to less than half that. As the Bank of Nova
Scotia *Monthly Review* pointed out, "In [these] circumstances, it [was]
not surprising that Canada's interest [in Britain had] waned."[27] At
least one Canadian official believed that "Britain ... had missed the
boat."[28]

The British were told that Canadian interest in exports to their
market would continue to decline unless London adopted a more

"reasonable" posture. And reasonableness was certainly not evident during the May UKCCC discussions: much to the disgust of the Canadians, Britain quibbled over the insignificant amount of $30 million per year of additional expenditure in Canada. If that policy were maintained, John Deutsch said, "it did not seem improbable that ... Canadian exporters might be forced to [continue] to re-direct their trade to other markets."[29] By 1951, the government had concluded that such redirection was probably inevitable. After years of trying to push back into the UK market, Canada had little to show.

As it had since the war, a similar situation existed with British exports to Canada. Ottawa had made strenuous, and at times successful, efforts to ensure that UK products had a market in a country where, by value, total imports had increased by 600 per cent between 1938 and 1951 and volume had gone up by 250 per cent. As well, tariffs had been progressively reduced through the GATT and Canada, as a member of the British preferential system, remained relatively open to Commonwealth exports, with the exception of certain dairy products. But despite that, as R.P. Bower, the commercial counsellor at Canada House in London, wrote to G.A. Newman, the director of the export division of Trade and Commerce, "it [would] be a difficult, if not impossible, task to maintain [British] exports at the 1950 level." He cited as reasons raw materials shortages, defence commitments, lengthening order books, and the relative difficulty of selling consumer goods in the North American market. The Canadian government could only do so much – after that it was up to UK exporters, who were failing miserably. For example, capital equipment such as machine tools was desperately needed by Canadian business. This was also one of the strongest potential dollar earners for UK industry, but its priorities lay elsewhere, usually within the sterling area. The capital-equipment market was also one of the most likely to suffer from the effects of UK rearmament which would, Bower suggested, "weaken for all time the interest of Canadian organizations in obtaining their capital good requirements from sources of supply so frequently subject to interference by international developments."[30]

Recognizing the Canadian interest in maintaining trade with Britain, Howe, in the House of Commons, decried the lack of zeal with which UK exporters regarded the Canadian market for machine tools. He noted that, despite vigorous efforts in the United Kingdom, Canadian purchasers had been largely unsuccessful. Of the $80 million worth of machine tools Canadian companies bought in 1951, $8 million had been produced within the country, $2 million came from Western Europe, $64 million had been purchased from the United States, and only $6 million had been sold by the United Kingdom, largely because of unavailability. "Surely," the minister complained, "Canada cannot be blamed for that situation."[31]

London's fixation with the RSA and its continued efforts to make it a viable organism were largely to blame for the UK disdain for dollar markets – or so Ottawa believed. Certainly, from the latter's perspective, the RSA had proved to be exceedingly costly to maintain in terms of wasted resources, misdirected trade, and inefficient production. Area discrimination was "self-defeating [and] one of the basic reasons why the [British] 'dollar shortage' had become chronic," a Canadian memorandum explained.[32] Moreover, sterling balances remained a troubling irritant in Anglo-Canadian commercial relations. The British continued to release blocked balances which gave rise to unrequited exports and drained off the United Kingdom's hard currency export potential. As well, the RSA had always demanded the right of partial repayment from the bloc's dollar reserves pool, which put a tremendous strain on the United Kingdom. The *Economist* noted that in the more than four years since the convertibility disaster of 1947 Britain's external deficit had been a relatively small $600 million that had been more than covered by borrowings from the colonial empire. However, this had been dwarfed by the dominions' external deficit of over $2.5 billion, which had swallowed up more than 80 per cent of US aid. In effect, the weekly noted, "Britain's share of European Recovery Programme dollars [was] absent-mindedly poured down the drain of Australia's high cost industrial boom."

Going on to speculate on what *could* have happened had the United Kingdom not been so intent upon spreading its Marshall Plan aid around, the *Economist* pointed out that "the dollar reserves in London would have increased in these four and one-half years by well over three billion dollars (if the colonies are included with Britain) or nearly 2 and one-half billion dollars (if they are divorced from it)."[33] The bottom line remained that the UK could not afford such generosity. As a Canadian government memorandum had observed earlier, those "habits of largesse which Britain [exhibited were] more in keeping with past achievements than with present resources."[34] It was a misguided effort, based on the belief that the sterling area represented "the UK's future trading partners and as such must be kept reasonably well-satisfied with their UK connection." At some later date, when the sellers' market had ended, Britain expected to "reap its reward."[35] To further complicate matters, another dollar crisis hit in 1951. Canadian queries about discrimination and inconvertibility were once more shunted into the background while Britain again sought an internal solution to its dollar problem.

THE DOLLAR CRISIS OF 1951

Between June 1951 and March 1952 the United Kingdom experienced a dollar crisis for the third time since 1945. During that period, gold and dollar reserves fell by more than $2 billion to $1.7 billion, enough to cover a mere two months worth of British imports. This occurred partly because American importers greatly reduced purchases of RSA products for which they paid in gold and dollars, and partly because London saw its position as a substantial creditor with the European Payments Union (EPU) – a multilateral clearing house which involved a number of countries – change to that of a debtor. In June, its EPU deficit was about $50 million, rising to over $250 million by October. As well, the sterling area's position with the non-sterling world worsened, while the entire affair was made worse by "doubts about British exchange policy."[36]

The Labour government and, after its October 1951 victory, the new Conservative government of Sir Winston Churchill preached the doctrine of dollar conservation to the sterling area. In November, the Conservative chancellor of the Exchequer, R.A. Butler, instructed his officials to recommend where dollar cuts could be made; he intended to cut imports "good and hard."[37] In December he announced his government's policy: trade liberalization measures were to be revoked on a selected list of fifty items, import licensing was again *de rigeur*, food rations in 1952 were to remain at 1951 levels, softwood imports were to be limited, the strategic stockpiling program was to be reduced, and tourist rations would be cut from £100 to £50 per person. As well, the open general licenses for private trade imports from Europe and other non-sterling countries were to be revoked and import quotas substituted. The package was designed to save £350 million annually out of a total import bill of £3.6 billion.[38]

The Canadian government was not at all pleased with the British resolve to cut imports. The faces had changed, but the liturgy remained the same. While reducing Canada's exports to the United Kingdom again, Butler's speech, G.E. Freeman of the Bank of Canada told Towers, was "little more than window-dressing designed to impress upon the United States that Britain is now a deserving claimant for further assistance."[39] Freeman was echoing at least part of the advice given the chancellor by a trusted advisor, Philip Cunliffe-Lister, Lord Swinton. Almost the last of the old "Ottawa hands," Cunliffe-Lister had based his prewar career – and made his reputation – by advocating "Empire" development, an idea which, in a number of ways, burned brighter among many in the cabinet and bureaucracy in the 1950s than it had twenty years previous. Swinton pressed for import cuts by the Commonwealth of the same magnitude as those in Britain in order to restore confidence in sterling. He ended by noting that "if the whole Commonwealth has clearly put its house in order, that makes us an insurable proposition, and that is the best way to bring in the US to underwrite the policy."[40] Clearly, the Conservatives were treading that well-worn Labour path of sterling area trade. Indeed, the similarities between the policies enacted by both governments were so striking that the *Economist* coined the word "Butskell" (after Butler and Gaitskell) to describe it.[41]

Towers agreed with Freeman, clearly disgusted with the UK penchant for restricting trade with dollar countries at the slightest sign of trouble. To his mind, that policy was the strongest possible evidence that Britain and the RSA were reluctant to face the unpleasantness that corrective action required. Implicit in such behaviour was:

(a) ... an unwillingness to face the requirements of competitive efficiency;
(b) a desire on the part of individual sterling countries to live beyond their means at the expense of other countries in the area and;
(c) on both counts ... the individual and collective [in]ability ... to export outside [the sterling area's boundaries undermining] the prospects for maintenance of any degree of balance that might be temporarily established.[42]

There were also no indications in the chancellor's address to the House of Commons that he was seriously considering anti-inflation measures. As Towers and Freeman, among others, all too clearly recognized, the British hope was that the Americans would again ride to the rescue. If that were to happen, however, there would be the usual US demand for a *quid pro quo* on imperial preference and that, Freeman noted, was most unlikely. There appeared to be no way out of the maze: the new UK government would "rely on much the same remedies as its predecessor – a further instalment of import restrictions ... plus a fresh appeal for US dollar aid."[43]

That was the general position propounded by the British at the January 1952 Commonwealth finance ministers meeting. As Deutsch observed to Max Freedman of the *Winnipeg Free Press* following the meeting, he had travelled to London in 1947, 1949, and in 1952 "to hear that Britain faced a new crisis and that England had to continue her discrimination against dollar imports."[44] Certainly, the entire Canadian delegation had no hope that meaningful trade action would be taken as the litany of British economic woe grew steadily: North American, but especially American, tariffs remained a discouragement; Korean War rearmament continued to create supply problems in the fully employed UK economy; and supply and quality problems still affected exports. Under those circumstances, the British were constrained by external conditions. As the Canadians had suspected, that was Butler's position: the reason for the meeting, he had informed his cabinet colleagues, was to stop the drain on the central reserves, restore the position of the sterling area, and make it viable.[45]

The conference rehashed past history but, unlike the old Labour government, the Conservatives appeared more willing to consider the role of the sterling area in the present crisis, a position that J.C.R. Dow has called "novel."[46] They went so far as to agree that the causes of the 1951–52 dollar problem lay within the sterling area itself, which was in a state of fundamental imbalance that could well bring catastrophe in its wake. As a result, convertibility was announced as an important objective. Much of the impetus for this pronouncement had come from certain officials in the Treasury, the Commonwealth Relations Office, and the Bank of England who had succeeded in convincing ministers that nothing less than Britain's future was at stake.[47] Unfortunately for Canada, the new cabinet, despite a willingness to consider the possibility of convertibility, would not be rushed, much, it seemed, to Butler's regret, and Deutsch was correct in claiming that the January meeting had only one purpose: "to tell Britain's sterling partners to tighten their belts."[48]

One of the results of the discussions, however, was the establishment of a committee of officials, the Working Party on Steps to Convertibility, under Sir Arthur Salter, the minister of state for Economic Affairs. Its mandate was to report on the intricacies and implications of convertibility. From the Canadian perspective, this hopeful indication of a new British resolve was dashed by the committee's decision to place convertibility and discrimination in separate categories. To Canadians it had always been clear that inconvertibility and discrimination "went hand in hand and [were] really different aspects of the same problem."[49]

Soon after the Commonwealth conference, however, a Canadian trade official at Canada House charged that the British were dealing with the issue "with a certain lack of crusading zeal."[50] It almost appeared that Butler had had second thoughts about the establishment of the Salter Committee and now saw it as an unwelcome diversion from the main task of getting Britain's balance of payments in order. At least one official was disappointed about the lack of movement on convertibility – Clarke wrote with some bitterness that "Cabinet [had] refused to take the plunge."[51] There was also some suspicion that the committee was a sop to respond to certain RSA criticism of Britain and, quite possibly, that of Canada as well. As a result, Ottawa now felt that the time had come to press its case with greater vigour, to express "views more forcefully than [it had] hitherto done."[52] The departure from precedent was partly the result of greatly intensified sterling area restrictions on dollar imports, which became more severe than at any time since the war, and partly a result of the readiness of certain RSA countries to undertake a basic examination of the bloc's trade and financial policies.

Canada's resolve to become more involved in Commonwealth financial matters was well-received in many quarters in the UK. The *Manchester Guardian*, for one, had long urged the country to abandon "its posture of Olympian detachment from Commonwealth affairs" and the *Economist* echoed this sentiment.[53] The new strategy entailed immediate discussions with British civil servants over the future viability of the closed sterling area "while the official UK attitude ... [was] nailed to the mast of convertibility and non-discrimination."[54]

Clearly, by mid-1952, the UK assertion that non-discrimination and convertibility remained the objective was becoming difficult for Ottawa to accept. In the sellers' market that had existed since 1945, Canada's "frustrated exports had found a ready market in the United States and at home."[55] But sellers' markets were not guaranteed, and the country's security and prosperity rested on the fragile base of international trade. As well, by mid-1952, economic conditions in Canada were levelling off. The boom associated with the Korean crisis had worked itself through and increased unemployment was an unpleasant prospect. In Western Canada, a poor 1951 harvest and an outbreak of foot and mouth disease were politically trouble-some because of the economic hardship caused Prairie voters. With few western members of Parliament, the Liberals had hoped to increase their support in the region, a task now made more difficult. The government was also hard-pressed by a Progressive Conservative opposition convinced that it was intent upon wiping out the last vestiges of "the British connection" which, a popular opinion poll had revealed, 80 per cent of English Canadians wished to maintain.

Accordingly, Ottawa welcomed a UK announcement that promised a change of policy. There was a genuine concern about the United Kingdom's economic future but, more important, there was also a perception that "UK weakness threaten[ed] the position [Canadians] wished to maintain between themselves and the US."[56] It was a concern that had certainly troubled Ottawa during the postwar period. The new initiative seemed to address that anxiety by holding out the promise of sterling convertibility. However, before officials could meet to plan ministerial talks, agenda problems had to be worked through. These suggested a British orientation which was a great disappointment to the Canadian government. Much of Ottawa's concern revolved around the impression created by the British-drafted agenda: it appeared that the British were trying to shift the emphasis from what Canada considered to be the fundamental problem of *internal* finance and *domestic* economy to the *outward* aspects of the United Kingdom's difficulties. Following several meetings with Butler, Norman Robertson cabled External Affairs that the chancellor was well aware of Canadian concerns and welcomed Canadian interest at least in part, Robertson, Canada's high commissioner in London felt, because "he expected to have his own difficulties with some of his cabinet colleagues and would be glad of any reinforcement or stiffening which our representation of the general Canadian interest and viewpoint would give him."[57]

Despite Butler's encouraging words, the published agenda did not address the Canadian interest in the slightest. Neither there nor in the accompanying explanatory memorandum was there any specific provision for discussion of the subject which seemed to the Canadian government to be the key to the whole problem – there was no mention of the internal economic policies of Britain or other sterling countries. Rightly or wrongly, Robertson cabled Ottawa, "the impression left here by the documents sent here from London is that the British government is looking for a cure to sterling's recurrent crises in external rather than domestic measures."[58] That was most discouraging.

At the September preparatory meeting for a Commonwealth Economic Conference to be held in December 1952, the British tabled their proposals for comment by assembled delegations of officials. Convertibility was given top billing. Even following Canadian input during the earlier stage, the document still bore the unfortunate marks of bureaucratic and political compromise, or so the Canadians thought. Sir Leslie Rowan of the UK Treasury led off, briefly outlining the government's conception of what its implementation would require:

(a) Anti-inflationary measures continuously and firmly applied in sterling area countries, coupled with sound development;

(b) Cooperative action designed to remove import restrictions on the widest possible scale;

(c) Good creditor policies by the USA;

(d) Fortification of dollar reserves and;

(e) Reform of GATT and also of IMF.[59]

What the British envisaged was some sort of "collective approach" to non-resident convertibility to be taken in concert with such other important trading countries as Belgium, Canada, France, and the United States. Rowan noted that this nucleus would "form a group where effective discussion could take place on major economic matters."[60] It would be the prime mover in developing and implementing a comprehensive program that would ensure the successful operation of convertibility and also ensure the future of multilateral trade.

While this idea went part way toward addressing some Canadian skepticism about future sterling area policies, Ottawa remained critical. As presented, the British proposal entailed the maintenance of import restrictions against the United States, but a relaxation or elimination of restrictions in trade relations with other members. While the sterling area would eventually take the necessary steps that would result in convertibility, it would do so only when *all* conditions were ripe. In short, the sterling area would continue to rely heavily on the direct control of imports. Indeed, by 1952 the degree and extent of restriction and discrimination were more severe than at any time since 1945.

To the Canadian delegation the collective approach proposal sounded too much like past prescriptions for the "British disease" and these, the delegation pointed out, had not proved effective: discrimination had not achieved international balance for the sterling area and, a memorandum tabled at the conference noted, there was "no apparent reason for supposing that further intensification would be any more successful."[61] There was also the sneaking suspicion that the British had a hidden agenda – the enlargement of the sterling and EPU groupings and a concomitant widening of British economic influence. Moreover, Ottawa found it difficult to believe that London expected the Americans to foot the bill for this rather ambitious plan while the United Kingdom continued to discriminate against US products. That course had been tried at various GATT meetings and, as the Americans had made clear each time, it was a definite non-starter.

When asked to respond to Rowan's presentation, the Canadian delegation found this to be "quite a difficult problem."[62] At a minimum, it was adamant that the United States would not agree to many of the points raised, nor would Canada. The highly protectionist policies outlined by the British would economically weaken collective approach participants and pose serious political implications. And finally, Ottawa could not support "any policy which [did] not make at least some move toward the elimination of discriminatory measures and a facing up to dollar competition."[63] What Ottawa wanted, and this was emphasized at the officials' meeting, was "a major shift in policy."[64]

The Canadian delegation was also dismayed by what it considered to be the excessively political orientation of the paper, figuring that it had emanated from the depths of Prime Minister Winston Churchill's cabinet room rather than from Whitehall. Rowan admitted as much: the "hands of United Kingdom officials [were] closely tied by the wishes of Ministers."[65] And as a Canadian staffer in the Embassy in Washington was told, "many Ministers, apparently, [were] unwilling to take any action which might result in by-election losses."[66] Harsh internal "corrections" might provoke that result, further discrimination against dollar goods would not. The result was, the Canadian delegation felt, a "collective approach" draft that did not in any material way further the progress of convertibility.

Both Secretary of State for External Affairs Pearson and Towers wholeheartedly agreed with their delegation's condemnation of the conference. Neither had any idea what the British were attempting to accomplish, and both suspected that convertibility and non-discrimination would be a long time coming. As Pearson later told Howe, there seemed "to be an atmosphere almost of political naivete about these 'Rowan proposals,' if it is seriously thought that in their present form they could be accepted in Washington, or that we could join in presenting them there." It would be "unwise ... to confront the Americans with any proposals which put them on the defensive."[67] Meanwhile, Towers advised the delegation to maintain at least an arm's length distance from the proposal and the "incompetent officials" who were involved in the process. His final word on the issue was a warning to cabinet which repeated Pearson's remarks: "Unless further elucidation changes our understanding of the proposals, they would seem to me simply to be reaching toward the ideal cherished by right-wing Tories and many elements of Labour since the end of the war, namely a world in which all or most countries discriminate against the US. The new idea brought forward is that this should be done with US help and blessing. Do they really believe this is possible?"[68] Apparently not, for the document circulated at the December ministers' conference was substantially different from the one discussed in September and it incorporated some the Canadian concerns that had been expressed at the officials' meetings.

The 1952 conference signified a watershed in the postwar development of the sterling area, or so the Canadian delegation believed, and the revamped collective approach, however badly introduced, was a concrete indication of a new attitude. It was not all internally driven, however, as a number of factors had intruded upon the regional system established and supported by the United Kingdom. As long as London remained able to support RSA development programs through capital exports and some dollar transfers, the area could function reasonably well. But the 1951 dollar crisis had provoked some serious thought among sterling area governments. It was becoming all too obvious that the United Kingdom could not continue to provide for the increasing demands of the bloc. With the end of the ERP and the flow of US dollars into Britain, the RSA could be caught in an unenviable predicament: at the same time that its receipts of dollar aid would be drastically reduced, demands for investment capital were likely to increase. If the United Kingdom could not meet those requirements, then some parts of the area would look elsewhere, most probably to the United States. The collective approach was an attempt by London to deal with a changing international situation in order to maintain its hegemony among RSA countries.

The conference, Canada included, finally passed a collective approach resolution that reflected the new official attitude. Certain Western European countries and the United States were invited to be a part of it. In its revised form, the policy envisaged " positive international action for the progressive removal ... of import restrictions."[69] In this resolution, there was none of the high-handedness and stridency of the ealier one, and the leader of the Canadian delegation, Prime Minister St Laurent, indicated Canada's willingness to help where it could. The collective approach proposals encouraged him to believe that the conference would consider a serious effort to change the general direction of the sterling area's trade and currency policy. However, St Laurent also warned that general agreement on broad principles was not enough: "The measures taken should carry conviction and should leave no doubt that there was in fact to be a basic reorientation of policy." General statements of objectives "would have to be accompanied by some indications of concrete action."[70] Even so, the Canadians were well pleased with the results of the conference. For the first time since 1945 there was a wide-spread feeling that "the British [were] on the right line and [were] sincere."[71]

THE COLLECTIVE APPROACH TO FREER TRADE AND CURRENCIES

The collective approach resolution could not have been passed at a more propitious moment, it seemed, as its adoption coincided with a rising tide of British prosperity. The United Kingdom's balance of payments position improved throughout 1953 and by April sterling area gold and dollar reserves were in a very healthy condition. In terms of its balance with the dollar area, the bloc achieved an overall surplus of about £400 million in 1952–53 as compared with a deficit of some £1 billion in 1951–52, and the forecasts were for even better numbers. As well, many of the raw materials controls that had been extended during the 1951–52 crisis were being removed. The various exchanges were also going back to work: the wheat exchange opened in December 1953 while the cotton exchange renewed operations in May 1954, after a thirteen-year hiatus. This restored the last of Britain's major commodity markets to private trade. Food rationing was also reduced during 1953 and ended completely in July 1954. By that year, Butler could boast of "a healthy balance in the economy as a whole" where even trade liberalization with the dollar area "was not unpromising".[72] But most significantly, the 1954 US recession did not spill over into the United Kingdom. American industrial production fell by ten per cent between July 1953 and April 1954, while sterling area gold and dollar reserves rose by nineteen. As Gaitskell pointed out, "If anyone in the middle of last year had forecast this combination of per centages he would have been written off as an optimist or an ignoramus – possibly both."[73] Given these conditions, it seemed only a matter of time before Britain would once again subscribe to the tenets of multilateralism and non-discrimination that had been promised with the new policy.

Despite the hopeful opening, however, the collective approach languished during 1953. The Europeans were not interested, largely because of uncertain economic conditions on the continent. Also, since convertibility threatened the operation of the EPU, there was some speculation in continental capitals that Britain was preparing to back out of European cooperation. As the president of the Board of Trade noted in a memorandum circulated to cabinet, in Europe, "there was a widespread distrust of our intentions as regards the Collective Approach," especially because of the adverse implications for the EPU.[74] That impression was difficult to dispel and, as a result, London was "sadly disappointed" in its efforts to encourage OEEC countries to think seriously about the initiative.

The Americans were similarly suspicious, especially given their proposed role in the establishment of the convertibility support fund and the necessity of maintaining good creditor policies. The British raised the issue with the US government in a memorandum in February 1953, and again in a more pointed way in March, but without much success. The newly installed administration of President Dwight Eisenhower favoured the proposals in a general way, but certain members of his cabinet had very contrary opinions. They, as Butler remembered in his memoirs, poured "cold water on the collective approach."[75] Congress was also unwilling and had little inclination to back Britain's conversion operation.[76] Moreover, Eisenhower had just appointed Clarence Randall to undertake an analysis of US foreign economic policy and he would not report until January 1954. During the remainder of 1953, the collective approach was the subject of conversation between Washington and London but, as Rowan told Deputy Minister of Finance Ken Taylor, the British had not been able "to pin them down to any firm views upon [it]."[77]

That was partly because the Americans were dealing with economic problems of their own. For example, they were contemplating budget reductions on the order of $6 billion in order to slash a projected deficit of $9 billion. Indeed, Randolph Burgess of the US Treasury told Sir Robert Hall, Butler's chief economic advisor, that he felt 1954 was "going to be a bad year for progressive policies" and that "it would be quite an achievement if there were no retrograde movements."[78] Washington felt it could make no promises; Sir Pierson Dixon of the UK Treasury called that "depressing."[79] As a result of these and other communications, speculation was rampant in the United Kingdom that the United States "was moving in the direction of restricting trade."[80] That, if true, had obvious implications for the collective approach in particular and world trade in general.

Even with this lukewarm American response, however, by 1954 the UK government appeared ready to move beyond generalities to specifics. That was surely a reflection of Britain's prosperity and the different attitude that now seemed to animate its government. London wanted general agreement on long-term policies among the United States, Canada, the RSA, and certain European countries. Given the renewal of interest, a Canadian delegation in Sydney, Australia, for a January 1954 Commonwealth meeting was prepared for a British announcement. It was disappointed, however, because, according to Louis Rasminsky of the Bank of Canada, sterling convertibility "had no political sex appeal in the UK."[81]

Therein lay the crux of the matter. Given Britain's relative prosperity during early 1954, the government was loath to take any precipitous action. In a telegram to Towers, Rasminsky said that Rowan and Sir Frank Lee, the permanent secretary of the Board of Trade, did not challenge the case he made in favour of immediately introducing convertibility on economic grounds. Rather, political considerations were paramount: the Conservatives wanted to be in a strong domestic position to deal with the certain political opposition to convertibility, especially if the US recession of early 1954 spilled over into Britain. The attitude of the RSA also had to be considered: certain countries were proving to be very protectionist. Despite all these reservations, Rasminsky concluded his telegram on an upbeat note. Unlike past conferences, "British views, at both the officials' and Ministers' meetings have been much closer to our own ... than they have to the pukka sterling countries."[82]

Moreover, despite the lack of movement toward the collective approach, the Sydney meeting was important for a number of reasons. Unlike earlier Commonwealth gatherings, it did not take place in a crisis atmosphere but was a calm evaluation of the sterling area's economic situation. There was also no suggestion of further import cuts from the dollar area, even given the United States recession and its possible effects on the United Kingdom. Indeed, Deutsch, now assistant deputy minister of Finance, told the Interdepartmental Committee on External Trade Policy in February that the British "had ... maintained that they might consider the use of some of their reserves to ride out a short-lived recession rather than resorting to restriction of imports,"[83] a very important policy change, at least from the Canadian point of view.

The Ottawa correspondent of the *Economist* reported that Canadian representatives had found the meeting to be "one of the most successful conferences of Commonwealth Finance Ministers there has yet been." The primary importance of Sydney was that British doubts and reservations about the collective approach had "now disappeared."[84] Even given some RSA reluctance, the direction was no longer in question, only the pace of the advance. Several months later the *Economist*, perhaps caught up in the very favourable economic conditions then prevailing, went so far as to suggest that the government's "generalized expectations to make sterling convertible when it proves possible are maturing into a definite intention to do so by or before next spring."[85] In short, all indicators, including general opinion in the international financial and business communities, suggested that non-resident sterling convertibility would be put in place in the very near future. In that regard, Ivar Rooth, the IMF's managing director, let it be known that he felt that "conditions were ripe for further progress towards currency convertibility and the abolition of restrictions and trade discrimination maintained for balance of payments reasons."[86]

As a result of the heady atmosphere generated by the conference, Ottawa felt it should develop an outline of post-convertibility trade policy. A memorandum prepared in the Bank of Canada noted that, although sterling earned by Canadians was already convertible, exporters were likely "to derive some trade advantage from arrangements under which all non-resident sterling is convertible." The British would no longer have any exchange reason for discriminating in favour of the RSA: by buying "in the cheapest market [the sterling area would] bring pressure on the British to do the same to maintain their competitive position." As well, the RSA would ease up on its own dollar restrictions because otherwise "non-residents [would] derive the entire benefit of sterling convertibility." These reasons were probably sufficient to force London to relax its own trade restrictions. The consensus in Ottawa was that it would be a mistake to attempt to tie the United Kingdom to anything like a phased program or specific commercial undertaking. In any event, Washington would almost certainly demand something of the sort, so the Canadians reasoned, as a *quid pro quo* for financial assistance.[87]

However, these plans proved to be premature – the British were not interested in the immediate abolition of trade discrimination, an unpleasant reality conveyed to Ottawa in August by J.H. Warren, the financial attaché at the Canadian Embassy in Washington. Contrary to Canadian hopes, an American suggestion that an undertaking to remove discriminatory measures against the dollar area should be written into any agreement had been refused by the British. The UK government did go part way, stating that for a *transitional* period after convertibility was established, "countries should retain the right to maintain trade restrictions and to discriminate."[88] The Canadian position was that any such period "should not be allowed to drag out." In Washington for meetings of the IMF and Commonwealth finance ministers, Walter Harris, Canada's new minister of Finance, said in September that he was concerned that such discrimination would check the momentum of the collective approach. He believed it was desirable "to have tighter trade rules, with more limited escape clauses," exactly the opposite of what the British were proposing.

At any rate, discussion over the possibility of sterling convertibility proved to be academic. Butler's attendance at the annual IMF meeting for the first time since he had become chancellor was not the favourable omen many had thought and non-resident convertibility was postponed once again. Press reports ascribed the delay to two factors: British politics and a lack of progress in the liberalization of American commercial policy. With regard to the former, Butler stated that any move toward convertibility had to be compatible with "high levels of employment, increased production and the highest standards of life."[89] With respect to the role of the United States, Butler repeated to the Conservative Party congress in Blackpool in October what he had said to the IMF: "If the Americans want convertibility, they must lower their own tariffs and other impediments first ... We have gone as far as we can go without proof from Washington that they not only understand the problem but will also act on that understanding."[90] An additional (and unremarked) reason for the go-slow policy lay in the deteriorating condition of the UK economy. Since 1953, sales had been growing faster than productive capacity, leading to an increase in inflation. The surge in domestic demand increased imports from outside the sterling area, resulting in a decline in British reserves of about £300 million. For all these reasons the British government felt it could not commit itself to a reduction in discrimination against dollar imports.

The Canadian ambassador in Washington, A.D.P. Heeney, was disgusted both at this turn of events and the conference's physical setting; as he cabled Ottawa after the British had announced their policy, "of all the meetings of Commonwealth Finance Ministers, none could have been less purposeful than the meeting ... in Washington." The heat was stifling "and the fans in the wooden sweatbox annexed to the UK Embassy [were] powerless against the heat, but quite powerful enough to muffle discussion so that much of what was said was inaudible."[91]

Heeney had correctly guessed that the British objective in convening the meeting was to explain to RSA ministers why London had decided to postpone changes. In large part, Butler declared, reiterating a favourite theme, this was the fault of the United States, which had not introduced good creditor policies. This failure meant that a permanent method of bridging the dollar gap was still lacking. Also, he was unclear about European plans, a further problem as "an orderly advance on a broad front" was a prerequisite of the collective approach. According to Heeney, the sighs of relief from RSA delegations over the decision "were like steam escaping from a boiler." Similarly, on the issue of relaxing trade restrictions, Butler promised little: "he could not hold out any hope of a further reduction in discrimination against dollar imports in the near future." Canadian reservations, as articulated by Minister of Finance Harris, were ignored. Heeney concluded his rather bleak missive by noting that "all in all, it is hard to resist the conclusion that the collective approach would be in a better position today if the meeting of ... finance ministers had never been held."[92]

The ambassador was worried, as were Harris and Towers, over what they felt were the shifting sands of British policy. Indeed, they went so far as to take Butler aside during the conference to tell him that they saw no reason to postpone again the implementation of non-resident convertibility. They offered some unsolicted (and certainly) unwanted advice:

If the international trade and financial situation in general and the attitude toward sterling in particular continued to be favourable, no pressure on sterling would take place. If, on the other hand, for reasons which we could not now foresee, sterling came under pressure, we suggested that the UK was in a most vulnerable position inasmuch as they had gone a long way in the freeing of commodity markets and widening of transferability of sterling while at the same time remaining on a fixed rate. If pressure developed, was there a risk that the Chancellor would have to retrace some of the steps taken in the last couple of years? Was it right to assume that the UK was better protected "as is" rather than by moving on to convertibility at a floating rate?[93]

In a personal letter to Norman Robertson, now back in London as high commissioner, Heeney wrote that "the first encounter of our new minister of Finance with the Chancellor of the Exchequer was hardly a case of love at first sight" – and there is little doubt that the manner in which the British minister chose to express the UK attitude on the collective approach did nothing to counteract the finance minister's adverse impressions. Butler was rigid, doctrinaire, and dogmatic with, it seemed to the Canadians, no clear understanding of the long-term effects of his policies. He realized that Ottawa was unhappy over the slow pace of the collective approach, "but almost pooh-poohed their disappointment ... [He] was quite obviously irritated by the suggestion that anyone else should presume to tell him how to protect sterling ... [and] would brook no interference."[94] The chancellor's patronizing attitude and his easy assumption that a "leave-it-to-father" principle held sway in the case of Commonwealth affairs grated on the Canadians.

Despite the generally bleak tenor of the Washington meetings, Butler and his officials were not completely discouraging or dismissive of the possibility that convertibility would be introduced

soon. In practical terms, however, no such commitment was demonstrated in 1954, nor was it evident in 1955 as Britain headed into
yet another balance of payments crisis. A briefing paper prepared
for Prime Minister St Laurent commented on the issue:

There can be no doubt that progress toward freer trade during 1954 was
limited and that several set-backs were suffered. During September and
October, Mr. Butler intimated in several public speeches that the achievement of convertibility might be somewhat further away than had previously
been anticipated. There is reason to believe that this attitude is dictated not
only by an assessment of the external financial situation but also by certain
considerations of domestic politics, which incline the United Kingdom Government toward caution in embarking on convertibility until such time as
they are confident that it would be a popular measure in the country.[95]

Achieving convertibility seemed to be ever farther away, to the
point where the Canadian government reacted with surprise to a
UK initiative to improve the GATT-IMF relationship in order to hasten
convertibility. As Rasminsky noted to A.F.W. Plumptre, the assistant
deputy minister of Finance, it was "encouraging to find that the
British still regard the 'Collective Approach' as sufficiently alive to
want to push ahead with these discussions."[96] How alive it was,
however, was not clear from Chancellor Butler's statement at the
annual meeting of the IMF and IBRD in Istanbul, Turkey, in September 1955: he did not contemplate any early movement on the
collective approach, especially given the rather alarming deterioration in the sterling area's balance of payments from a surplus of
£300 million in 1953 to an estimated deficit of £200 million in 1954.
   To the Canadians, events were equally unclear with respect to
trade liberalization. London was retreating from its commitment to
eliminate discrimination within a definable transitional period after
convertibility – its earlier ideas had been "too optimistic." The British,
backed by studies on the subject, were firmly of the opinion that
non-discrimination would involve immediate and heavy purchases
from North America and precipitate further balance of payments
problems. There was also more than a sneaking suspicion in Ottawa
that London's position was at least partly the result of a desire to
protect UK industry against North American competition.
   At the 1955 Commonwealth Finance ministers' meeting in Istanbul,
held in parallel with meetings of the IMF and IBRD, the Canadian
delegation told the British that they would not accept any declaration
"which promised or half-promised easy approval of discriminatory
restrictions in circumstances of convertibility." As at the Washington

conference, Canada was prepared to see discrimination dismantled over a *brief* interim period following convertibility, but it was not about to support a statement that contemplated the continuation of discrimination for a prolonged period of time. Canada would "prefer no policy statement to one which made explicit reference to the approval of discrimination."[97] Any discrimination seemed a departure from the collective approach principles announced in December 1952. If that were the case, Rasminsky asked the United Kingdom's economic secretary at a private lunch, "what point [was there] in Canada participating in the Collective Approach?"[98]

While the Istanbul discussions indicated that there would be problems in the future, there were also pressing problems in the present. Indeed, Britain's commercial problems with Canada intensified over the course of 1955 to the point where even London became concerned about declining trade volumes. During the first six months, when total Canadian imports expanded by seven per cent, British sales to Canada declined by 2.5 per cent. R.P. Bower pointed out the obvious to the deputy minister of Trade and Commerce, Frederick Bull: "The UK's hold on the Canadian market [was] slipping."[99] He could easily have said it had slipped. As a per centage of total UK exports, a steady downward progression in imports from Canada was evident. In 1953, it had been six per cent, in 1954, five per cent, and from January to June 1955, it fell to 4.4 per cent. The reverse was also true: exports to Britain fell from 23 per cent of the total in 1949 to roughly 15 per cent by mid-decade.

Nor were forecasts any more encouraging. R.W. Low, minister of state, Board of Trade, was succinct in dampening Canadian hope. With respect to UK exports to Canada, which Ottawa had encouraged, British domestic demand was absorbing too large a proportion of national production to have much left over.[100] As well, British industry was simply not interested in a sustained effort in Canada: it could dispose of output more easily in Europe and the RSA. The years of comfortable selling in a protected and lucrative sterling area had taken its toll on the willingness of British manufacturers to develop more difficult dollar markets. While prices were often good, UK exporters were notorious for lax delivery times and low quality products. As Bull noted at a December 1955 UKCCC meeting, the RSA was an "easier [market] that tended to look for soft currency goods and [was] therefore prepared to wait for delivery. In Canada the pattern was different."[101]

But even where markets had been established for UK business in Canada, there was no certainty that they would be regularly supplied. For example, after encouragement by the Iron and Steel Board to "Buy British," Canadian steel users were very critical of an abrupt cancellation of UK steel exports to North America in late 1955. They had contracted to purchase 16,000 tons annually but were informed that they would receive nothing in the fourth quarter – instead production was going to fuel the 1955 boom in the sterling area. Canadian users would have to turn to American suppliers. As one observer of the situation correctly noted in the letters column of the London *Financial Times*, "once custom has been transferred elsewhere, it is extremely difficult, if not impossible, to regain."[102] At the December meeting, however, Lee was unsure that his government could accomplish more:

It was extremely difficult to know what further action, in a free economy, the UK Government could take. Hints or threats to industry were not efficacious; and in the circumstances all the Government could do was to make industry aware of the problem and its own long-term interest in cultivating a market where demand was likely to remain at a high level. [It had] been ... a disappointing year but ... given freer trade conditions, it was difficult to do more except by encouragement and exhortation.[103]

The Canadian delegation refrained from saying that it had heard that speech for the past ten years. And, while Lee could point a finger at the uncooperative attitude of British industry, the government was not above reproach. London put no end of obstacles in the path of Canadian exporters, such as those who tried to sell chemicals. This was an area of some promise, and the British had indicated in the past that they were willing to introduce a modest amount of competition into the chemicals industry by way of opening the market to Canadians. In fact, Lee had told Bower in August 1954 that in the future Whitehall would consider importing chemicals from dollar sources when they were not available in Britain. Whatever the true intent of the communication, Canada's producers had taken it as an indication of "chemicals liberalization." As a result, fifteen Canadian firms had participated in the Plastics Exhibition held in London in June 1955.

By September, however, the British were refusing to import dollar chemicals and were encouraging UK manufacturers to enlarge capacity. Canadian producers were tremendously irritated by this *volte face*, as was Bower. It was a clear violation of the *intent* of the collective approach. He wrote to his friend Claude Isbister of the Department of Trade and Commerce that he was distressed by "the complete lack of any sense of guilt or regret on the part of the Board of Trade at their proposed actions. It does not seem incompatible to them that their import licensing machinery should be used in this way. Instead of looking upon this legislation as something to be discarded as soon as possible, it is treated as an instrument to be used whenever it is convenient."[104]

It was clear that the collective approach was becalmed. When Ottawa pointed out that British policy was inconsistent with the spirit of the 1952 initiative, the same arguments were given: London needed a current account surplus in the range of £200–300 million in order to meet commitments and it had to build up the central reserves. That remained a difficult task because the sterling area, especially Australia and New Zealand, was a continuing drain, while India's second five-year development program would also surely prove taxing. While this was probably true, the British, as Rasminsky said at the UKCCC meeting, should not wait for perfect conditions before beginning the move toward convertibility; they should act when conditions were good. And, he pointed out, "conditions by and large were good at present."[105]

The hoary chestnut of dollar scarcity was simply not as compelling in 1955 in justifying import restrictions as it might have been in 1947. Canadian officials had consistently urged the relaxation of discrimination and controls as quickly as possible. But despite those efforts and the public pronouncements of British officials and ministers, controls remained an integral part of Britain's commercial life. As one critic of that policy noted in 1955, "ten years ago those who were best able to predict what the future held for world trade would never have believed that at this date convertibility would still be something of a planner's dream and that many of the larger trading nations of the world would still be operating highly effective import restrictive machines."[106]

CONCLUSION

There was no improvement in the UK performance in 1956. Britain's share of world trade was steadily dropping and it had been granted an emergency loan of $561 million from the IMF and a $500 million line of credit from the Export-Import Bank. Indeed, the next few years were to prove very trying for London as the government grappled with serious problems and issues. For example, the ill-conceived Suez adventure provoked another crisis of confidence in sterling and the loss of almost $280 million in November 1956, 15 per cent of the United Kingdom's total gold and dollar reserves, was attributable to the invasion. It also claimed as a prominent casualty Prime Minister Anthony Eden.

Moreover, disagreement developed between the United Kingdom and its European allies with respect to the collective approach. Much of the problem centred on exchange rate policy: the Europeans were especially concerned over Britain's desire to achieve a greater flexibility in its exchange rate – as much as three per cent on either side of a pegged figure. Organizational difficulties were also evident: OEEC countries were anxious that the close links between Canada and the United States implied in the collective approach might threaten the organization's authority. As well, the United States was increasingly reluctant to support schemes like the collective approach. Secretary of the Treasury George Humphrey was graphic in his description of the decline he saw in American strength. As he told Harold Macmillan, then chancellor of the Exchequer, in 1957, the United States "had lost gold every year [since 1948]. It was spending too much at home and abroad" and the litany went on. [107] And, even though throughout the 1950s, the United States ran a large current account surplus with the rest of the world, balancing the budget was "an absolute fetish" for Humphrey. [108] As a result, very little progress was made on the collective approach.

Canadian attempts to draw attention to a lack of progress with respect to the initiative were ineffective. The British would decide the convertibility timetable. In that spirit, a Canadian official said of a May 1957 UKCCC meeting that "it was an ordinary thing, there were no surprises, nothing startling developed and nothing was accomplished except the 'usual' better understanding resulting from a really exhaustive examination of the facts of life of UK-Canada economic relationships."[109] At another UKCCC meeting a year later, a mere five months before the implementation of non-resident UK convertibility, Rasminsky appealed to the British to make some definite move toward the collective approach. As he noted, "hope deferred turneth the heart sick."[110] The UK response was to ask for understanding.

Thirteen years after the end of the war, and eleven after its first abortive attempt to restore non-resident convertibility in 1947, Britain finally implemented the policy in 1958. That Canadians were disappointed by the delay was undeniable, although Canada had prospered immensely, even with reduced sales to the United Kingdom. The "dreaded loss of the British market"[111] had occurred, yet not many Canadians seemed to notice. By the end of the decade, the importance, both political and commercial, of exports to Britain had largely disappeared. Prosperity had made Canadians less sensitive to the pitfalls of continentalism and dependence, and even the election of the more Commonwealth-oriented Progressive Conservative government of John Diefenbaker in June 1957 did little to alter the pattern of Canada's trade.[112] As A.F.W. Plumptre has so evocatively noted, "The croaks of the few Cassandras who dared to question either the economic or the political desirability [of such a condition] were drowned in the Hallelujah Chorus."[113] The collective approach, announced with so much promise in December 1952, had been a casualty of shifting circumstances and cautious British governments. And Canada was not to blame: the King and St Laurent governments had both tried hard to maintain trade with the United Kingdom but with little success. They could only exhort and encourage their British colleagues toward convertibility – they could not, nor would they have wanted to, dictate. The intensified development of Canada-us trade during the 1950s was the obverse of the difficulties that Ottawa experienced in gaining untrammelled access to the UK market. The future of Canadian trade had been determined as much, if not more, in London and Washington as in Ottawa.

4 The Organization for European Economic Cooperation, Dollar Restrictions, and Canada, 1948–57

One of the more important aspects of the ERP was its emphasis on a common European approach. When in June 1947 Secretary of State George Marshall announced his government's intention to partly fund Europe's dollar shortage, assistance was made contingent on interested countries submitting a single proposal. Most of Europe complied, applying for Marshall assistance through the ERP office in Paris and pledging themselves to expand production, reduce barriers to trade, and establish internal financial stability. The OEEC established and promoted by the United States, initially to disburse assistance through the Marshall plan, was to be, in American minds at least, "the midwife attendant on ... the economic unification of Europe."[1]

As Alan Milward suggests, however, this hope was not realized. Instead, "in the place of a liberal, unified Europe came a closely regulated Little European common market whose twin purposes were to provide for French national security by containing West Germany and to permit its members to continue to pursue a very limited range of common economic policies in a few specific sectors of the economy, which would otherwise have become impossible."[2] While this failure of US policy in Western Europe is not the theme of this book, it is instructive with respect to Canadian policy. Even with its military and political power and huge reserves of gold and dollars, Washington was unable to orchestrate developments on the Continent to its satisfaction. Ottawa, with much less influence and power, was even less successful in increasing its volume of trade in Western European markets. Citing dollar shortages and the imperatives of reconstruction, Canadian goods were largely kept out as intra-European trade gathered momentum.

To the trade commissioners, it seemed that "a curse [had] been placed on Canadian exports" to Europe. It became painfully obvious that Canada rated far down on the list of possible suppliers: OEEC countries avoided buying in Canada "if it were possible to do without, to produce themselves, or to buy in Europe." Similarly, "the feeling [was] that trade with the extra-European sterling area ... [was] more desirable than trade with Canada." Only with great difficulty (if ever) could Canadian exporters expect to "find [their] place in the OEEC sun."[3] Ottawa was aggressive in pushing the Canadian interest because the government could not envisage Canadian prosperity without Canadian participation in a prosperous European market during the later 1940s; indeed, there were "few subjects of greater importance to Canadians than the recovery of Western Europe ... Canada [needed] European markets."[4] Despite that effort, the expenditure in terms of personnel and resources was largely wasted.

Exports to the Benelux group, France, Germany, and Italy, told the sad story – from eight per cent of total Canadian merchandise exports in 1947, the last pre-ERP year, they declined to less than four per cent in 1950, and to only six per cent by 1955. As a corollary, Canadian exports to the United States boomed, from 38 to 65 to 60 per cent, respectively. The sobering reality, of which decision makers in Ottawa were only too well aware, was that Canadian prosperity depended on export markets – anywhere and everywhere, even if that meant focusing Canadian trade almost exclusively on the United States.

CANADA AND THE ORGANIZATION

The OEEC was a complex organization made up of a council of all the participating countries, an executive committee of seven, and a secretariat of about 300 technicians. Stemming from the council were a number of general and technical committees. The general committees included those on program, balance of payments, inter-European trade and manpower, and budget. Each of these had a corresponding directorate in the secretariat. Separate technical committees and subcommittees were formed to examine such areas as iron and steel, coal, oil, electricity, timber, pulp and paper, and non-ferrous metals.

Completed proposals were sent to the program committee, which passed them to a working party of statisticians. At the same time, the program committee invited a subcommittee of four or five of its members to recommend a total allocation per country of the available us aid.[5] As soon as this allocation had been approved by the program committee, the proposed import programs of the separate countries were adjusted so that the total amount of aid being requested for seperate commodities was not in excess of the amount allocated by the program committee. When the proposals had been adjusted, they were returned to Paris where they were evaluated by the technical committees in order to ensure the countries needed the commodities for which they had submitted requests; these commodities could not be obtained from other participating countries; and the volume of commodities being requested from the western hemisphere was in fact available.[6] The final step in this long and involved procedure was to send the collected data to the administrative arm of the ERP, the Economic Cooperation Administration (ECA) in Washington.

It was clearly in Ottawa's interest to determine precisely where Canadian business could fit in to take maximum advantage of this system. The ERP also offered Canada an opportunity to trade with Europe for dollars which, the government hoped, would help to redress the heavy drain on Canadian reserves that had resulted in part from the credits that Ottawa had extended to the United Kingdom, France, and a number of other European countries. In August 1948 Sydney Pierce, the Canadian liaison man in Paris for the OEEC and the ERP, called together the European representatives of the Department of Trade and Commerce for a strategy session soon after the passage of the program by the us Congress. The meeting, held at the Hôtel Scribe, was to discuss the Canadian interest in the ERP and explain the mechanics of the OEEC. Fourteen members of the department attended – one trade commissioner for each OEEC participant. The method of ERP operations was explained, from the country-by-country beginnings through to Paris and on to Washington. It was up to these men to ensure that Canada was chosen as a source of supply in the initial stages of the ECA process because, if it were not, it would be difficult, if not impossible, to change that later. Pierce pointed out that it needed to be emphasized to national officials in each country that the ECA gave "complete freedom to ERP countries to nominate Canada as a source of supply if price and other conditions of sale were comparable."[7] If some countries showed a preference for nominating American goods out of gratitude for American aid or for political reasons when a better price could be gotten in Canada, then Trade and Commerce representatives must make a compelling case for the Canadian commoditiy.

There was reason for concern. It had been anticipated that approximately 40 per cent of all ECA funds, about $5 billion, would go for off-shore purchases. Canada's share could be about $750 mil-lion.[8] However, relations with the Europeans were problematic. Canadian economic assistance to Europe, while generous in the case of countries such as France and the United Kingdom, was of little consequence when compared with that of the United States. And Western Europe, never free from the fear that it might not get the next ERP instalment, did not want to jeopardize access to those billions of hard dollars. In consequence, it did its best "to buy in the United States at a hint that the United States [had] something it want[ed] to sell."[9] While the Canadians could cite specific examples where that had happened with Belgium, Holland, Greece, and west-ern Germany, they were powerless to change the trend, especially when ERP officials encouraged it.

During the first eleven months of the ERP, a disappointing per-centage of OEEC imports came from Canada, and the great bulk of those sold were purchased by the United Kingdom. Further, coun-tries of the OEEC appeared to be contemplating Eastern Europe as a larger source of supply. In a memorandum to Norman Robertson, Canada's high commissioner in the United Kingdom, A.E. Ritchie, head of the economics division at External Affairs, commented on a report prepared for the OEEC secretariat that dealt with the relations with the Communist bloc. As he bleakly noted, "there is nothing in this report to give us comfort. If arrangements were to be developed along the lines suggested and Canada were to remain outside, the result would be, from our point of view, merely to extend the area from which we shall be excluded (or at least in which we shall be subjected to discrimination) from the sterling area plus Western Europe, to the sterling area plus Western and Eastern Europe."[10] The unpalatable result would be that a geographically large and potentially very important area would be subject to dollar discrim-ination of one sort or another and Canada's exclusion would almost be total. The British example was all too clear in Canadian minds: the West's Cold War enemies had taken over "Canadian" markets in Britain for commodities such as eggs and cheese (Poland) and timber (the Soviet Union). Given such a situation, the chance to break into new markets would be, it was thought in Ottawa, lost forever.

As the decade drew to a close, the condition of world trade gave thoughtful members of the Canadian cabinet and bureaucracy cause for despair. The Europeans were increasingly drawing inside the walls of their continent, commitments made under the GATT not-withstanding, and Canadian exporters more often than not found themselves on the outside looking in. That became even more likely when, in July 1949, in the midst of their second postwar dollar crisis, the British announced that they intended to seek a waiver from the non-discrimination obligation under Section 9 of the American loan agreement and Section 5 of the Canadian agreement order to relax restrictions from OEEC Europe at the same time as they greatly intensified them *vis à vis* the dollar area. As a memorandum submitted by the president of the Board of Trade to the Economic Policy Committee of cabinet noted, Ottawa was alarmed over the British request which, it felt, if permitted would be a highly symbolic act, and would be "taken by world opinion to mean a widening of the gulf between the dollar and non-dollar worlds."[11] Despite that concern, however, there was little else that Ottawa could do. Clearly, under the circumstances the British could not implement the loan agreement's non-discrimination clause. It was also another mark of Canadian generosity that the waiver was freely given.

The Canadian government was also becoming concerned over talk of European integration, assiduously encouraged in Washington. The issue was thoroughly disussed in the ICETP, the forum where views were aired among the senior mandarinate in Ottawa. Decision makers were not opposed to European integration *per se*, but instead opposed to plans which would greatly reduce the possibility of increasing Canadian exports to the Continent. The committee was unanimous in its recommendation to cabinet that there was no good reason why Europe should be built, even temporarily, "into a discriminatory trading bloc – no reason why there should be any exception ... to the general policy of multilateralism [and] non-discriminatory trade and policies."[12]

Fear of Canadian exclusion made Ottawa less than enthusiastic about European integration. For example, the Franco-German agreement to merge their iron and steel sectors, and the Stikker Plan, named after its sponsor, Dutch Foreign Minister Dirk Stikker, both placed a tremendous emphasis on European self-sufficiency. While Norman Robertson, now back in Ottawa as cabinet secretary, felt that Canada could have it both ways – "a Europe stronger economically and at the same time a better customer of ours" – that result did not seem likely. Even though a founding member of the NATO in 1949, and an associate member of the OEEC (along with the United States) by 1950, Canada had little influence in terms of helping to shape European action. Indeed, even the Americans, the dominant economic power, had little effect on the Europeans.[13]

On the issue of European integration, Ottawa and Washington diverged: not nearly as dependent as Canada on exports and wanting a united and prosperous Europe as a bulwark against international communism, the United States encouraged and assisted the sort of integration about which Ottawa had serious reservations. This schizophrenic American attitude, on the one hand stenuously pushing for tariff reductions in the GATT while, on the other, promoting protectionism in the OEEC, confounded Ottawa. Indeed, Canadian policy-makers had complained for several years that Washington "seemed to be scarcely aware that [this] sort of regional grouping ... [was] sharply at variance with the universalist theory of world trade."[14]

During the next several years, examples of trade restrictions and discrimination multiplied. Even among the OEEC countries themselves, there was some difficulty in moving beyond the 75 per cent liberalization of intra-European trade that had been established as a goal at the organization's meeting in October 1950. Progress had been uneven at the best of times, and the reimposition of emergency import restrictions in late 1951 by both the United Kingdom and France as a consequence of another dollar crisis meant a further serious set-back in the trade liberalization program. But the malaise went further than periodic dollar crises. There remained a "deep-seated conflict of interest among Western European countries ... and their traditional concern for national protection."[15] In those states, "vast vested interests sheltered behind national barriers to trade" which resisted any suggestion that they be exposed to the "chilling blasts of international competition" both within Europe and without.[16]

Even the British, with a foot in each world, the sterling area and Western Europe, wished to keep them firmly planted at some distance from each other. London chose not to support an Australian–New Zealand initiative to press for the extension of OEEC liberalization measures to the RSA, in part because of exchange implications but also because it would result in an increase of manufactured exports from Europe which had hitherto come to the Antipodes from the United Kingdom.[17] As was later pointed out, when ERP assistance ended in 1952 a disappointing 66 per cent of intra-European trade was free of restriction while a mere 11 per cent of OEEC countries' imports from the dollar area had been so liberalized.[18] That statistic spoke volumes as far as the Canadian interest in the European market went.

From its inception the OEEC was a European institution, even after Canada and the United States became associate members in 1950. Its primary purpose in its first half-decade was to disburse Marshall Plan aid to prime the European pump and set the continent back on the road to recovery. In that task, it was a success in economic terms – among OEEC countries, industrial production rose by

39 per cent between 1948 and 1952, while the volume of exports doubled. Because of those developments and others, Europe was in a much healthier economic state after ERP. However, the fact remained that the OEEC did not operate as Ottawa had hoped. While Canada did receive a share of off-shore purchases, this was mainly because of American largesse and not because of any rational program of European purchasing in Canada. Indeed, as noted above, the OEEC, for economic or political reasons, actively discriminated against Canadian exports, despite efforts by Ottawa to promote Canada as a source of supply.

A further complicating element in the equation after 1950, as far as Canada was concerned, was the operation of the EPU, which eliminated all bilateral relationships in trade between OEEC countries and provided for each state to settle its trade account with the EPU. It balanced intra-European trade credits and debts, and a state became a net debtor or net creditor to the EPU only, which settled accounts in gold and dollar credits. In short, the EPU provided machinery for fully multilateral settlement between its members. Moreover, as Brian Tew points out, "the effective area of multilateral settlement under EPU was very much greater than that comprised by its European members,"[19] because the currencies of several members were the usual medium for making international settlements in other areas of the world. The British-dominated sterling area, the Belgian, Dutch, French, and Portuguese empires were all included within the operation of the EPU.

Since the EPU provided facilities for multilateral settlement, Tew observes that "we [can] reasonably speak of a 'binary system' of two multilateral settlement areas, kept apart until December 1958 by exchange controls." [20] These were, of course, the dollar area, which settled its accounts in US dollars, and the soft currency area, which used sterling or the EPU machinery to settle accounts. The implications of the operation of such a system were obvious to Canada as the EPU countries and their colonies/dependents/dominions, which included a good part of the globe, actively discriminated against Canadian exports for currency reasons. As far as EPU countries were concerned, there was little incentive to embark upon the sometimes slippery and treacherous path to currency convertibility and non-discrimination. And if one of their number were to withdraw from the EPU as the British, however fleetingly, contemplated the introduction of convertibility in 1952 and 1953, then the most likely result, so the experts claimed, would be " the return to greater trade restriction and bilateralism."[21] There was tremendous pressure put on Britain to remain a consistent EPU player and not undertake a precipitous program which could destroy the EPU. That pressure, of course, meant that the United Kingdom would continue to discriminate against Canadian exports.

Canada also had to contend with a most inconsistent US policy with respect to European integration. Even as late as the 1950s Washington alternately supported and opposed Ottawa. Inter-departmental squabbles within the administrative and bureaucratic sectors in the American capital left their mark on policy. Moreover, international communism was a much more obvious target for Congress than European restrictionism, especially in the heated atmosphere generated by the senior senator from Wisconsin, Joseph McCarthy. And if trade restrictions would result in stronger "free" European economies to better resist Moscow, then they were well worth supporting.

DOLLAR RESTRICTIONS, 1951-4

A constant theme espoused by Canadians in the postwar period was that restrictionism bred inefficient economies behind high barriers to trade. The protected industry that grew up and prospered behind these walls ultimately cost the host country in terms of production costs, quality, and competitiveness. Ottawa's standing instructions to its OEEC mission in Paris were to constantly stress that point and generally encourage the Europeans to liberalize *vis à vis* the dollar area. Given Canada's limited power and influence, however, the policy did not extend to demands for action on specific commodities. The Canadian argument remained that it was "in the interests of the European countries themselves to liberalize their import restrictions."[22] The strategy was to advocate the desirability of more liberal treatment for raw materials and foodstuffs from the entire dollar area, not simply those from Canada. Ottawa cloaked its self-interest in general statements about the desirability of freer trade.

Unfortunately for those Canadian exporters with an interest in the European market, the Continent remained content with its situation throughout the period under investigation. The French had never evinced an interest in the process and some countries, such as Belgium, Britain, France, and Italy, actually moved away from dollar liberalization at various times. The case of Belgium was particularly galling to Ottawa and, some thought, demonstrated a rather bleak future for dollar liberalization. After having reduced restrictions on a wide range of hard currency imports, Brussels increased them in late 1951 because, Canadians believed, of quintessentially *political* pressures.[23] By late 1952, Britain, France, and Italy were also well onto the "deliberalization" trail. While it remained likely that the British would reduce restrictions as soon as possible following the 1951–52 dollar crisis, the intentions of the the other two were more problematic. Neither expressed a particular interest in dollar liberalization; in Italy some ministers, after having been so precipitous as to publicly favour a liberalization policy, were forced to beat a hasty and undignified retreat after a very hostile popular reaction. It was the belief of the OEEC's secretary-general, Robert Marjolin, that, given that situation, the Italian government would be tempted to go too far in the other direction "and start a series of new restrictions" to prove that it was responsive to popular opinion.[24]

In the OEEC, the steering and management boards dealt with the question of dollar restrictions and, according to Dana Wilgress, the head of the Canadian delegation in Paris, they were extremely lax in the interpretation of their mandate. In a meeting with Marjolin, Wilgress emphasized his government's concern "at the apparent failure of [the boards] to deal with their terms of reference in the field of dollar import restrictions." Certainly, Wilgress believed, the OEEC could "go a bit farther and faster ... in removing restrictions." If Europe was ever to become competitive it had to "buy cheap" and "sell dear" by purchasing raw materials from efficient and low-cost economies like Canada's. The organization's objective, so the Canadian said, should be to remove "disparities between prices of similar goods in different markets."[25]

The Europeans were not oblivious to the obvious and various reports produced by the OEEC throughout the earlier 1950s recognized the logic of the Canadian position. For example, a preliminary report drafted by Managing Board officials pointed out that "further attention should ... be given to the removal of restrictions on imports from the dollar area ... In particular, greater freedom for imports of raw materials, basic foodstuffs, semi-manufactured goods, machinery and equipment, the cost of which enters into the cost of production of finished goods in Europe, would also assist the increase of productivity in European agriculture and industry."[26]

The report mirrored the Canadian position very accurately and the delegation used it and similar OEEC studies to its advantage. Always stressing freer trade, Wilgress took the opportunity presented by consideration of dollar discrimination at an executive committee meeting in June 1953 to make the point once again. Buttressed by studies, he was of the opinion that implementation of a new set of trade rules permitting freer dollar imports into OEEC countries would not result in a sudden tidal wave of dollar goods deluging the Continent, a rationale many other delegations had cited for going slowly. In this, at least, Wilgress had the support of a number of international civil servants such Marjolin, who believed that Europe was unduly frightened by the prospect of reducing restrictions. Marjolin confidently expected that many North American goods, such as refrigerators and automobiles, were simply not suited to European conditions or needs and would therefore not be purchased, even if they were available. And, by 1953, when Continental supply had caught up with demand, there was slight chance that North American products could compete effectively in a whole range of products.

However, the OEEC was not interested in even investigating the prospect of increased dollar imports. At a top-level ministerial meeting, held during October 1953, Continental delegations made that position crystal clear. As the Europeans saw it, their policy was a result of Washington's trade practices. They had earlier told American officials that if the US government could not or would not adopt a more liberal trading policy, Europe could well be forced to adopt further restrictions which would, of course, adversely affect Canada.[27] As well, the OEEC made plain its disinterest in Canadian participation in its dollar restrictions study even though, as an associate member, Canada had the right to attend. Only after top-level protests was it included. Even so, Wilgress claimed, attendance at Managing Board meetings was such "a jealously guarded prerogative" that there was no sense in trying to force his way in, regardless of the recent victory. The Canadian delegation would wait, only pushing for admission if the situation took a turn for the worse. At the ministerial meeting itself, the only bright spot for the Canadians was the marked divergence of opinion over the desirability of dollar liberalization. As Wilgress noted, "having in mind how OEEC countries have tended in the past to adopt a rather regional point of view, perhaps this division of opinion should be considered a healthy development."[28]

Given the different perceptions of how fast the Europeans could liberalize trade and implement convertibility, Canada and the OEEC were unlikely to reach a rapid consensus. Moreover, liberalization was uneven across the OEEC, being pushed more forcefully by some countries than others. On a common list of dollar imports, percentages ranged from from a low of 24 for Italy to a high of 98 for Switzerland.[29] Much remained to be done and it was the self-

appointed task of Canada's delegation to encourage and exhort reluctant members in the direction of freer trade to the limit of their
ability.

A DOLLAR RESTRICTIONS STUDY, 1954–56

All these themes were brought together in early 1954 when the OEEC
study of dollar import restrictions, requested by the ministerial council the previous August, was undertaken with Canada and the
United States participating as observers. This study seemed crucial
to Ottawa, with much of Europe now completely recovered from
the effects of the war and becoming once again the economic pow-
erhouse it had been in times past. An added feature was the contemplated move to convertibility by many countries in Western
Europe.

Members of the dollar restrictions working group, which was
chaired by the chancellor of the Exchequer, R.A. Butler, included
ministers of Finance or Economic Affairs from Belgium, France,
Greece, Italy, Norway, the United Kingdom, and West Germany
with support from officials of those countries. This group would be
solely responsible for the final report to the OEEC's council, although
the North Americans would be given an opportunity to present their
views. Such a loose connection with the process was not what Ottawa had expected: as a result of the resolution adopted on dollar
import restrictions at the ministerial meeting that had agreed on
Canadian and American participation, the former had assumed "that
Canada and the United States would be invited to play the part of
full members in the working group." That they were accorded a
second rank position appeared to stem from the fact that there was
"a good deal of reticence on the part of some countries in carrying
out this study," and these did wish to be pushed and prodded by
North American carping and sniping over the slow pace of dollar
liberalization.[30] And while the American-Canadian status in the exercise would not hinder the actual mechanics of participation, to
Canadians it was an unsettling and highly symbolic commentary on
the attitudes with which many of the member countries were approaching the coming investigation.

However, the working group's preliminary report, prepared by
the officials' group, favoured the Canadian position on dollar liberalization. The report was to be considered first by the Joint Trade
and Payments Committee and then, or so F.G. Hooton of the delegation in Paris hoped, would be placed on the agenda of the ministerial council. The report was highly critical of the maintenance of

dollar import restrictions. Indeed, Hooton noted that it was opposed to the creation of "economically unsound" industry that promoted inefficiency and hindered the development of a modern industrial infrastructure. In strong and forceful language it made case in favour of the relaxation of quantitative restrictions on products from Canada and the United States. Moreover, the report continued, one of the first consequences of dollar liberalization would be "to force some prices down for the benefit of European consumers and discourage any unjustified price rise."[31] In short, the Canadians themselves could hardly have penned a better indictment of quantitative restrictions. The obvious political problem now facing Wilgress and his delegation was how best to contain the hostility that would be generated by such a document among a large number of OEEC Ministers who had no wish to move with speed and purpose.[32]

The delegation's work was clearly set out when the preliminary report was considered by the Joint Trade and Payments Committee – the document received short shrift. A number of countries, among them Britain, France, Italy, and West Germany, expressed a strong preference for killing the report at that stage. It was far too optimistic and did not "develop the disadvantages and dangers of lifting dollar import restrictions to the same degree as it [developed] the advantages." According to the UK member, the report was "naive." However, both Canada and the United States pressed hard for its inclusion on the council agenda. The Canadian feeling was that it would provoke discussion which would, "on the whole, be favourable to the relaxation of dollar import restrictions."[33]

Neither the British nor the Germans, two very large and very influential participants in the exercise, agreed with Canada, feeling instead that the report would provoke a most antipathetic reaction from the ministerial council. The result, according to both delegations could, (and probably would), be "retrogressive." However, Bonn's delegation suspected that the British wished "to stall the work on dollar import restrictions ... since it [had] become increasingly embarrassing to the United Kingdom to have some continental countries adopt a much more liberal policy than the United Kingdom [had] adopted." Certainly it was the Canadian sense that their Commonwealth colleagues would work to keep the report off the ministerial agenda for their own reasons; the latter's position was "difficult to understand" and "not helpful."[34] However, the Canadians pushed on, as did the Americans who, under specific instructions from the Department of State, had taken a very strong position that the report should be considered.

The reservations of the less committed members of the working group were overridden and the report was considered by ministers on 5–6 May 1954. Both the Canadians and Americans viewed it as a vitally important step toward convertibility and non-discrimination and both made statements, coordinated by Wilgress and the US delegation chair, Harold Stassen, in order to ensure that the right points were addressed, to the ministerial council. In his presentation, as he had done on many occasions since 1945, Wilgress emphasized the necessity of eliminating dollar restrictions. Because Canada was such an open country and so dependent upon foreign trade, it was concerned about the implications of creating permanent artificial conditions of trade in Western Europe. Reports such as the one under discussion showed that the OEEC was aware of the dangers of high-cost and uncompetitive economies and that it was not too late to take "corrective" action. The experience of certain countries that had liberalized to some extent, such as West Germany and the Benelux group among others, had not been bad – their imports had not risen appreciably. Indeed, in some areas they had actually declined. In short, as Wilgress noted, in many instances the net effect of reducing dollar discrimination had been "to reduce prices in the EPA [European Payments Area]." He ended by saying,

I need hardly emphasize the importance of the relaxation and removal of these restrictions as a preparatory step to currency convertibility. Because of the inevitable uncertainties involved it is important that time should not be lost ... The forecast for the next year ahead appears to be favourable for such moves. Activity is holding up in North America and Europe, and United States extraordinary expenditure abroad, on the basis of present plans, is due to increase. Thus the dollar deficit is not likely to present a serious problem during this period.[35]

The Americans echoed the Canadian analysis: Stassen noted that European dollar reserves had increased by about $2.2 billion in 1953, despite an American recession. Forecasts of US economic activity were now good which, he noted, made it "an appropriate time for adopting basic measures for strengthening the economies of the free world."[36]

At least partly as a result of North American pressure, the OEEC ministerial council decided to press ahead with the work being done by the Trade and Intra-European Payments Committee. Member countries would be asked to submit the necessary information to the organization so that work could progress. However, the Department of External Affairs was not sanguine that this course would yield results. It hoped that in answer to any questionnaires sent out,

OEEC countries would be "more forthcoming than they were with the previous questionnaire." In this case, however, the OEEC secretariat had decided to lose no time in proceeding, and External believed that that in itself was a good sign. Certainly Wilgress and Stassen were not unhappy; a final report would be submitted by 1 October 1954, and it appeared that the great majority of members were fully cooperating with the OEEC.[37] But the Liberal government, removed from the scene of the negotiations, remained more cynical – it would wait. And that scepticism, as events developed, was more appropriate: France and Italy were adamant that they would not join in any early convertibility operation that would signal an end to non-discrimination, with the West Germans, while not as categorical about liberalization, also hesitant.[38]

In a move that surprised Ottawa, during the summer of 1954 the Americans approached the Canadians through their embassy in the national capital and also through their Paris OEEC delegation to determine the possibility of the two delegations working together to steer the Europeans along the "proper" path. Washington's suggestion was that Canadian and American experts together examine submissions by European countries in order to ensure, whenever possible, that continued discrimination against commodities generally imported from the United States or from Canada had an economic justification.

Both Ottawa and the delegation in Paris were sceptical about American motives. Wilgress cabled External Affairs that his group had not "been able to decipher exactly what the US authorities wished to study jointly." He wanted more information before committing himself in any way to work with the United States. Indeed, he felt that the American interest in this case was almost entirely self-seeking. As he said, "one need not look far to find reasons why the United States is seeking our cooperation ... the United States is in a weak position whenever the question of discrimination arises, since European countries would like to bargain the removal of discrimination against the introduction of a more liberal United States commercial policy and it is no wonder they are looking for an ally with a clean copybook."[39]

The Departments of Finance and Trade and Commerce were similarly perplexed by the American request. The former saw it as American scheming to make the OEEC a forum which would adopt a commodity approach where dollar restrictions against specific products which were drawn to the administration's attention by affected US industry would be discussed. As Assistant Deputy Minister of Finance A.F.W. Plumptre pointed out in his reply to the question

posed by external affairs, the United States was "much more concerned with specific complaints made by their domestic industries
than they were with the broad objectives of obtaining maximum and
continuing progress in removing restrictions and discrimination as
a whole."[40] Indeed, at the same time that Washington was making
its request to Canada, it was clear that the US government was
intending to subtract from its GATT obligations in the upcoming
review session, slated to begin in early November 1954. The self-
interest of the American position was too much for Plumptre to
accept. Similarly, Claude Isbister, the respondant for Trade and
Commerce, claimed that his department was "somewhat puzzled as
to the nature and intent of the United States' proposal."[41] He, too,
was opposed to the American suggestion, believing it to be plainly
undesirable given the US record on trade liberalisation. As a result,
as far as the Canadian government was concerned, the matter was
ended. The formal reply to Washington was negative.

As the 1954 study by the Joint Trade and Intra-European Payments
Committee progressed, some Canadian fears were realized. For example, the data received from some countries were inaccurate and
unreliable: from Paris, Wilgress reported that per centage figures for
dollar liberalization were "almost meaningless." Similarly, the attempt to determine the effect of removing dollar import restrictions
on balance of payments fell short of expectations. The OEEC wanted
"to compare the per centages of dollar and European imports into
European countries for 1938 and 1949 and thereby draw some conclusions as to the effects of removing all QRs."[42] Wilgress felt that
there were too many drawbacks to that sort of analysis, and that it
could not be used as a basis for European decision making. Faced
with what appeared to be an increasing mass of inaccurate information and a very suspect methodology, the Canadians took the
position that the ministerial council should make a general recommendation that OEEC members eliminate all discrimination as soon
as possible. The officials' working party agreed to this to the extent
that the *principle* of non-discrimination within the organization
would be established.

The terms of reference of the working party also required it to
address the specific problem of dollar restrictions *vis à vis* Canada
and the United States. On this count, a number of proposals had
been made, none of which were entirely acceptable to Canada or,
it transpired, to the Continent. Among the suggestions were the
establishment of a common list of liberalized products, the establishment of a per centage liberalization target, and the introduction
of a procedure for periodic justification of dollar restrictions. With

regard to the first, Simon Reisman, a member of Canada's delegation to the OEEC, advised "no," to the second he appended "questionable," and the third he wrote "really the job of the G.A.T.T."[43]

The Europeans were fundamentally in agreement with Canada on these points. For various reason, there was no support in the working group for a common list or for the establishment of targets. For example, the British were opposed because they considered that the OEEC should not undertake commitments to non-OEEC countries. The Canadians were concerned because, given the great differences in per centage liberalization among organization members, any attempt to make all conform to one figure "might well retard the advance of the stronger countries." Wilgress ended his report from Paris by observing that progress thus far, while not totally satisfactory, was also not entirely without promise. Still, as he said,

The most helpful line for the OEEC to take, in our opinion, would be to relate the desirability of the removal of dollar discrimination to the probable, if not inevitable, economic effects of the introduction of convertibility – which imply that discrimination must end with convertibility. A forthright ministerial principle on the desirability of removing discrimination as an essential step toward preparing the country economies for convertibility would be a useful keystone for future work.[44]

The report itself, although given to the OEEC in late October, was not discussed by the council until late the following month. The importance attached to these council meetings was considerable. Reflecting that, Stassen and Randolph Burgess, the Deputy to the US secretary of the Treasury, made a special trip from Washington to represent the United States, and there were also observers from the GATT, the IBRD and the IMF present. Despite the intense interest shown, the Europeans refused to play along, which the Canadians did not appreciate. A draft council resolution concerning the relaxation of quantitative restrictions on imports from the dollar area was distributed for general consideration in early December 1954. The resolution, drawn up by some of the smaller OEEC countries, urged that while member countries should undertake to the best of their ability the removal of dollar discrimination, such a policy should not be allowed to interfere with or endanger progress made thus far on intra-European liberalization.

A Canadian counter-resolution did not achieve much success. The proposal reiterated Canada's view that it was in the European interest to eliminate dollar QRs and also pointed to the danger which Ottawa saw in attempting to relate European trade policy liberalization to further liberalization of American trade policy. In a telegram to External Affairs, Wilgress observed that such a situation "would make it more difficult for the Canadian Government to resist demands from Canadian producers for increased protection if specific reciprocity were made a condition of QR relaxation." The Canadian objective in submitting an alternative resolution was two-fold: first to separate the examination of trade practices in the two associated countries, Canada and the United States, and thereby reduce the risk of demands for reciprocity and second, to restrict liberalization and remove any suggestion of substracting the liberalization list.[45]

Certainly Canada was not prepared to accept any resolution that made an improvement in commercial policies of dollar countries toward Europe a *quid pro quo* for relaxation of dollar import restrictions which the Canadians maintained was in the interest of the Europeans. If satisfactory changes were not made in the draft, then it was quite possible that Canada would abstain. Officials in External Affairs notified the delegation in Paris that under those circumstances, they had "no alternative to reconciling ourselves to such a situation since we are not prepared to participate in the sacrificing of the important principles involved."[46] Those important principles translated into markets on which Canadian prosperity could well rest. If the country's position was seen as unhelpful, because North American, especially American, protectionism was an important barrier to a Europe anxious to pay its way, it should be remembered that Canada's tariffs had fallen dramatically since 1947, and Ottawa was prepared to do more.

Neither the Americans nor the Europeans, however, believed that there was any chance of the Canadian counter-resolution being accepted. Furthermore, Wilgress felt that if Canada persisted in its opposition to the European course of action, there was the possibility of a number of unhelpful results:

One possibility is that all studies of dollar restrictions might be dropped. This [British delegate Sir Hugh Ellis-Rees] thinks would be unfortunate since the subject is so closely allied to convertibility [which the United Kingdom was considering through the collective approach]. Another possibility is that all references to Canada might be deleted and the wording adjusted so as to make it acceptable to the United States and passed without our approval or participation in future studies. This result would be bound to have most unfortunate and uncomfortable repercussions on our position in OEEC.[47]

Pressure was being brought to bear by the European and the Americans to get Canada to conform to the wishes of the majority. Facing a solid wall of opposition, the delegation sent to Ottawa for instructions.

Wilgress's message had been discussed in cabinet and with the deputy ministers of Trade and Commerce and Finance, while the advice of Louis Rasminsky, deputy governor of the Bank of Canada, was also canvassed. Clearly, Canadian ministers and officials were very worried about the atmosphere in which the dollar liberalization discussions were taking place. It appeared in Ottawa that the OEEC's member states were intent upon reneging on GATT commitments to free trade and reduced discrimination as their domestic economic situations improved. A better name for the exercise could well turn out to be dollar de-liberalization.

The cabinet's view was that the delegation should stand its ground. The senior mandarinate in Ottawa held the very strong opinion that Canada would not "agree to a resolution which would imply that the liberalization of dollar import restrictions by member countries ... should be made conditional or dependent on the commercial policies of the North American countries or on the avoidance of any significant disturbance in the present pattern of European trade." Under-secretary of State for External Affairs Jules Léger elaborated, noting that,

In holding this position we are not merely being purists. We are certainly not underrating the importance or urgency of an improvment in US commercial policies. We are also not moved by any reluctance to have our own policies examined critically. We are, however, genuinely worried by the use which might be made of the principles involved in this resolution in subsequent discussions in the OEEC, in the consideration of related matters in broader bodies such as the GATT and the Fund as well as in any bilateral talks which we may have with individual European countries.[48]

If the Europeans rejected Canada's resolution, then the delegation was not to stand in the way of the passage of the OEEC resolution favoured by member countries: it would abstain from the vote. However, it would also make plain its desire to participate in any related discussions or studies of the matter. Here the Canadians stood alone, but they could not afford to be left out of OEEC deliberations, whatever the principles involved.

The American Department of State also put pressure on External Affairs to change its views, but ultimately to no avail. Indeed, the Canadians played a crafty game in turning back US overtures. Clearly, for political reasons, Canadian participation in the dollar liberalization exercise was important to Washington. Secretary of State John Foster Dulles and Stassen, for example, wished to be able to point to this OEEC activity "as a mark of the Organization's vitality" when dealing with Congress[49]; Canadian reservations about the exercise could well arouse congressional suspicions that American interests were not being projected as assiduously as they might be. In a sense, Washington needed Canada's participation. But Ottawa had very serious reservations about the usefulness of dollar liberalization exercises in the OEEC. The dangers were very real that the organization could decide upon a more restrictive policy and there was also the very real Canadian concern that the Europeans would come to view the OEEC as a more legitimate forum than the GATT for the discussion of trade problems. Ottawa was emphatic that this should not be allowed to happen and no amount of cajoling could sway it from that point of view.

Canada did participate in the program, although not because of American pressure: it was demonstrably in Ottawa's own interest to do so. As Wilgress said to the OEEC council on accepting the obligations imposed by the dollar liberalization exercise, he did not need "to emphasize the Canadian interest in the removal of quantitative restrictions on imports from the dollar area." He reiterated Canadian policy that countries which maintained QRs should remove them "as soon as their individual financial situations permit, in accordance with their international obligations and in accordance with their own interest in rationalizing and strengthening their economies, reducing costs and improving standards of living."[50]

The dollar liberalization exercise itself had been almost anticlimactic. After its vigorous fight during the Christmas period over the wording and intent of the resolution laying out what would be studied, it was unsettling, but certainly not surprising, for the Canadians to realize that the OEEC was not as interested in the Canadian situation as it was in that of the United States. Indeed, the questionnaire asking for details of economic policy sent by the organization to both North Americans was almost specifically directed toward the United States – it had little bearing on Canadian policy. According to Wilgress, none of the OEEC delegations claimed to have any complaint with Canada's commercial policy. The main reason the country was being asked to submit a response at all was "so as not to single out the United States for special attention" which, the OEEC worried, would make Washington more suspicious and intransigent.[51] As Wilgress and his delegation were becoming more and more aware, Canada mattered less and less in the larger context.

Even so, Canada remained watchful of OEEC transgressions and periodically intervened in order to inject what it believed to be some proportion into the organization's affairs. For example, Canada was called upon to defend the supremacy of GATT and IMF obligations over those of the OEEC. In early June 1955 Wilgress made a very strong statement to that effect, prompting the French to denounce Canada as having "taken too rigid a line."[52] Both the Americans and the Germans welcomed the Canadian statement, with the head of the American delegation, despite his previous attitude, claiming that "he wished he could have made a similar statement."[53] Unfortunately, he was barred from doing so by his superiors. To the Canadians and several of their OEEC allies (of which there were a few), the statement was "both appropriate and useful." "It is true that it was introduced into a delicate and many-sided negotiation in which the tactics of dealing with the French were important. The results of the Ministerial Council, however, would not appear to indicate that our intervention disrupted the European negotiations and a firm restatement of our views will have done no harm and perhaps some good."[54]

Whether or not that was the case, the shape of the final report was not likely to recommend it to Canada. Indeed, after reviewing the replies to the OEEC questionnaire on dollar import restrictions, External Affairs observed that the concern which the Canadian delegation had expressed as to the council's December-January resolution was justified. Certainly it appeared to the Interdepartmental Committee on External Trade Policy that the terms of reference as laid down by the resolution had encouraged "a negative view of dollar liberalization in which they attempt to justify a go-slow policy and place the onus on the United States and ourselves."[55] Furthermore, several OEEC members had adopted the attitude that dollar restrictions were in themselves good, which prompted External Affairs to once again repeat Canadian concern over that attitude.

In particular, the French had adopted that position. As External Affairs uneasily noted, Paris believed that "import restrictions provide the necessary protection to higher cost economies."[56] This was antithetical to the generally accepted principle that import and exchange controls were justified only as a temporary expedient to safeguard a country's balance of payments position. Also, it appeared that France was of the opinion that any dollar liberalization program should not disturb the pattern of trade among the OEEC's members and underdeveloped areas which had been constructed through regional and bilateral agreements. This was in direct conflict with Ottawa's objective of global multilateral trade and ran counter to the thrust of such international organizations as the GATT.

Despite evidence that their position did not make economic sense, the French persisted. When an *ad hoc* meeting of American experts and European officials was held to discuss dollar liberalization during the several days following 26 September 1955, Paris, unlike the great majority of other OEEC members, did not send a senior bureaucrat. Consequently, whether out of design or not, it played a very limited role in the proceedings. Nevertheless, the French response to certain questions elicited a sharp rebuke from both the Canadian and American in attendance. When asked whether the French government could remove a few quantitative restrictions against dollar imports, its delegate had observed that this would be difficult: "For example ... the French Government might wish to allow the importation of certain types of chemical products which were not produced in France. A year or so later after production had been built up in France, they would wish to cease importing from the dollar area. Accordingly, it was preferable to keep such categories under quantitative control."[57] As Wilgress noted, "This gratuitous disclosure given in a frank but tactless manner drew sharp criticism from both our representative and from the US representative."[58] But that merely reflected the reality of the French position, where even with respect to OEEC trade, about 55 per cent of imports were still covered by restrictions in the form of import taxes. When Edgar Faure had announced in mid-January 1955 that by 1 April, his government would move to the 75 per cent liberalization figure that had been attained by most organization members, it remained more of an April Fool's prank – soft currency imports were liberalized but the taxes remained.[59]

The September meeting of experts had been called largely at the behest of the United States, which believed organization countries were not taking full advantage of opportunities to press forward with further dollar liberalization and felt that an exchange of views would serve to allay European fears. The initial reaction of the Europeans had been cool and the American delegate felt compelled to offer the OEEC countries the opportunity to quiz three American experts on US commercial policy if member countries would agree to meet and exchange information on the effects of dollar liberalization.

American reasons for convening the meeting were largely borne out by the results. Indeed, with the exception of the French and British, the latter of whom gave a very contradictory presentation, the majority of OEEC members came out in favour of dollar liberalization. At the end of the meeting, the Germans, a "pivotal power" in any dollar liberalization exercise, were visibly impressed by what had transpired. The German delegate went so far as to claim that "Maybe the problems [of dollar liberalization] have been over-estimated and the advantages under-estimated."[62]

Canada took an active part in the discussions in support of the us position. All in all, Wilgress found them to be most satisfactory. Certainly it appeared that European misconceptions had been cleared up with rewarding results, while countries opposed to the North American position, such as France and the United Kingdom were forced to resort to shaky argumentation in defence of their positions. Indeed, when Isaiah Frank of the us delegation concluded that dollar liberalization had not had any harmful effects on European trade, most of the Europeans concurred. However, the real test of strength would come when the report itself was tabled in the ministerial council.

Its consideration was delayed for several months until early 1956 as revisions were sent from various oeec capitals. Some of these revisions made Canadians suspect that politicians had not taken to heart criticisms levied and accepted by officials at the September meeting. Ottawa was concerned about a number of points raised in the penultimate draft report. While noting that it was an improvement over earlier versions, Ottawa still recommended a number of revisions. For example, chapter 5 still placed "too much emphasis ... on obstacles to further progress, and this almost obscures the fact that the balance of payments situation of each individual country should be the sole criterion. Some of the "obstacles" to which considerable detail is devoted ... appear to us to be more imaginary than real, and would not, in any case, provide justification for continued restrictions."[61] The delegation in Paris was instructed to take up such points with the oeec.

After this period of hectic activity, the oeec appeared to become almost somnolent by late 1955, perhaps a result of the new objective undertaken by six of its members, the European Economic Community (eec) initiative of that June. However, the Canadians were concerned that there was slight chance that there would be any developments on convertibility and dollar liberalization. Even the freeing up of intra-European trade "was in the doldrums" and the 90 per cent liberalization measure undertaken in January 1955 would not be realized.[62] The Canadians in Paris worried that these developments, when combined with the mild inflation then afflicting Western Europe, would have a disproportionate effect on the final report. In spite of the goodwill expressed during the recently completed exercise and the September *ad hoc* meeting, a negative attitude now prevailed in most European capitals with respect to the limitation of qrs. Wondering whether or not a salutary shove could be given to the whole dollar liberalization exercise "in light of the somewhat barren outlook for the oeec," the Canadian delegation answered its own question – it was difficult "to see what further decisions the OEEC might take at the present time."[63] As a result, the delegation was instructed to wait for the final report, when it would be in a better position to assess what might be acceptable to the Europeans.[64]

Unfortunately, what was acceptable to them was not acceptable to Ottawa. Officials in the capital believed that the draft report's findings were extremely prejudicial to the Canadian interest. For example, serious questions were raised over the report's contention that the need for protection against North American imports was a legitimate reason for continuing discrimination and also that the liberalization of US commercial policies was a necessary prerequisite to dollar liberalization. The Europeans challenged the American practice of subsidization of some exports, their penchant for tied loans, and the generally punitive nature of US customs administration. As well, economically stronger OEEC members, such as West Germany, were not prepared to agree to the elimination of quota restrictions. There was also no sign of unanimity on the need to adopt non-discrimination as a principle in conducting world trade. To countries such as Canada which thought in terms of a world system in which convertibility and non-discrimination were inseparable, it was surprising to discover that others whose currencies were, in some cases, on the road to being convertible still had some reservations about the abandonment of discrimination, at least against the products of the dollar area. Those reservations lent support to those, such as the French, who attached great importance to the continuation of discrimination because they were opposed to any general move toward convertibility.[65] Finally, many Europeans, but especially the French and Italians, favoured a bilateral policy that was consistent with much of the above.

In short, the report gave more emphasis to alleged obstacles and dangers in the way of further liberalization than it did to "any clear recognition of balance of payments criteria as being the essential justification for the maintenance of quantitative restrictions."[66] Furthermore, it gave no indication that OEEC countries had any sense of commitment or obligation to liberalize trade as a result of their membership in GATT. This was what Canada had most feared and what it had sought to avoid by constant repetition that the GATT took precedence over the OEEC.

The "Final Report on Dollar Liberalization," tabled in January 1956, had obviously not paid even lip service to the consistent Canadian criticism, bringing home once again Ottawa's relative powerlessness in the larger context. Not surprisingly, the report made no attempt to disguise a particularly Eurocentric view of arrangements. Still, the Canadian delegation felt that the exercise had not been a total failure in that the report contained some valuable statistics and indicated that the European experience thus far was that dollar imports did not swamp liberalizing countries. To the contrary, as Canada had maintained, it helped them become more efficient and productive. In his statement to the OEEC's ministerial council in mid-February, Wilgress emphasized these points. He pointed out that "these results of past stages of liberalization should serve to encourage Members to take new steps." He went on to note that the Canadian government

would stress the importance of Member countries seizing on these favourable circumstances and in their own interest to adjust their economies to outside competition and reduce discrimination as quickly as their individual balance of payments positions permit ... [But chapter 5] places too much emphasis on the obstacles to further progress and tends to obscure the fact that the balance of payments situation of each individual country should be the sole criterion for maintaining QR's. Most member countries have commitments with respect to Quantitative Restrictions in other organizations and an acceptance of this report is predicated on the understanding that it in no way implies a derogation from those commitments.[67]

The long dollar liberalization exercise, lasting nearly eighteen months, had been unsatisfactory for Canada. Its delegation participated in meetings, yet the Canadian vision of international trade did not have much impact on the Europeans, even though the economic and political climate was not unfavourable and their actual experiences with respect to dollar liberalization had been favorable. By 1956, although a significant percentage of European imports from North America were now free of restrictions, it had been a long, slow process with many detours and much backsliding. The reluctance to liberalize had forced Canada to turn to the United States as a market of last resort.

Similarly, later dollar liberalization exercises did not live up to Canadian expectations, although this mattered less by the later 1950s when a huge percentage (65 %) of Canada's trade was done on a continental basis. For example, during a trip to Paris in late 1956, Plumptre felt that the exercise then underway, which has been started that year, was "all pretty hasty and superficial" and he doubted that it would "influence the rate or direction of dollar liberalization."[68] The exercises did provide a forum more amenable to the Europeans in which to discuss their trade restrictions and American commercial policy. They also provided "objective" proof of European progress to date on dollar liberalization, always important when dealing with the United States. Canadian hopes that the exercises might translate into direct Continental tariff-cutting legislation were not realized.

And while the conclusions of another OEEC dollar liberalization exercise undertaken in 1956–57 were generally more positive and outward-looking than those of the year before, Plumptre nothwithstanding, another factor had influenced their pace and direction. As a result of the uncertainly caused by the Suez crisis, the Canadian delegation reported home that "no general advance in removing dollar restrictions is contemplated or recommended this year."[69] But more to the point, the 1956–57 exercise seemed designed almost exclusively as an American-European one, with Canada involved only tangentially and then only because of the strength of its delegation. The Europeans seemed unwilling to take advantage of a rapidly expanding Canadian market for manufactured goods and semi-manufactured products that the Continent turned out in great abundance. Indeed, one of the major Canadian concerns with the dollar liberalization report issued in March 1957 was its preoccupation "with the proximity of the USA" as an explanation for the poor showing of European exporters in the Canadian market.[70] But, as Ottawa was well aware, it was far more than that: the Europeans were simply disinterested.

Future dollar liberalization exercises were planned, the most immediate to report to the OEEC by July 1958. By that time, however, discussion was largely academic as the European Common Market had come into being with its range of barriers to trade and the European Free Trade Area was threatening to do likewise. While the exercises did provide some insights into the operations and rationales of European countries with respect to dollar liberalization, they ultimately accomplished little; certainly there was nothing in their results to suggest that they propelled the Continent forward down the road of freer trade. Ottawa put much energy into the meetings and played its part to the hilt, operating under the mistaken impression that the earlier exercises would have some moral, if not executive force. For Canada, the stakes were high: European reluctance to lower trade barriers was one more factor that contributed to the development of a continental North American market, much against the wishes of the Canadian government. Unlike Nebechanezzer, however, Ottawa did not need a Daniel to translate the writing on the wall: the starkness of the statistics was difficult to miss.

Beginning in the earlier 1950s, the OEEC undertook a number of dollar liberalization exercises, which included Canada and the United States in their capacities as associate members of the organization, that stretched over a number of months. Canadians used these exercises to encourage their Continental colleagues to reduce tariff restrictions against dollar goods and implement convertibility, but to little avail. Indeed, it was not until the Fifteenth Session of the GATT, held in late 1959 in Tokyo, that war-induced restrictionism was no longer an issue. There, the American delegation shared the Canadian view that the session "marked the end of a period when discrimination was a major issue."[71] But by then it mattered little to Ottawa; Canada was firmly a part of a continental North American economy. The country's exhortations, encouragements, and proddings had met with such resistance in Europe that it had had no alternative but to turn to the United States as the only secure market for many of its products. As had been the case in its bilateral relationship with Britain, Ottawa's policy in that regard was guided not by the subjective preferences of politicians and officials but by necessity. As a result, Canada remained, by and large, on the outside looking, not so much in, as south.

5 Canada and the GATT, 1952–56

Since the first round of tariff negotiations at Geneva in 1947, Canada had relied in large measure on the GATT to provide the leverage necessary to prod other countries into lowering tariffs and liberalizing trade. Through Geneva and the following rounds held at Annecy (1949) and Torquay (1950–51), Canada met with other contracting parties to encourage multilateral reductions. However, as a result of British and European use of non-tariff barriers against dollar imports, the primary benefit to Canada from the exercises came from agreements made with the United States. At GATT administrative sessions, held at least once per year, Canada's delegation continued to press for some form of dollar liberalization to give effect to the tariff reductions negotiated in GATT. The British and the Europeans began to move toward liberalization in the early 1950s, but progress was halting, circuitous, and sometimes contrary. Because of this scenario, the GATT did not live up to Canadian expectations during the early 1950s. Nevertheless, it remained one of the cornerstones of Canada's economic policy, reflecting the country's economic vision and the hope it held for the future.

However, by the mid-1950s the GATT itself was in an ambiguous position. Following the rather lacklustre results of the Torquay round, it seemed that the multilateral spirit had dissipated and, along with it, the determination to see the GATT experiment through.

Of some concern to multilateralists, the agreement remained an interim organization only, with no real official standing. Throughout its brief history it had been applied provisionally on the basis of an understanding reached after the untimely demise in 1950 of the ITO at the hands of its archenemy, the Congress of the United States.[1] That in itself had been a sobering reminder to internationalists of the power of protectionist sentiment in the United States.

There were other actions that drained strength from the GATT. One of these, the 1951 Belgian decision to impose import restrictions on dollar imports from North America, provoked a reaction from Ottawa and Washington that was out of all proportion to the potential rewards to each. Both insisted that Belgian policy was purely discriminatory and had little justification other than to give certain sectors of the Belgian economy added protection. In an additional twist, the Canadians were also convinced that Brussels had implemented the restrictions at least partly at the behest of the British, who wanted to reduce North American competition in that market.[2] To Canada and the United States, the policy contravened both the letter and the spirit of the GATT and the former especially was "very much on the war-path."[3]

In concert with Washington, Ottawa pushed Belgium to reconsider its decision, citing the damage being done to the agreement. The Canadian government was only too well aware that the case created substantial risks in the United States which threatened the continuation of relatively liberal US import policies. These were "already under heavy pressure" by protectionist interests and it was clear to policy makers in both capitals that the Belgian decision was "not defensible on balance-of-payments grounds [and] may well provide the basis for further actions by Congress limiting opportunities for foreign countries to export to the US."[4] But despite intense North American pressure, the restrictions remained in place for more than eighteen months, ultimately at a not insignificant cost to the credibility of the GATT.

Two initiatives that the British Conservative government undertook following its election in late 1951 also aroused the ire of Ottawa and Washington and proved very unsettling to the GATT. The first was "deliberalization" with respect to the non-sterling world, the result of Britain's 1951 dollar crisis. The policy, started by the Labour Government and carried forward by the Conservatives, saw the per centage of dollar imports that entered Britain free of restriction decrease while open general licenses were revoked on a wide range of imports from Western Europe. Although the GATT was not directly involved, any policy enacted by any government, however justified, that subtracted from obligations under the agreement redounded to its discredit in Washington.

The other initiative, which was much more worrisome for multilateralists and contained the potential seeds of destruction for the GATT, was the internal British debate over the advisability of securing a waiver which would permit them to raise any most-favoured-nation (mfn) rate without at the same time raising the British Preferential (BP) rate. London was determined to escape from the confines of the no-new-preference rule, agreed to in 1947, which had bound margins of preference (the difference between the mfn and BP rates). This was in part because of the United Kingdom's attempt to substitute a system of tariffs for a system of quotas, but also because the Conservative Party believed in the principle of imperial preference. As well, the political side of government (as opposed to the bureaucratic) felt the GATT to be increasingly unsuited to Britain's context in the early 1950s: as a UK memo noted, it "was getting more and more unrealistic, chiefly because its Articles were designed to regulate trade in a much more stable world economy."[5] What was needed was some other type of world trade organization or, as some in cabinet suggested, for Britain to withdraw completely from the agreement and "go it alone" with the sterling area.[6]

Within Britain itself the debate provoked some unsettling issues. For example, in discussions in the cabinet, two positions were staked out by opposing factions. The first, most popular with government, the Conservative Party, which had a long history of viewing imperial preference as the apogee of civilization, and the country at large, was presented by the president of the Board of Trade, Peter Thorneycroft. Strongly opposed to the liberal doctrines enshrined in the GATT its supporters advocated abrogating the no-new-preference rule, whatever the consequences. As Thorneycroft's group insisted, "Her Majesty's Government should proceed as if the waiver had been granted." This faction believed that the system could not work until the imbalance in world trade was addressed, in which the United States would have to play a major role. The other position, led by Foreign Secretary Anthony Eden, maintained that such a policy would be an unmitigated disaster "and could not be confined to the forum of the GATT." It would antagonize all concerned and "play into the hands of protectionists in the U.S.A." to the detriment of UK interests.[7]

While the British attack was divided, it was still perceived as dangerous in Ottawa. As an indication of how seriously the Canadians viewed the situation, the minister of Trade and Commerce,

C.D. Howe, travelled to Geneva to address the eighth session of the GATT in Geneva in September 1953, the first time a minister in his position had done so. While not singling the British out for attention, he surely had them in mind when he claimed that "it is common ... to blame trade difficulties on the General Agreement ... Those who feel that their interests are adversely affected by the General Agreement are inclined to be more vocal than those who benefit."[8]

The disharmony among the GATT's important members had a very debilitating effect as neither the Canadians nor the Americans could accept a waiver of the no-new-preference rule without compromising one of the GATT's most important provisions. The latter called the waiver "undesirable,"[9] while the former wanted to bump up the level of representation at the Commonwealth pre-GATT meeting for the eighth session in order to properly deal with the problem. As a British bureaucrat then noted, "the Canadians [were] itching to have a discussion about the future of the G.A.T.T."[10]

In the end, little of the hard-line scenario of the North Americans was realized and the British did get a waiver, although not the blanket one requested. It was subject to two conditions: that any resort to restrictions not unfairly divert trade from foreign to Commonwealth sources and that the decision apply only in respect to goods which had traditionally enjoyed duty-free entry into the United Kingdom when imported from the Commonwealth.[11] However, the lengthy debate within the government by a very important member of the GATT (to say nothing of the award of the waiver) again served to compromise the agreement's integrity and prevent the development of any basic consensus. Indeed, in Britain, in the words of a Foreign Office official immediately following the eighth session, "GATT [had] gone to ground."[12] With brush fires springing up which threatened to turn into raging infernos, the North American governments were forced to react rather than initiate. Moreover, the result helped to strengthen protectionist forces in both countries. And when one of those countries appeared set to desert the cause of liberalization and non-discrimination to seek its own waiver, alarm bells sounded in Ottawa as never before.

Washington had always been less consistent than Ottawa in its commitment to the GATT, but multilateralists in the Department of State had been in control for most of the postwar period. However, after Torquay, it increasingly appeared to many in Ottawa that support for this position was decreasing as the United States implemented some procedures that contravened its GATT obligations under Article XI 2(c)(i), which allowed quotas on agricultural imports only when domestic production was being restrained to the same degree. That was not the case when quotas were imposed on imports of butter, cheese, dried milk, and a few other agricultural commodities under the authority of Section 22 of the Agricultural Adjustments Act, first implemented in August 1935 and renewed periodically thereafter, which *required* the secretary of agriculture to invoke such restrictions where low prices tended to undermine domestic agricultural programs. Since the Americans had spent more than $90 million supporting producers in these areas since 1952, it was automatic that the affected sectors would receive additional protection. Congress had had the last word here and had included a rider in the Trade Agreements Extension Act of 1951, the legislation that empowered the president to enter into commercial agreements with foreign countries, to the effect that no international agreement could be administered in a manner inconsistent with the requirements of Section 22.[13] These restrictions were illegal under the GATT, but CPs could do little, given the position of power from which the United States operated. As Robert Hudec has pointed out, "all GATT could do in the last analysis was to demonstrate, as sharply and as precisely as possible, the community's view that the United States has sinned."[14]

The strength of the "protectionists" in departments such as Agriculture, the Treasury, and Commerce was clearly waxing as the decade progressed. Reflecting that, US Secretary of State John Foster Dulles was told in mid-1954 that the government's recent foreign economic policy record was "one of inaction at best or retreat."[15] This change in tone in the United States was the result of a number of factors, including traditional congressional hostility combined with the demands of constituents and the election of a Republican president, Dwight Eisenhower, in 1952.

The change in US administration was the reason for the August 1953 establishment of the Commission on Foreign Economic Policy (CFEP), also known as the Randall Commission after its chairman, Clarence Randall. It was struck to investigate and recommend appropriate policy on Washington's foreign economic relations to President Eisenhower. The commission heard submissions from interested groups in the United States and also travelled to Paris for four days. There Dana Wilgress presented a statement in his capacity as chair of the GATT which also reflected policy in Ottawa. He reminded the Americans of their obligations, noting that many CPs were very anxious over the use of agricultural import quotas. This had had not only "a serious practical adverse effect on the economies of some countries but it [had] created doubts about United States import policy as a whole." Moreover, those doubts could not have come at a worse moment; for the first time in six years, Wilgress felt, there was "concrete evidence that countries were prepared to dismantle their restrictions against the dollar." He also pointed out, however, that any substantive forward movement depended on the participation and cooperation of the United States. Indeed, while 1953 had been held out as a year in which further tariff cuts would take place, that had not been possible, largely because the United States did not feel it was in a position to engage in further tariff reductions. If, Wilgress finished,

the recommendations of your Commission and the resulting trade policies of the United States are positive, I feel the prospects are good for making a real advance towards an effective system of multilateral trade and payments, from which all countries, including the United States, would benefit. If United States policies are not encouraging, I very much fear a progressive deterioration in world trading relations, a resumption of restrictionist and discriminatory policies, and a revival of autarky and economic blocs in many parts of the world.[16]

This "not encouraging" scenario drew shudders from the mandarinate in Ottawa, which fully subscribed to Wilgress's ominous predictions.

Hume Wrong, Canada's ambassador to the United States, suggested that his intervention had gone largely unheard by Randall and in Washington. Indeed, Wrong thought that "the wind [seemed] to be blowing [very] strongly here against GATT," which was worrying. That anxiety was heightened by Raymond Vernon of the Department of State who, with the support of some senior people in his department, was active in encouraging Wrong to tell Ottawa to deliver a toughly worded note against possible American backsliding on the GATT. As suggested by Vernon's activity, liberal-minded elements in the US Administration and bureaucracy saw Canada as one of their few allies in the fight against more restrictionist colleagues and congressmen.

Vernon also offered the rather startling opinion that the secretary of Commerce, Sinclair Weeks, was flatly opposed to the GATT, the secretary of the Treasury, George Humphrey, was sceptical about it, and the powerful secretary of State, Dulles, had shown very little interest in it. Given this rather sobering analysis, Wrong agreed that Ottawa should make its concerns known, suggesting to External Affairs that "a statement ... by Mr. Howe of Canada's interest in the GATT would certainly have a salutary effect." The ambassador proposed a number of recommendations for the minister's consideration:

- that a note on GATT should be presented to the State Department within the next few days;
- that the importance attached by the Canadian government to GATT should be reiterated;
- that the value of having an international code of commercial conduct should be emphasized and;
- that questions should be asked about the views of the Administration on the future of the GATT.[18]

The note from Ottawa went out on 1 March, emphasizing Canada's "deep concern" over Washington's developing attitude toward the agreement. Clearly, as Assistant Secretary of State Samuel Waugh noted, Ottawa was "especially interested in preserving the strength of the General Agreement."[19]

The timing of the Canadian note was undoubtedly influenced by the release of the CFEP's report, the general thrust of which called for a more liberal trade policy. However, its recommendations were hemmed in by restrictions and political expedience and were cautious and limited in scope. From the Canadian perspective, it could have been much better: Claude Isbister of Trade and Commerce found certain sections "had been written in great haste as a political compromise and did not represent the outcome of any deep or prolonged thought."[20] The Canadian embassy claimed the report was "discouraging,"[21] while from his vantage point in Paris, Wilgress also expressed concern about the possible effect of some of the recommendations made with respect to the GATT.[22]

Specifically, the report questioned the underlying basis of the GATT. It proposed that GATT's organizational provisions "should be renegotiated with a view to confining the functions of the contracting parties to sponsoring multilateral trade negotiations, recommending broad trade policies for individual consideration and providing a forum for consulation regarding trade practices."[23] Ottawa did not want an organization whose power was to be confined merely to jurisdictional matters – it wanted one that would continue to establish a code of international commercial behaviour. In short, the Randall Commission suggested weakening the GATT just where the Canadian government wanted it strengthened.

What followed from the CFEP's recommendations was US determination to push ahead with a general review of the GATT, in large part to make the agreement's provisions more closely parallel American legislation. Washington was concerned over the possibility that the CPs might act collectively to change US prerogatives without the agreement of the United States. Clearly, Congress would not tolerate such an intrusion into American policymaking and, if the situation was not changed in favour of the United States, it would be very difficult, perhaps impossible, to obtain congressional ratification for the GATT, which would mean its demise. The objective, so an American memorandum maintained, was to find a formula that would allow an accommodation of GATT and US interests without totally impairing the former's effectiveness.[24]

As well, the United States was adamant that the review session should take place by November 1954 at the latest because of Washington's legislative timetable. Given one of the Randall Commission's recommendations, that any of the GATT's organizational provisions be submitted to Congress for approval, it meant that any review session would have to meet the deadline imposed by the president's decision to submit his program to Congress by March 1955 in order to have it dealt with before the presidential election year of 1956. And regardless of the disadvantages of having an early review session, the United States had to be accommodated, given the carrot of the president's intention to secure congressional approval for the GATT. That was the aspect the agreement's secretary-general, Eric Wyndham-White, emphasized to more reluctant members such as Canada: "In view of the importance of securing congressional approval for United States participating in a GATT organization, I feel there is a great deal to be said in favour of arranging the review time-table in such a way as to meet the legislative requirements of the United States."[25] Power carried with it benefits as well as responsibility.

Wyndham-White, however, was not sure that any new tariff legislation submitted to Congress would be ratified. As he told Isbister, "a number of competent observers consider that in the present temper of Congress it is unlikely that even the modest proposals put forward by the Administration can be adopted."[26] In other words, any advance in US commercial policy could be very limited. However, he was also at pains to make clear that, despite potential US problems, attending countries should approach the negotiations in a positive spirit: if they were regarded in a negative way from the outset, the results could be most unpleasant, serving no other purpose than to strengthen restrictionist elements in Washington.

The Canadians did not necessarily agree with the secretary-general's interpretation nor with the order in which the Americans proposed handling the review. Indeed, Ottawa was convinced that the us approach would only end in bad results. Rather than having the Americans negotiate changes in the agreement and then submit legislation to Congress, the Canadians felt that the United States should state their trade policy and then proceed with the GATT negotiations. As A.R. Kilgour, one of External Affairs' men at the embassy in Washington, pointed out to his department, the embassy "was inclined to doubt that it would be practicable to hold a useful review session before us trade policy legislation has been passed or at least until there is more convincing evidence than is available now of a real determination on the part of the us to move forward."[27] As he rightly observed, to attempt a review of the GATT in the present circumstances would be to risk a us demand that its obligations under the organizational and agricultural provisions be completely reworked. Moreover, to try to negotiate on those questions without holding out any definite hope of concessions in other respects would be to risk disintegration of the agreement.

There were a few added twists in the equation. The State Department had lost most of its GATT experts through sabbaticals or retirements, while the us Department of the Treasury, which would presumably have to take up some of the slack, had demonstrated little interest in the agreement. There also remained the omnipresent problem of a struggle which would pit the executive arm of government against the legislative. This had been brought out most clearly when the Eisenhower administration withdrew from consideration legislation sponsored by Representative Robert Kean that provided for the extension of the president's authority to enter into trade agreements: the president had wanted the Reciprocal Trade Agreements Act extended for another year "without strings."[28] This was an absolutely basic and vital point and, as a result of the withdrawal, the United States would have no effective power to enter into another round of tariff negotiations.

Finally, to make matters worse from the Canadian point of view, the United States had announced that it intended to obtain a waiver from the agricultural obligations of the GATT. Despite the popular impression, agricultural goods were included under the agreement's provisions, but rules governing their implementation had more often been observed in the breach. Indeed, rules governing agricultural products had proved so ineffective as to make them a mockery. Because of this, John Jackson has written that "some writers or practitioners have made the error of stating that the GATT does not legally apply to agricultural goods."[29] Certainly the Section 22 requirements imposed earlier in the decade by the United States had been a graphic indication of that. Article XI governing agricultural imports was powerless in the face of us determination to pursue its own course, undeterred by the legal niceties of GATT membership. While the Americans had been operating in this area as if their GATT obligations did not exist, the waiver they demanded, if granted, could have immediate and disastrous implications for Canada's large trade in agricultural products with the United States and also give permanent *de jure* status to an unenviable situation. Despite their close economic relationship, Canadian and American interests were not similar. And if Washington was unaware of that fact, Ottawa certainly was not, preferring to keep its options open as much as possible. By 1954 a large percentage of Canada's trade was done on a continental basis, but the government nevertheless held out hope that a strong and effective GATT would eventually force other CPs to conform to its rules, opening up their markets without restriction. Given that fervent hope, the *principle* of the waiver would be a very unhealthy precedent, especially if granted to a CP that had once numbered itself among the agreement's biggest promoters.

By mid-decade then, it seemed that the GATT was in serious trouble. The uncertainty of the pending review session, the contrary policies implemented by some CPs, and the interim status of the agreement proved debilitating and supporters were never certain that the bells would not toll for them. Indeed, the rising crescendo of disharmony among agreement members, threatened to deafen politicians and bureaucrats in Ottawa, and the government mobilized political and bureaucratic resources on a grand scale to minimize the damage as much as possible. The Canadian government saw the review session as nothing less than a frontal assault on the organization on which it had based much of its postwar economic policy.

THE AMERICANS

Ottawa decided that one of the main thrusts to be emphasized at a March 1954 meeting of American and Canadian ministers was the GATT's indispensability: whatever its defects, a memorandum prepared for the conference noted, it was "the best institutional safeguard yet devised to control and limit discriminatory trading practices and to encourage countries to ... move towards a free multilateral trading system."[30] Without the GATT, Canada thought, the almost certain result would be the establishment of regional trading blocs and greatly increased discrimination. The Canadian delegation was determined to force home to the very senior American ministers attending the meeting the necessity of maintaining the GATT in, at the very least, its present form.

It knew this would be an uphill battle. On the American side, the meeting was attended by Dulles, Humphrey, Weeks, Secretary of Agriculture Ezra Benson, Gabriel Hague, Eisenhower's economic minister, and Sherman Adams, the president's right hand man and a person of some influence in Washington in his own right. Minister of Finance Walter Harris, Howe, and Secretary of State for External Affairs Lester Pearson were the Canadian representatives. Howe led off, stressing the importance of the GATT as an agency to enforce an international commercial code. He also emphasized that the United States must be above reproach in its dealings with the agreement, because if Washington attempted to subtract from its obligations, it would "offer an unfortunate example to the rest of the world."[31] The GATT had relied a great deal on the leadership of hard currency countries such as Canada, but especially on the United States, and while adherence to the agreement certainly raised some difficulties for the United States, the benefits far outweighed the disadvantages, especially through the GATT's supervision of an internationally recognized code of commercial behaviour. In short, Howe hoped that Washington would postpone the GATT review session until, as the Canadians saw it, some of the internal inconsistencies affecting policymaking in Washington were dealt with.

Howe, Pearson, and Harris also launched a frontal assault on US disposals policies, claiming that the methods used disrupted Canadian markets abroad. Indeed, Ottawa regarded surplus disposal as one of the most important problems of world trade and had long lobbied for the inclusion of provisions in the GATT setting forth principles to be observed in the disposal of surpluses. As the Americans were told, until the CPs developed methods of dealing with this problem, there would continue to be a serious gap in the agreement which could only harm relations between Ottawa and Washington.

Howe finished the Canadians' presentation by situating the GATT firmly in the North Atlantic matrix of defence, political, and economic relations – a move Canadians often made when hoping to impress the Americans with the seriousness of a problem.

It is important that the United States continue to provide an example of forward movement and leadership in this field, and I would like to draw your attention to the serious results of any other impression being given to the outside world. Economic cooperation in the western world, and particularly amongst our allies, most of whom are members of NATO, is of crucial importance to our whole system of defence relationships. If the western world is to be divided up into separate currency blocs, with restrictive and discriminatory trading systems, it is very difficult to see how these other matters of political cooperation and defence can be worked out at all satisfactorily.[32]

Howe and his colleagues did make an impression on the American ministers, especially Benson, who "had been astonished at the vehemence of Canadian complaints about [United States] disposals policy."[33] The biggest revelation for secretary of agriculture was the realization that US external relations were involved in this matter, when he and his bureaucrats had always considered it to be a purely domestic matter. However, it was not readily apparent that American policy would change.

Canadian officials followed up the ministerial conference, meeting with US officials in late May to discuss the agreement's problems (especially the timing of the review session) and an American proposal to further restrict agricultural imports under Article XI. In bureaucratese the discussions were "very open and frank," but in reality the US delegation left Ottawa, in the words of their leader, "severely tested."[34] The Canadians were single-minded in outlining their interpretation of the issues and the necessity of establishing what they termed "sound economic relations" among the countries of the free world. Echoing Howe's comments, the delegation explained that Ottawa wanted the United States to undertake "a significant, purposeful and timely advance in the removal of barriers and uncertainties so as to provide reasonable opportunities for mutually advantageous trade with other [free] countries to widen and expand."[35] The primary sticking points there were US escape clauses, customs procedures, administrative practices, the "Buy America" Act, and the US use of agricultural QRs. Moreover, the Americans were bluntly told that their suggestion that they should be given *carte blanche* in the imposition of import restrictions on agricultural products was outrageous: "a GATT on those terms was of little interest to Canada."[36] But it seemed that the United States was already operating on that basis. Washington's restrictions on imports of cheese and dairy products had been violently criticized by Canadians, who considered their American neighbours to have violated GATT regulations. Following their rather harsh condemnation of US policy, nothing more was heard from Washington on the subject for a number of months and Isbister was of the opinion that the delegation had returned home greatly displeased with the Canadian attitude. Other than irritating the Americans, the delegation was not sure what impact, if any, it had.

There were a number of reasons Canadian officials felt it worthwhile to provoke their American colleagues and disrupt a usually harmonious relationship. For example, since 1945 the United States and Canada had been the two countries which most consistently advocated freer trade, non-discrimination, and currency convertibility. GATT was an integral part of the overall scheme and progress in the desired direction was made only when US commercial policies appeared encouraging to other countries. The climate prevailing in 1954, however, was not conducive to trade liberalization. The Eisenhower administration appeared to have suffered a major defeat in its trade policy legislation with the rejection of the Kean Bill. The outcome of that defeat was likely to be a reluctance on the part of other countries to accept a tightening of trade rules.[37] Indeed, to the Canadians, "experience showed that it was very difficult to conclude satisfactory negotiations on [trade] matters when there was not a fairly good idea of what the United States might do." [38] The possibility clearly existed that the United States was now moving in the direction of restricting, rather than liberalizing, world trade.

Further, to try to renegotiate the GATT in the climate prevailing in 1954 would be a very difficult exercise which, Ottawa feared, might do irreparable harm. In proposing to demand a waiver to legitimize its past actions with respect to agricultural products the United States was attempting to subtract from its GATT commitments. In the past Washington had provided leadership at GATT rounds, now no longer possible because of congressional hostility. That would have a depressing psychological effect throughout the world and, following the American lead, other countries would surely attempt to renege on their obligations with the "net effect [approaching] disaster."[39]

There was also the inherent inconsistency of the American position. Given that international trade was becoming more competitive, the United States would be asking other countries to bind themselves concerning manufactured goods but to leave the United States free on agricultural products. It also wanted to strengthen balance of payments provisions, making it more difficult for countries to discriminate against American exports on that basis. Washington insisted that QRs for balance of payments reasons should not be permitted, except to the extent necessary to give effect to exchange restrictions authorized by the IMF which was largely controlled by the United States. As the Americans later told the British, if the GATT was to be defensible in Congress, they had to be able to point to substantial concessions from developed countries "in the form of a virtual embargo on the balance of payments Q.R.s"[40] And while Canada fervently agreed with that policy, having preached it for a number of years, it was also unrealistic, given the US request for a waiver. As one Canadian official remarked following the May meeting, if the United States was successful in ramming its objectives through, he could not hold out much hope for the GATT.

Canada also had a special interest in the US campaign to gain some breathing room with respect to its agricultural obligations. Canada's trade with the United States contained a significant proportion of agricultural commodities and any attempt to justify US discrimination against those imports was bound to cause trouble. Moreover, because of the trade and exchange restrictions of various countries with which Canada had exchanged offers at Geneva, Annecy, and Torquay, the tariff reductions negotiated at these rounds had not, by and large, been practically applied, remaining for the most part statements of intent. The main benefits for Canada had been obtained from the United States and, if Washington resorted to the increased use of escape clauses for agricultural products, many of the concessions that Canada had negotiated would be of little value. Given such a situation, it would be very difficult to defend, or even to participate, in future trade negotiations that were subject to this caveat. In all likelihood Canadians would demand equal concessions, which would have adverse implications for Western cooperation, for NATO, and for North American relations. As was pointed out to the Americans, Canadians were quite rightly suspicious that "their" sales abroad could be undercut by a United States operating under different rules. Canadian sales were already dropping off as customers in Asia, the Middle East, and South America bought US wheat instead. For example, during the first eight months of the 1954–55 crop year, exports of wheat and wheat flour by the four major exporting countries were up about 25 per cent over the comparable period of the previous year. However, Canadian shipments were up only two million bushels, while exports by the United States represented a gain of 64 million bushels, attributable entirely to American disposal programs.[41] According to the US ambassador in Ottawa, "Canadian resentment over US agricultural surplus disposal policy is [the] outstanding issue today between [the] two countries and one which easily could be inflated to unmanageable proportions."[42]

With these global issues cropping up to plague the GATT it was extremely problematic if the effort of a review session would be commensurate with the results. In any event, the United States did not demonstrate any willingness to consider Canadian objections with regard to either its agricultural policy or with respect to the timing of the review session.

THE BRITISH POSITION

As they had with the Americans, Canadian officials met with British colleagues over a number of months to determine how the latter felt with respect to the timing of a GATT review session and items on the agenda. UK officials also appeared somewhat anxious. The British generally claimed that they had only reluctantly fallen in with the American proposal – the consensus in London was that it was far more desirable to postpone the exercise until early 1955. The government wanted to establish tougher trade rules, such as tightening up escape clause provisions to make it more difficult to impose quantitative restrictions, an instrument that the United Kingdom now believed to be "a pernicious obstacle to international trade."[43] It also wanted a rule designed to make Article XIV of the GATT, which allowed restrictions to be administered in a discriminatory fashion, much less available to CPs. This new attitude was in preparation for convertibility of sterling and London was very concerned that the United States, through its wish to put revised proposals to Congress as soon as possible, would opt for a much less searching review. However, since the Americans were insistent on a November 1954 start, the British capitulated.

As befitted their role as a major trader, British GATT policy was moving increasingly close to Canada's now that the prospect of convertibility was looming ever larger on the horizon. As the chancellor of the Exchequer, R.A. Butler, noted on various occasions, "progress towards freer currencies must go hand in hand with progress towards freer trade."[44] The GATT was becoming an "essential instrument" for maintaining "order and fair play" in international trade and affording "valuable safeguards for export trade."[45] The differences between the United Kingdom and Canada were now more of degree than of kind. And given the British government's new-found commitment to an agreement, it joined with Canada in protesting American agricultural support policies, claiming there was basically "no difference between the United States protection of agriculture and other countries' protection of their agriculture."

Moreover, if a special case were made for American agriculture, it would be impossible to resist protectionist pressures in Britain that could compromise the GATT.[46]

It seemed ironic to Canadians that, while the British were now talking of more "executive" sort of agreement, the Americans were beginning to discover the virtues of a relatively more emasculated one. This difference of opinion had the potential to cause trouble for Canada. Since 1947, the Canadian government had relied upon the GATT to smooth out trade differences between Washington and London, allowing the two to get along more equitably in other areas. Some policymakers believed that had the United Kingdom and the United States been forced to deal with trade arrangements directly, their whole relationship would have been quite different, in all likelihood marked by discord, denunciation, and rhetoric. Canada would certainly have been affected by the hostility generated.[47] In short, the GATT had provided a forum for conciliation and discussion, resolving disputes and defusing tensions which might otherwise have led to diplomatic reprisals.[48] And as Canadians well knew, trade disagreements during the 1930s had created a tremendous amount of discord between the United Kingdom and the United States.

THE REVIEW SESSION

With no way of avoiding a review session, given the Anglo-American intention to proceed, Ottawa's main objective was to minimize any damage by restrictionist-minded countries. The Canadian government felt that other countries should be apprised of the depth of its concern over the possibility that the GATT could be destroyed. One protection involved binding tariff rates beyond 30 June 1955, the date to which the GATT schedule was bound. At the ninth session of the contracting parties, which would begin on 28 October, one of the first items of business would be the status of the tariff schedules. A memorandum prepared in the Department of Finance by its assistant deputy minister, A.F.W. Plumptre, for consideration by cabinet suggested that "the question will be: what action should be taken regarding all the many tariff rates which, as a result of negotiations at Geneva (1947), Annecy (1949) and Torquay (1950), and the temporary prolongation of last year, are 'bound' until, but only until, June 30, 1955?" Since a number of governments had already indicated that they intended to withdraw concessions after that date. Ottawa envisaged a downward spiral of withdrawals and counter-withdrawals to the point where "much of the fabric of tariff concessions laboriously built up [at other rounds] might be quickly torn down."[49]

These negotiations and their results embodied, so the paper maintained, the commercial policy of Canada. Ottawa was reluctant to tamper with them, especially if that meant reducing their effectiveness. The memo urged that Canada should continue to champion "the liberal cause" at the ninth session in 1954–55 just as it had at the other rounds. The Canadian delegation was instructed to "seek a re-binding of tariff schedules on the broadest base acceptable to the Contracting Parties." The problem was that that base might be very narrow: many CPs had severe balance of payments problems and protected industry in those countries would not willingly acquiesce to lower tariff rates that reduced protection. Plumptre's memorandum, to which cabinet completely subscribed, ended by suggesting that the Canadian delegation in Geneva should seek to:

(a) achieve a general re-binding for a further three years of tariff schedules on the broadest base acceptable to the Contracting Parties, and;
(b) avoid any general tearing down of the existing structure of tariff concessions, such as might be involved in a special round of tariff re-negotiations under Article XXVIII.[50]

It was up to the delegation to do what it could to limit deviation from the GATT's basic principles while supporting the promotion of trade.

More specifically, the Canadians were to encourage their GATT colleagues to limit the use of QRs, especially with more widespread European convertibility on the horizon. A new era would be opening up with its restoration and Ottawa wanted new, and preferably tougher, rules in operation. While it would be necessary to continue to allow countries with legitimate balance of payments problems access to QRs of a *non-discriminatory* character, the delegation was instructed to determine whether or not more satisfactory arrangements could be devised "with respect to the circumstances in which these may be imposed, the length of time for which they shall remain in existence, and the role of the Contracting Parties and the International Monetary Fund in effectively supervising them."[51]

With respect to QRs for *protective* purposes, Canada was adamant that they should not be allowed.[52] Many GATT countries maintained these to placate industry long used to protection and to create jobs. While Ottawa was willing to contemplate a transitional period for countries faced with this problem, it would also do all in its power to seek some solution over which the GATT would have some authority. At the ninth annual meeting of the IMF and the International Bank for Reconstruction and Development, held in Washington in September 1954, Harris had stated that he was concerned lest the move toward convertibility and freer trade be checked by an excessive desire to maintain import restrictions. His government wanted "to have tighter trade rules with more limited escape clauses,"[53] a fervid wish that Howe emphasized to the review session's plenary session in December.[54]

Finally, Ottawa hoped to reach some sort of compromise with the United States over the scope given to agricultural import restrictions. In its original form, the GATT contained limited provision for the imposition of import restrictions on agricultural products. The American objective at the review session was to gain more latitude while the Canadians wanted to examine "alternatives," although it was unclear what that meant.

The session quickly bogged down under the weight of its own inertia. Discussion, of which there was much, was inconclusive and debilitating. In a report to the UK Treasury from his position in the British delegation in Geneva, D.A.V. Allen encapsulated the myriad of problems and some of the dynamics that were operative from the first day of the session. A part of his report, although lengthy, is worth quoting here:

The Review Session proper was opened this afternoon. The Chairman's opening remarks were followed by a message from President Eisenhower ... which did not seem to offer very much ... He was followed by M. Faure for France, whose speech was so cleverly worded that it meant all things to all men and seemed equally incomprehensible in both French and English translation ... So far as we could make it out he was pretty negative about the idea of France accepting tighter rules on quotas, he wanted tighter rules on tariffs and he made some obscure remarks about the problems of developing French colonies which seemed to imply that he had increased preferences in mind and which have already made Edgar Cohen [of the UK delegation] smack his lips in anticipation of a joint Anglo-French fish extracted from these troubled waters ... He was followed by M. Larrock for Belgium, who stressed the problem of low tariff countries and called for a commitment that tariffs would not be raised; and by Mr. Corea for Ceylon, who appealed for extensive rights for underdeveloped countries – a wholesale re-writing of Article XVIII.[55]

The Canadians with whom Allen spoke could not have agreed more, although they reserved most of their vitriol for the Americans.

The delegation from Ottawa found their us colleagues to be rudderless and obstructionist. As Louis Couillard of the Canadian delegation told Allen, his continental neighbours "had come empty handed."[56] Further, the position of the United States, with its demand for an agricultural waiver to allow it to impose QRs on agricultural imports, flew in the face of rationality: Washington wanted the waiver at the same time that it was holding out for a strengthened agreement in other respects. However, the Canadians morosely conceded, it would probably be accepted since the United States could offer a few concessions to gain the support of most of those presently opposed. More important, it would be supported by the Belgians, the French, and the Germans, all of whom were interested in the *principle* of a waiver. And given the American precedent, it was felt in the ICETP that a flood of requests for waivers might come to GATT after convertibility had been introduced and countries such as those mentioned could no longer impose restrictions for special balance of payments reasons. Finally, since most of the contracting parties wanted a successful review session and the only way to achieve that was to give the United States what it wanted, there was a general willingness to do so.

It was left to the Canadians to denounce American policy, an opposition that emanated from the top levels of cabinet. For example, Prime Minister Louis St Laurent told Commonwealth colleagues at a prime ministers' meeting in London that the waiver, if awarded, "might weaken the confidence of the world in United States' intentions."[57] Harris was resolute in his detemination not to condone the us request,[58] while Howe was also irritated by it, writing to his friend George Bateman that "GATT is not going well" and that he wanted the Americans to "modify the very unreasonable attitude [they] are taking there"; the us negotiating position at the session was "so unbalanced and negative as to overshadow everything else."[59] For the first time in many years of Canada-us cooperation in trade liberalization, their views now diverged so sharply as to constitute an impasse.

As well, the United States now seemed to place more faith in the IMF than it did in the GATT, because of the weighted vote in the former which gave Washington the greatest amount of influence. Therefore, the Americans wanted to redraft the agreement in such a way as to make it clear that the IMF had the sole right to determine whether the circumstances of a country justified the application of balance of payments restrictions and, if so, whether the magnitude of restrictions was justified. Needless to say, that position was untenable in Canada and indeed, with many other CPs. Ottawa felt that the fund's voting provisions were not suitable for the determination of trade questions. That position, with support from other countries prevailed. Instead, the majority felt, some sort of bridging organization was needed.

As a result of what the Canadian government considered to be a crisis waiting to happen to the GATT, it was decided that forceful representations should be made at once in Washington to set out Canadian concerns. Ministerial representatives would:

(1) Express the concern of the Canadian Government that the US request for a waiver would have a damaging effect on the continued development of healthy commercial relations between the two countries and upon the Review Session of the GATT, and;
(2) Urge that the Government of the United States should not press forward with a request for a waiver which the Canadian Government would have no alternative but to oppose.[60]

Pearson, Howe, and Harris carried the message to the US capital, meeting with Dulles, Humphrey, and a number of senior bureaucrats. They went, according to Conservative John Diefenbaker, to protest "against the gutting of the GATT by the United States."[61] The *Economist* called it a "curious escapade" and one which graphically demonstrated Canadian anxiety over the course of the session. The weekly's Ottawa correspondent surmised that the three went "to impress upon the 'highest levels' of the US Administration the damage which is being done to Gatt in general and Canada in particular."[62]

Diefenbaker and the *Economist* were certainly correct: Ottawa was deeply concerned about the proposed American waiver, feeling that such a blanket request "would strike at the foundations of Canadian-American commercial relationships and of the General Agreement."[63] Throughout the eight years following the first round of tariff negotiations at Geneva, Canada had made substantial concessions to the United States. In return, the latter had lowered tariffs on a number of items, among the most important of which were those on agricultural products. As the aide-memoire delivered to Washington pointed out, North American trade in its entirety, as well as Canadian support for the agreement, could be jeopardized if the waiver was awarded: "much of the support for present commercial relations with the US under the General Agreement comes from those sections and interests which rely on these traditional exports."[64] Protectionist pressure was building in the country and fuel was added to the fire because of the request for a waiver. Other sectors were also becoming uneasy: as Pearson told the Americans, it appeared in Canada that tariff concessions made by the United States in previous GATT rounds were "becoming increasingly flexible."[65] Neither Canadians nor Parliament could accept or condone such an instrument. And if it was granted, then it would "be most difficult for the Canadian Government to take part in further tariff negotiations under the Agreement."[66]

These were hard, but justified, words. Much of Canada's prosperity now depended on continental trade and to Canadians, quite apart from the importance of Canadian agricultural exports south of the border, it was a distinct possibility that other sectors in the United States would resort to a GATT waiver when faced with adversity. Moreover, Canada was also worried about the establishment of a precedent that would compromise important principles enshrined in the agreement. A waiver such as that demanded by Washington involved a fundamental departure from the spirit and practices of the GATT and would seriously, perhaps fatally, upset its balance. Even more worrisome, Canadian unemployment was at its highest level since 1945. Unfortunately, the ministerial trek to Washington yielded no comfort.

In January 1955, the cabinet steeled its Geneva delegation's will. It was not prepared to accept the US demand, even in the slightly amended form the Americans offered to make it more palatable. Practical politics and principle remained the basis of Ottawa's decision. Even when, on instructions from Washington, the American delegation invited the Canadian to suggest modifications to its proposal, the Canadians declined. A telegram from Harris, Howe and Pearson told the delegation to reiterate that the government had no alternative but to oppose the blanket waiver requested by the United States. They instructed their representatives that in the Canadian statement at the end of the Conference, Canada would "reserve [its] freedom subsequently to take whatever steps seemed appropriate with respect to US exports to Canada in the event that, contrary to our hopes, actions are taken under the waiver which injure our trade or impair concessions which we had previously secured."[67] As a country dependent on external trade, Canada was worried about the possibility of having its multi-billion export market to the south closed off even partially – too much in terms of economic growth, and Liberal votes, was at stake.

Quite apart from its effect on Canada, the US request was also having a detrimental effect on events at the review session in general and American inconsistency was at the root of most of the dissension. As a result, by early January 1955 the exercise seemed to be going from bad to worse. According to the Canadian delegation, many variables contributed to this impression. One of the most persistent was regionalist tendencies among many European countries which felt that the GATT should not be interpreted in such a way as to interfere with European liberalization. Some, such as the Germans on agricultural products and the French on manufactures, wanted to maintain QRs permanently on dollar goods. They were also on record as suggesting that, if forced to be non-discriminatory, they would have to withdraw liberalization measures altogether. (By early in the new year, that position had been brought to a head by a Benelux paper circulated to the agreement advocating, on the one hand, an immediate tightening of the rules relating to discrimination and, on the other, a specific exemption from the tighter rule for European liberalization.[68]) As well, there was the insistence of underdeveloped countries, because of special problems affecting them, on greater resort to QRs than the Canadians felt was healthy for the GATT. There also remained the desire of many countries to have continuing access to QRs even when balance of payments difficulties had been overcome.

All of these, and the American attitude toward the session, had a detrimental effect on the development of the GATT. The United States, the United Kingdom, and Canada had all intended to begin the process of renegotiating GATT rules; the intention had, however, "fallen into the doldrums." The United Kingdom had not sufficiently thought out its long-range policy, while a number of European countries felt themselves too weak economically to be able to reduce discrimination, so they resisted even discussing new trade rules. And given the general pessimism demonstrated by certain countries that had, in times past, set the tenor for the agreement, many of the CPs who were interested and capable of moving ahead "were not getting very excited about the new rules."[69] Under such circumstances, it was a serious possibility that the whole skein of compromise that was the GATT would be unwound.

However, as bleak as the session was perceived to be by Ottawa, valuable progress was made in certain areas. For example, the CPs agreed to establish an Organization for Trade Co-Operation (which still had to be ratified by Congress) to administer the agreement and give it some permanent shape. There were also a number of substantive changes agreed to which would help the GATT. Among these were those strengthening the procedures of Article XII for consultation regarding the use of QRs for balance of payments purposes, additional provisions in Article XVI regarding export subsidies, and the revised provisions of Article XXVIII relating to the withdrawal or modification of tariff concessions. Article XVIII, which established conditions and procedures for under-developed countries with low standards of living to deviate from the GATT in order to promote economic development, was also revised. As well, the CPs adopted a resolution on surplus disposal, the old Canadian bugbear. While not a very strong statement, it did provide for consultation among interested governments to avoid damage and disruption to normal commercial trade which was a step, at least, in the "right" direction.

GRANTING THE WAIVER

The waiver on agricultural restrictions was accepted by the CPs in March 1955, in the process making the GATT consistent with US legislation. Ottawa was very disappointed but, as the *Canadian Banker* pragmatically noted, it "was necessary to secure even the consideration, let alone the passage, of the new and permanent GATT by the United States Congress."[70] Canada was potentially more affected by the waiver than any other country: two-thirds of its trade went south and a substantial proportion of this was agricultural products. As well, the various tariff rounds had produced the most extensive concessions between the United States and Canada. As Wilgress told the ninth session following the approval by the contracting parties of the US waiver, "we wish to make one point clear ... Even though the waiver does not impose a firm obligation on the United States in respect to normal trade, we would regard it as unreasonable and unwarranted if the United States were to use this waiver to exclude normal imports ... The Canadian Government will be watching the course of events very closely."[71]

In addition to the US waiver, two other waivers were granted. The British obtained one to ensure the continued access of the UK market for colonial goods. This represented the last gasp of the imperial preference movement that had been re-launched in the early 1950s. Subsidies and QRs were to be used for such items as citrus fruits from the West Indies and Cyprus and bananas from the Cameroon. A waiver was also granted to certain European countries "emerging from balance of payments difficulties" for a limited number of commodities.[72]

The use of the waiver by the United States was a fundmental change in the GATT and the review session seemed to support a decision to use such waivers much more freely. To Plumptre this was disturbing and, while Canada had no choice but to accept, what it symbolized was not in the country's interest. Indeed, it "would be difficult to sell to Canadians since it would make GATT appear weaker." In his presentation to the ICETP, he pointed out to his colleagues the obvious fact that, given what had transpired at Geneva, pressure would build in Canada "to follow the US procedure to obtain a waiver at any time that this might seem to be needed. With the pressure from farmers, etc., the Government would not be able to use GATT as a reason for not introducing trade restrictions."[73] Certainly it seemed that US impetus toward the policy of freer trade, which had its origins in the 1930s, was virtually exhausted.

For that reason, among others, Canada was hesitant of involvement in a fourth round of negotiations proposed by the United States for early 1956. Indeed, the ICETP noted that there could very well be "public criticism of Canadian participation in further tariff negotiations with the US in the present circumstances." The ICETP also believed that any negotiations undertaken in the prevailing climate would be very difficult and the results probably meagre. However, Canada decided to take part in the upcoming tariff negotiations, despite recent developments and setbacks. As the ICETP noted, one of the most compelling reasons for participation was that Ottawa could not afford to refuse to cooperate with a move, however slight it might be, towards lower tariffs sponsored by a Republican president in the face of widespread opposition from protectionist elements in Congress and industry. And although new American legislation might be limited and disappointing, it set forth "a more attractive policy where the alternative would possibly be large and widespread tariff increases."[74] While it might be done under protest, Ottawa would send a delegation.

That was the message given to American secretaries when they travelled north for the second annual meeting of the US-Canada Joint Committee on Trade and Economic Affairs in September 1955. The Canadian government reserved the right to reconsider its decision if events in the United States worked against the GATT. It had in mind definite criteria against which it would measure its decision, such as restrictive legislation enacted by Congress, the use that might be made of new and revised escape procedures incorporated in recent legislation, and the use of the waiver on agricultural products granted to Washington by the CPS.[75] What Canada really hoped for was a commitment by the United States to remain a consistent GATT player. Repeating their old arguments, the Canadian ministers maintained that without increased trade standards of living and prosperity, North Atlantic security and defence and a raft of other items could be jeopardized by the ensuing isolationism and regionalism with attendant "economic and strategic consequences which would be intolerable."[76]

At the US-Canada meeting the American delegation gave the Canadians slight cause to believe that they had made their point. For example, secretary Dulles pointed out that countries wishing to export to the United States "should endeavour to show a certain amount of self-restraint." After all, the United States could not be the "dumping ground" of the North Atlantic community. He went on to note that "everybody must recognize that an indefinite increase in imports was not possible. If other countries attempted to take too large a share of the US market, there would be a political revolt against liberal trading policies." Treasury secretary Humphrey also noted that the rest of the world (and presumably Canada) could and should do much more to attract American investment.[77]

Other countries would simply have to recognize these facts. But despite the Americans' denunciation of foreign trade practices, a sigh of relief must surely have escaped from the Canadians present when the Americans ended their presentation by noting that, for trade purposes, the continent of North America was considered as a single unit. Still, that in itself was a double-edged sword and the prognosis for the GATT did not seem good.

The next few years did not promise to be easy ones in terms of the liberalization of trade and payments. A disappointed United Kingdom and a newly combatative United States made the self-appointed Canadian task of reconciling disparate points of view in the agreement, and especially Anglo-American differences, that much more difficult. The forthcoming tariff negotiations seemed certain to tax Canadian patience and ingenuity – prospects for the GATT remained problematic, an unhappy state to which Wilgress devoted much time in his opening statement to the CPs.

THE FOURTH ROUND, GENEVA, 1956

The tariff round began on 18 January 1956, with the dreary Swiss winter providing a perfect backdrop to the negotiations themselves. The session ended in late May, and although it was relatively short-lived and quite narrow in scope, did provide Canada with certain benefits, not the least of which was the unintended reaffirmation of the GATT as a viable instrument. This round was the first in which new US trade legislation had come into effect following the review session. Prior to the actual beginning of negotiations, Ottawa discussed the likely impact of the new regime on the success (or failure) of the round. The effective ceiling imposed by legal limits on the powers of American negotiators through the Reciprocal Trade Agreements Extension Act meant that certain items of interest to Canada would not be dealt with in any meaningful way or, even worse, would not be dealt with at all. In a memorandum to Harris, Plumptre pointed out that "when Trade and Commerce compared the original Canadian list of requests for US tariff concessions with the preliminary list on which the US administration was prepared to negotiate, they found that quite a number of items of interest to Canada were eliminated." The request lists received from the United States, however, asked for reductions in the Canadian tariff on approximately 235 products, "including many sensitive ones." This was not a negotiating position, so Ottawa felt, but an insult and Plumptre doubted that "the Americans could pay for half the reductions they asked for."[78] Moreover, the ICETP pointed out in a memo to cabinet that any tariff concessions resulting from negotiations with the United States were of a more questionable value than formerly because of the possibility of a subsequent withdrawal of concessions. With this sort of negative attitude prevailing, the ICETP was of the opinion that there could well be public criticism of Canadian participation in further tariff negotiations with the United States.

According to the Reciprocal Trade Agreements Extension Act, a duty in effect on 1 January 1955 could be reduced by only 15 per cent of the effective rate over the course of three years, at an annual rate of 5 per cent. And, as Plumptre observed to Harris, where US tariff rates were more than 30 per cent, "a 15 per cent reduction is so small as to be almost irrelevant." Given such a situation, Canada could not offer any substantive reduction in return. Conversely, where the US tariff was already low, as was the case of with certain raw materials already exported by Canada to the United States, "a reduction of 15 per cent of the rate is not likely to have any significant impact on Canadian exports." Given Plumptre's memo, with which cabinet agreed, it was difficult to see how Canada could benefit in negotiations with the United States based strictly on an analysis of the mechanics of the operation. But there were also other considerations that were relevant. Among these was the fact that the US delegation would be under tremendous pressure to "bring home the bacon": Washington had in fact already informed Ottawa that it would bargain "to be paid in full for any tariff concessions the US may make."[79] The Americans thought that the forthcoming negotiations with Canada would take place in a less favourable climate to tariff reductions than at any time since the GATT was initiated.[80]

As in the past, the United States was the principal country with which Canada would negotiate: the other twelve negotiations it entered into at Geneva were very small. Indeed, in the cases of

Austria and the Dominican Republic it was "very difficult to find concessions that [would] be of any value … There really are very few products for which the United States is not the principal supplier to Canada." For that reason it was important, as Pearson and Harris agreed, for the Canadian delegation to take a "hard line."[81]

Still, by the midway point in late March the negotiations had not been marked by the rancor of Torquay and appeared to be progressing well. Canada had submitted its final position to the Americans, although it was still too early to project any conclusions as the offer still had to run the gauntlet of the Trade Agreement Committee, the multi-member body that rode shotgun on the US negotiators. As far as agreements with European countries were concerned, the delegation reported back to Ottawa that these would largely be "of a goodwill character, containing relatively painless concessions on both sides."[82]

Surprisingly, considering Canadian fears prior to the round, the agreement eventually concluded between Canada and the United States was again one of the major single agreements resulting from the conference. Of the 650 tariffs on the US schedule of concessions, approximately 150 were of interest to Ottawa, representing imports into the United States totalling $200 million in 1954. Included in the new schedule were revised rates on chemicals, aluminum, steel, certain types of wire, mining machinery, auto parts, agricultural and fisheries products, and paper. Canada also concluded agreements with Austria, Benelux, Denmark, Germany, Sweden, Italy, and Norway.

Equally surprising in light of its second most important status in terms of Canada's trade statistics, Ottawa did not even negotiate with the United Kingdom, although the country benefitted from British sensitivity over some issues. For example, reflecting its own interests as much as Canada's, the United Kingdom was reluctant to negotiate a concession on canned salmon with a third party, even though the Canadian government had agreed to release them from the preference which was bound only to Canada. A memo produced in the bowels of the Board of Trade suggested that the strain on the economy of British Columbia, the source of the salmon, would be too severe if the preference were negated. However, it was, in all likelihood, the *quid pro quo* in which the British were interested far more than the effect on British Columbia. As the paper noted, "insofar as we can show consideration for Canadian views on preferences they enjoy here, we are the more likely to get consideration from them in dealing with the widespread attack on our preferences made by foreign countries and by the United States in particular."[83]

Still, Geneva had not proved to be the unmitigated disaster some had feared. Grasping a marginal victory from the jaws of almost certain defeat, Howe told the House of Commons that the tariff agreement was not "as strong and effective ... as I hoped last October when the review session began ... [However, amendments to the GATT] do add up to a more satisfactory agreement than I had feared when I returned from Geneva last December. The result is not as good as it might have been, but it might have been much worse."[84] That masked a true unhappiness with the evolution of the proceedings, which senior government officials made clear to the Americans. The *Globe and Mail* reflected the dominant Canadian attitude in an editorial, claiming that the United States stood "as the leading advocate of dog-eat-dog policy."[85]

In short, the next few years did not promise to be easy in terms of trade and payments liberalization. Moreover, it was felt in some quarters that the weakening effects of the various waivers would postpone the implementation of convertibility for some time.[86] Certainly that was what Wyndham-White believed. He also felt that the tariff reduction exercise had run out of steam entirely and that QRs and subsidies would continue to plague the operation of the GATT. GATT obligations were "considered very light-heartedly in the Organization for European Economic Cooperation" whose governments referred "without inhibition to quantitative restrictions which [were] maintained solely for protectionist purposes or for bilateral bargaining ... In fact, a general air of polite scepticism prevails generally in OEEC circles."[87] Given that situation, Canada could easily remain caught between a bilateral rock and a discriminatory hard place. Its interest lay in breathing some life into an organization that its own secretary-general claimed to be seriously compromised because of the blatant disregard for its principles. Clearly, "the king's horsemen [were now] pulling in different directions and it [would] take generalship of a high order to discipline them that it may become possible to re-establish a liberal régime of world trade."[88]

Ironically, however, the Canadians were to discover in the late 1950s that the "new" agreement would to suit them far better than the old. Increasingly hard-pressed in the years following 1956 by competition from newly industrializing countries and those now completely recovered from the effects of World War II, Ottawa, too, would want to make use of tariffs and other barriers to trade. Indeed, the Royal Commission on Canada's Economic Prospects, the Gordon Commission, suggested that the days of tariff reductions were now over.[89] The United States had faced the new reality of changing world trade and Canada would soon follow suit.

But that remained in the future. For the present, Ottawa had fought a rearguard action against the United States and other countries for nearly a year. With little hope of success in the face of the United States' tremendous economic power and political influence over other members of the agreement, and the very keen European interest in and support for the US position, it maintained its opposition to the very end. The year also marked another disappointment in Canada's dealings with the agreement. Certainly one of the most internationally minded countries in commercial terms in the mid-1950s, Ottawa felt itself once again "let down" by the very organization ostensibly dedicated to furthering the freer movement of goods and services throughout the world.

The 1956 tariff round also represented one more continental linkage in a series that began in 1947. With many Canadian exports still shut out in Western Europe and the United Kingdom because of quantitative restrictions, Canada's agricultural products and raw materials continued to travel south more than east at a rate of approximately 3:1. Whatever the problems associated with the US market, it still represented the best, and in many cases the only, destination for a number of Canada's exports. The GATT did not open up other markets because of QRs. And there was another development on the horizon that, beginning in 1955, would further restrict Canadian possiblities in Europe. In June of that year six countries met in Messina, Italy, to discuss the possibilities of a common market that would hinder the development of export markets by Canadians among that group.

6 Canada at Sixes and Sevens

In terms of foreign economic policy, the Liberal years in office ended in June 1957 much as they had begun with the renewal of Mackenzie King's mandate twelve years previous. Trade discrimination had been a way of life then and, by 1957, it had become, in certain ways, even more deeply entrenched. For example, the six countries that formed the European Economic Community (EEC) – the Benelux group, France, Italy, and West Germany – had agreed to establish a common market which would reduce barriers to trade among themselves. The EEC gave formal recognition to a situation that had existed since 1945 *vis à vis* Canadian exports to Western Europe. With only 6 per cent of Canada's total merchandise trade going to the Continent when a new Progressive Conservative government, led by John Diefenbaker, squeaked into office, the Conservatives hoped to increase that figure. However, Diefenbaker's government was to be no more successful than St Laurent's in diverting trade away from the United States.

Generally, Canada had been chary of schemes for closer European economic cooperation, a caution that had its origins during the Great Depression of the 1930s. By the 1940s and 1950s, Canadian policy-makers remained opposed to regional groupings that threatened to keep Canada's products out of their markets. For that reason, certain European schemes for economic integration were opposed by Ottawa. Any program of closer economic cooperation was tested against one simple criterion: "whether or not it [would] lead to a progressively wider cooperation in trade and other economic matters between *all* the countries of the free world."[1] That was the Canadian objective but not necessarily the European, as the latter made no secret of the fact that they had little interest in developing trade with Canada. As noted in chapter 4, Ottawa had fought against that tide during the 1950s but with little success.

The program for what later became the European Economic Community (EEC) was first mooted at a gathering of the six members at Messina, Italy, in June 1955. There, this core group agreed that the meetings had been fruitful enough to warrant further study. An intergovernmental committee, known as the Brussels Committee of Experts, was established to draw up more detailed proposals that would "work for the establishment of a united Europe by the development of common institutions, the progressive fusion of national economies, the creation of a common market and the progressive harmonization of their social policies."[2] This committee, under the chairmanship of Belgian Foreign Minister Paul-Henri Spaak, reported in May 1956, and the report was officially accepted as the basis for the drafting of two agreements, one on atomic cooperation (Euratom) and the other on the common market.

Even though the Europeans generally paid only lip service to their GATT obligations, the initiative the six were undertaking was permitted within the agreement. As Article XXIV states, "the contracting parties recognize the desirability of increasing freedom of trade by the development, through voluntary agreements, of closer integration between the economies of the contracting parties to such agreements. They also recognize that the purpose of a customs union or free trade area should be to facilitate trade between the constituent territories and not to raise barriers to the trade of other contracting parties with such territories."[3] When that clause was written soon after the end of the war Europe was physically and emotionally devastated and it was hoped that regional trade associations would be a method whereby that unhappy state could be overcome.

THE INITIAL CANADIAN ATTITUDE

Canada remained relatively neutral during the early stages of the the EEC movement, as European integration remained a "motherhood" issue in Ottawa and was not opposed in principle. However, the Canadian government did have an agenda of its own in this matter; as a major exporting country, Canada was anxious about the possibility of losing markets if the Messina proposals were acted upon. As the secretary of state for External Affairs, Lester Pearson, said to the English Speaking Union in London in early 1956, Canadian approval was given "on the assumption that in this case the whole, while greater ... could not be ... more restrictive than its parts."[4]

It was almost impossible to conceive that a European common market would develop into the sort of institution that could enforce rules and regulations against outsiders. The relatively powerless Benelux bloc had set the pace of discussion with the initially hesitant French and West German governments. And when the motion was put to establish the Brussels Committee, it was agreed upon only reluctantly.[5] It was felt that the Six would enter into some sort of joint arrangement that would symbolize an economic union without embodying it and without a practical program to attain it. Ottawa confidently assumed that the lobbies of farmers and industrialists who would be affected by economic integration would fight the program and such vested interests would distort the principle of the common market into some unrecognizable shape. Moreover, it seemed in Ottawa that the movement was at least partially a reflection of French fear of Germany and that Paris wanted the United Kingdom associated with the community in order to better contain German aspirations. It was felt that the final shape of the common market would, at a minimum, be affected by that situation, which would mean a diluted agreement. In the end, so the Canadian government believed, despite brave talk and high objectives, "it was most unlikely that ... the Messina proposals or any other common market scheme would meet the need [of rallying Europe to a common cause]. The divergence of economic interest between the countries concerned, particularly in the important agricultural sector, is so great that it seems unlikely that a complete customs union ... could ever be achieved. It is more likely that a little progress in the less sensitive sectors could be made, and that the scheme would then bog down."[6]

There was some support for this scenario even among the delegations negotiating the EEC treaty. Joseph Bech, the elder statesman of Luxembourg and a man of some influence in the EEC process, was reported to have suggested that if those who were worried about the initiative could sit in on the ministerial discussions, "their worries would vanish."[7] The Netherland's foreign minister, Dirk Stikker, felt the same way. He was generally depressed over the pace and direction of negotiations, telling Canada's ambassador to Brussels that anyone who was "not a confirmed optimist ... would begin to lose hope. For every problem that is solved, two new ones bob up."[8] For example, basic and very difficult questions arose concerning the participation of French colonies and the contentious issue of the harmonization of social policies among the six plagued negotiations throughout.

But even if an EEC were established, Canadian analyses pointed out that the country's broad trading interests could be *enhanced* by a stronger Europe. At a minimum, Canada's exports to the common market countries would remain substantially unchanged. There was a possiblity that French wheat might displace some Canadian, but that would only happen "if the participating member [decided] not to provide any special arrangements in the field of agricultural products." Similarly, exports of raw materials would be relatively unaffected. The only area, official papers claimed, where Canada's export trade might be damaged would be in manufactured goods, and those, the statistics graphically demonstrated, accounted for a negligible per centage of Canada's trade with Europe.[9]

There were also strong arguments in favour of some sort of customs union among the countries of the Continent. Ottawa was in general quite concerned over the political, economic, and military situation there and any policy designed to bind parts of Western Europe together was justified and welcome. A briefing paper prepared for Prime Minister Louis St Laurent and Pearson pointed out that in the perceptions of senior officials in Canada, "there was a very real danger of Germany slipping away from the Western Alliance after [Chancellor Konrad] Adenauer's disappearance. In France, and perhaps elsewhere, there is the danger that Popular Front or neutralist governments may take over unless the political situation can be stabilized and set in order. Any of these developments would, of course, strike at the Atlantic Alliance and would gravely, perhaps disastrously, compromise the resistance of Western Europe to Communist domination."[10] The Departments of Trade and Commerce and Finance, as well as the Bank of Canada, agreed that the Continent "needed a rallying point."[11] Furthermore, the common market could also be a vehicle with which to contain German economic and political aspirations, a factor of some weight in the development of Canadian policy. That aspect, combined with the perception that Canada's interests would not be too adversely affected, led Ottawa to conclude that on straight economic grounds "Canada can well afford to support, or at least not to oppose, any ... program which would show real promise of contributing" to European economic strength.[12]

Accordingly, Ottawa went on record as being in favour of the movement but opposed to the development of a *discriminatory* free trade area in Western Europe, in large part because of the legitimation of a "bloc mentality" for the developing world. If it had a choice, the Canadian government did not want discriminatory common market proposals to stimulate the creation of like-minded groups elsewhere. Moreover, it wanted the Messina powers to take their program to what Ottawa believed was a logical conclusion, namely a North Atlantic–wide free trade area that would breathe some life into the long-moribund Article 2 of the NATO Treaty. [13] There was another consideration, relating to the degree of economic dependence of Canada on the United States: a new and large-scale European preferential scheme could certainly add to that concern. [14]

That was not the British attitude, however, and the common market movement figured heavily on the UKCCC agenda of meetings held in December 1955. The UK team, led by Sir Leslie Rowan of the Treasury, were especially concerned over European proposals. Alarmed at being left outside, they claimed to be unable (or unwilling) to participate because of Commonwealth and sterling area obligations. Rowan insisted that what the six had in mind was something very exclusive which, without British participation, could only be "a narrow regional bloc, dominated by Germany." It would also be very divisive and Canada "ought to give very careful thought to this and consider the danger it represented to the collective approach" and, by extension, to the whole matrix of Anglo-Canadian commercial relations. [15] Considering the state of the latter relationship, it seemed to the Canadians that that was a largely gratuitous concern.

With only vague proposals and inadequate information at hand, Canada felt it was unnecessary to do more than "sound a note of caution" at this early stage. [16] It was also important, as the country's high commissioner in London, Norman Robertson, said, to "not commit ourselves to a purely negative position." There were definite dangers for Canada in the common market proposals but they "could be neutralized and ... [the common market initiative] turned to advantage." [17] Certainly the Canadian delegation to the UKCCC meeting was not unaware of the dangers posed by the development of a regional trading bloc, but Canada had had to deal with that before, most importantly in the case of the British and the sterling area. While Rowan decried events in Europe, Canada was faced with largely similar problems in its relations with the United Kingdom.

The American response to the initiative was entirely supportive. Indeed, it was viewed in Washington as the realization of US policy in the postwar period. After all, this was what the ERP was supposed to achieve. As former British Prime Minister Harold Macmillan notes in his autobiography, the United States was working enthusiastically to promote the plan "on the general ground that if a United States of America was an almost divine plan for 'God's Own Country,' a similar constitution might revive a decadent Europe."[18] The United States was willing to accept the tariff discrimination that Continent-wide economic integration implied so long as it could be taken as a first step toward the political integration of the region.[19]

However, the British could not have disagreed more, and their response was to develop their own program for Europe, Plan G, a European Free Trade Area (EFTA) which, with London directing events, would include the six as a single unit and those OEEC countries which would join. Britain's entry into the EFTA would involve the removal, by defined stages, of customs duties on the products of its partners in the endeavour in return for reciprocal action. In order to protect its Commonwealth colleagues, London proposed that the free trade area would not apply to foodstuffs, feeds, beverages, and tobacco. As Macmillan, then chancellor of the Exchequer, told Walter Harris, minister of Finance, the United Kingdom could not in any circumstances join a customs union à la Messina because of external commitments; it went without saying that Britain's first purpose would "be to maintain our association with the Commonwealth."[20] The British also suggested that Canada had a special interest in these proposals, as the president of the Board of Trade, Peter Thorneycroft, explained to a meeting of Commonwealth finance ministers, Canada's own problem with the United Kingdom and Europe was not the effect of tariffs, but of dollar quota restrictions. So long as Europe remained divided, Thorneycroft noted, "she would not be strong enough to face competition from United States manufacturers and therefore would not give up discrimination."[21]

Ironically, in view of later developments, the Canadian government viewed the EFTA as a much more serious threat than the EEC, given that about 15 per cent of the country's exports went to Britain while only 6 per cent went to those countries comprising the EEC. The subject was discussed in the ICETP in late 1956 and the mandarins present tried to determine what motivated British policy. A. F. W. Plumptre, assistant deputy minister of Finance, felt that the EFTA represented an attempt by London to "control" Messina, while the senior civil servant in Ottawa, Secretary to the Cabinet R.B. Bryce, felt it to be more that the United Kingdom did not dare to be left out of events on the Continent but also could not, because of external commitments, join the common market. Louis Rasminsky agreed with both interpretations and added a further twist of his own: the free trade area was not based on economic reasons but rather was "a political move which was urged by the position of the

UK in the world today. The Free Trade Area was one aspect of an effort to create a Third Force."[22] And that, to Rasminsky, was at least one indication that the British had still not come to terms with their greatly reduced global status.

As with the common market movement, Robertson was more sanguine about the EFTA initiative; there was, he felt, a real danger in "exaggerating its effects on Canadian trade." Indeed, through the involvement of some of the Scandinavian countries, tariffs might even fall. As he noted, "the industrial competition which would result from the UK entering into a free trade arrangement would tend to create pressures for the removal of tariffs which raise the costs of production. Although it was difficult to forecast what would happen within the next ten years? ... [In all likelihood] under a Free Trade Area the overall European requirements for what Canada wanted to export would increase."[23] Rather than impede the flow of Canadian exports across the Atlantic, the EFTA might serve to increase it.

The Canadians heard the UK pitch about the EFTA at the Commonwealth finance ministers meeting held in Washington as the Commonwealth gathered to participate in the annual meeting of the IMF in September 1956. The Commonwealth was asked for its collective opinion and generally, the response was favourable. Certainly the UK delegation believed that most of its colleagues would approve the EFTA proposals. Almost alone, Canada was more critical, ironically given its past record in the GATT and behaviour elsewhere, because of a generalized concern over the possible elimination of UK preferences but also because of the political dangers posed. Among the latter, two items figured prominently. First, there was the concern that if Ottawa was too encouraging "many would feel that Canada cared little if the UK 'left' the Commonwealth," a very real worry for a government led by a French Canadian that had undertaken several initiatives perceived as weakening the "British tie." The other subject of discussion was the possible evolution of the Canadian-American relationship if the British participated in the EFTA. Some bureaucrats, such as the deputy minister of Finance, Ken Taylor, somewhat reminiscent of closing the stable door long after the horse had bolted, suggested in the ICETP that Canada should give "serious study to the possibility of joining the Free Trade Area to offset the danger of being completely driven into the US orbit."[24]

A paper analyzing the possible impact on Canadian exports of the implementation of the common market and free trade area schemes was written by Plumptre in late 1956. His most important message was that, whatever happened, Ottawa should do all it could to ensure that the United States and Europe continue "pulling together." That reflected the basic instinctive judgement that Canada would find it very difficult to stand alone if there where a split between the Americans and Europeans. He was most concerned with the political and military implications of integration: the more the world was bound together in common economic purpose, the less likely it would be to break apart under political or military strains. As he wrote, "European integration that is not carried through steadfastly and in the right spirit can have seriously damaging effects over the long run on the Atlantic Alliance and on the whole world." Canada, Plumptre felt, would be "stretched and strained" if the United States and Europe drifted apart.[25]

He was also in agreement with Robertson with respect to the possible threat Canadian exports might face in the European market. Hopes of a market for manufactured goods on the Continent had "never burned very brightly" and the possibility of being displaced from the very small market share that Canadians then held would "scarcely [cast] a shadow over the vast aggregate of our exports," especially since the United Kingdom was proposing to exempt agricultural products from its program.[26]

Plumptre also involved himself in the general discussion taking place in government with respect to Canada's foreign economic policy, outlining a few options for his minister in dealing with the proposed changes in Europe. The first, Canadian membership in the EFTA, was not feasible. He correctly pointed out that European countries could not be expected to dismantle restrictions against Canadian goods, which would limit export opportunities. The only way to deal with that condition would be to impose dollar restrictions against the United States, which was also a non-starter. The second possibility, a special arrangement with the EFTA, he also dismissed as unworkable as it would involve the extension of preferences and a departure from the most-favoured-nation principle that was fundamental to the GATT, on which Canada had based so much of its postwar foreign economic policy. Again, given the huge volume of trade with the United States, it would involve some painful (and politically impossible) decisions. But despite his effort to offer alternatives, Plumptre's evaluation of the EFTA was relatively benign – "no vital or sensitive Canadian exports were likely to be affected."[27]

THE GATHERING STORM

The interpretation of the Messina proposals, with respect to their impact on Canada, differed from Plumptre's conclusions about EFTA

Table 5
Increases in Western Germany's tariff

	West German Tariff in 1960		Proposed Common External Tariff of the ECC
		(percent)	
Automobiles	13–16		27–29
Motorcycles	11–14		24–26
Bicycles	9		21
Cameras	4		18
Machinery	0–9		4–17
Linoleum	4		20
Carpets	14–16		22–40

Source: *International Financial News Survey*, 6 May 1960.

and the Canadian government became increasingly alarmed. In both an aide-memoire sent to the six countries in late 1956 and a prime ministerial statement to the common market countries in mid-November, it was pointed out to those governments that their rhetoric did not match their actions. St Laurent's statement indicated strong support for the *principle* of economic integration on the assumption that it would more closely bind Europe's economy with the rest of the trading world. At the same time, however, he made clear Canada's increasing concern over the possibility that it might lead to increased restriction of trade and discrimination against outside countries. Certainly, the prime minister observed, as Canada had "learned more about the plans and intentions of the six countries [it] had become increasingly disturbed about the direction taken."[28] This concern was warranted, as the Table 5 which uses the example of West Germany, a moderate tariff country, illustrates:

An increase in tariffs was permitted under the rules of the GATT, but it was manifestly not in the Canadian interest and was a condition against which Canadians had fought since 1947. Written into the agreement was the concept that the average common external tariff of any customs union must not be higher or more restrictive than those prevailing, on the average, prior to the formation of any union. In general, EEC tariffs met this requirement, given the great disparity in tariff rates among the participants, some actually experienced increased tariff protection. As Sidney Dell has written, "in arriving at the common tariff, the pre-existing national tariffs were averaged arithmetically without regard to the value of goods imported in each case: had allowance been made for the value of imports by each country under every tariff heading, the common tariff would have been significantly lower."[29] The low-tariff Benelux group was treated as a single unit in the averaging process, while France, West Germany, and Italy were treated as another bloc, giving the high tariffs of France and Italy a disproportionately large weight in the final outcome.

The Canadian government was also concerned about the possibility of discriminatory provisions in the treaty. This was especially worrisome as these articles appeared designed to take priority over the relevant provisions of the GATT, which had no way of enforcing its code anyway. What the EEC treaty proposed was that the common market institution itself and the GATT would have concurrent jurisdiction over the reimposition of discriminatory procedures brought about, for example, by an adverse balance of payments situation. The Canadian note pointed out that "we should be very disturbed to see enshrined in a permanent treaty provisions whose real meaning and intent was that if members of the common market ever had to reimpose quantitative restrictions, they would, in principle, avoid adopting a non-discriminatory approach." Obviously, they would favour their EEC colleagues. Ottawa was also anxious over the the possible establishment of a common list of liberalized products being established within the EEC, as it only seemed reasonable to believe that such a list would reflect the position of the country with the weakest balance of payments position and, therefore, the country with the greatest stake in maintaining a high level of discrimination.[30]

However much the Canadian government might disapprove of their proposed course, its only option was to remind the six of their GATT obligations. They were committed under the agreement to remove quantitative restrictions as soon as their balance of payments situations permitted, and the movement toward a customs union should not provide any justification for retarding the process either on the grounds that the Messina countries felt they ought to bring their policies into line with one another or because they considered that the requirement to liberalize within the customs union area was too onerous to permit them to make progress on both fronts.

Such a slowdown, however, seemed to be happening. A number of the six countries were increasingly reluctant to liberalize their trade with hard currency countries, even after they were declared "sound" by the GATT – that is able to fully integrate into the global economy. For example, both Belgium (1955) and West Germany (1957) chose to ignore their GATT obligations, with the latter issuing a statement that it had no intention of "disinvoking" restrictions on agricultural production and some industrial goods. As Robert Hudec has noted with considerable understatement, "The candor of the German statement seemed to stun many the [GATT] delegations.[31]

In an ICETP meeting held in mid-January 1957 and in messages sent out by External Affairs, Canadian anxiety over the developing common market was evident. Ottawa was now troubled "about a number of elements ... which, taken together, could be substantial enough to affect the direction and health of this movement."[32] There was also talk among the trade departments in Ottawa that high level representations be made at once to the Messina governments to indicate Canada's concern over the direction in which the six were now heading. Unlike his earlier, more sanguine assessment, Robertson also agreed with the prevailing analysis. Moreover, time was of the essence because of a recent acceleration in the customs union timetable. Ministers and officials were in accord that Spaak, in his capacity as chair of the heads of delegations of the Messina countries, had to be apprised of Canadian concern over the evolution of the movement. Indeed, information being received in Ottawa during February and March 1957 demonstrated that, if anything, the final form contemplated by the six would be even more protectionist and restrictionist than the Canadian government had feared.

There were a number of areas affected, but policies on tariffs, QRs and agriculture were at the top of the list. Particularly with respect to the last, the Canadian government felt the EEC would not be consistent with the terms of the GATT. Robertson observed in a telegram to Ottawa that "I am inclined to think that when the dust has settled, we may find the agricultural provisions of the Customs Union the most difficult to accept ... and the most damaging to our trade with the Area."[33] It now appeared that, along with internally subsidizing agricultural production, the common market would also undertake serious discrimination against outside competitors. As a result, the ICETP prepared a tough submission for cabinet to be delivered to Spaak in an attempt to influence events before it was too late to have any effect whatsoever on the process. Both the associate deputy minister of Trade and Commerce, Mitchell Sharp, and Finance's A.B. Hockin encouraged that the statement not be "watered down."[34]

The aide-memoire, sent to Messina capitals in late February 1957, pointed up Ottawa's concern over some of the provisions of the proposed treaty. Among these were the establishment of a protected agricultural system, higher tariffs, import restrictions, and long-term preferential marketing arrangements. This would translate, so the note suggested, into high-cost and inefficient economies, much like those of the sterling area. But more to the point, as far as Ottawa was concerned, it would raise serious problems for Canadian exports of agricultural products as under the new regime West Germany and the Benelux would have to purchase subsidized and expensive

French wheat instead of wheat from Canada, a long-term and traditional supplier. If that attitude prevailed, then it was clear that the common market was not being launched in an "expansionist" fashion but would rather "restrict" trade.

Ottawa felt that much of the new direction of the common market movement was a result of French leadership. Prime Minister St Laurent agreed with an assessment of their role – many of the features in the proposed arrangement which would arouse concern in Canada were "the result of French demands."[35] In view of strong protectionist pressures in France, its dominant influence was seen by Canadians as destructive. There was also the chance that, in its consideration of the common market treaty, Paris would insist on even more stringent safeguards for French agriculture and industry against outside competition. And within the EEC, what was the case for France would be the case for all.

THE EFFECT ON CANADA: THE EEC AND THE EFTA

The proposed customs union was discussed at length during a UKCCC meeting held in May 1957. Unlike their last discussion in that venue, the Canadians were now quite aggressive. For example, Claude Isbister of Trade and Commerce said that Canada had been more active "both in public and private" against the shape the common market treaty was assuming "than most European countries." His country stood to suffer more than almost any other "from a growth of continentalism in any field on either side of the ocean." And while Canada might not have the power or influence to in any way threaten ratification, Canadians "might well be unable in [the] GATT to concur in those provisions of the Treaty which went beyond the essential principles of a Customs Union and which would unjustifiably impair Canadian interests." If forced, Canada would be prepared to consider the withdrawal of tariff concessions negotiated with the six over the course of four tariff rounds and to negotiate a different arrangement with them.[36] Perhaps it was merely brave talk, but it certainly emphasized the extent of Canadian concern.

In the latter half of the decade, the six countries involved in the movement, taken together, represented Canada's third largest market, absorbing approximately 7 per cent of the country's merchandise exports. But more important, for a number of traditional Canadian exports such as wheat, the common market was of major significance. Of Canada's total world sales of wheat, more than 30 per cent was sold to the six. In the case of flaxseed and polystyrene, the figure was more than 70 per cent, while for asbestos, synthetic rubber, pulpwood, and rye, it was about 25 per cent. As well, more than 10 per cent of Canadian sales of barley, iron ore, nickel, tobacco, and aluminum were to EEC countries.[37] These were important per centages and any adjustment or reorientation in European trade patterns had the potential to seriously disrupt Canadian farmers and industry.

Moreover, given very high EEC import totals, a potential did exist, Plumptre's analysis notwithstanding, to expand into other sectors. Canadians were doing this in sales of fabricated products and end products which were progressively larger following the gradual elimination of import restrictions levied against those goods. It had been expected, perhaps over-optimistically, that Canada would continue to increase its export of manufactures to Europe. Now, with the EEC, after their decade-long fight for less restricted entry into Western Europe, the future volume and pattern of Canada's trade would depend in large part on the decisions of the restrictionist-minded common market. And in most cases "restrictive decisions [were] to be feared."[38]

The EFTA also posed problems, but to a much lower degree. The British attempt to control the EEC through its association with a free trade area failed utterly. Confronted by this failure, with its concomitant loss of prestige, but unable "to afford to stay outside this powerful European economic movement," the United Kingdom, Austria, Denmark, Norway, Portugal, Sweden and Switzerland, finally established the EFTA. The EFTA Treaty was signed on 20 November 1959. Each free trade area country was free to set its own tariff rate on any product and to pursue an independent commercial policy. By comparison with the common market, the EFTA was a very loose arrangement. At least part of the rationale for this approach was the hope that the free trade area would provide "a stepping stone to new negotiations with the six, leading in due course to some sort of free trade arrangement between all countries of the two European groups." Indeed, it was thought in some quarters that there was no other political objective of the EFTA than eventual association with the EEC.

Canadian exports to the EFTA were largely unaffected. There were potential areas of concern with paper goods and chemicals, but these turned out to be unwarranted. Certainly, lacking the degree of economic integration of the EEC, the danger to Canada's trade was much less pronounced. The primary Canadian concern with the EFTA was not with that arrangement *per se* but that it might come to an agreement with the common market and form some sort of Europe-wide association. As a memorandum pointed out, there was "a danger that some of the more restrictive features of the Common Market would inevitably be carried over into any [European group], particularly in the field of agriculture and fisheries."[39]

Of most importance to Canadian calculations was the British position, for despite the problems that had plagued Anglo-Canadian trade during the 1950s, the United Kingdom remained Canada's largest overseas customer and largest market for some of her major exports. London had undertaken to reduce to zero its tariffs on imports of industrial equipment from its EFTA partners, which disturbed Ottawa because of the implications it seemed to hold for manufactured exports in general. Still, the seven countries in EFTA were among the world's "tradingest" nations, with imports worth some $18 billion in 1958, of which 16 per cent came from other EFTA countries, 28 per cent from the EEC, and 56 per cent from the rest of the world. Their exports in that year amounted to $16 billion, of which 18 per cent went to other EFTA members, 22 per cent to the EEC and 60 per cent to the rest of the world.[40] Those figures provided Canadians with some solace: the EFTA was internationally minded in fact and in spirit.

CONCLUSION

As the common market developed from the first concrete proposals at Messina, through the meeting in Venice and the establishment of the Brussels Committee of Experts, to its final form in 1958, so too did Canadian policy adapt to the changing environment. From their first, relatively unconcerned, approach in 1955 to the more focused approach adopted by 1957, Canadian officials and politicians developed a dislike for what the common market came to epitomize.

Certainly important issues were at stake. Unlike the United States, Canada could do little to influence the course of European events to better suit her conception of how the Continent should develop. But after spending the better part of a decade attempting to convince the Europeans of the benefits of multilateral and non-discriminatory trade, the disappointments attendant on the implementation of what was, in essence, a regional bloc, were immense. The end result of the Messina initiative was to place further roadblocks in the way of Canadian-European trade. Ottawa felt betrayed after its heavy commitment to Western Europe through the NATO and the extension of financial assistance to its NATO colleagues. Much good Canadian coin had disappeared into the collective defence effort in Western Europe with no real commensurate return.

In practical terms, the situation with respect to the EFTA was not as bad, but it, too, was symbolic of a certain mind-set. While it was an almost *ad hoc* arrangement, it drove home to Canadians how dependent they were on the goodwill of other states for their national wellbeing. Canada lived by its exports which, it seemed in the later 1950s, were under attack on a number of different fronts. The only reliable market, twelve years after the end of World War II, remained the United States, a fact brought out most clearly by the statistics: 60 per cent of Canada's exports went south, while a staggering 70 per cent of its imports came from the United States. For reasons of its own, Washington had exempted Canada from certain pieces of restrictive trade legislation and had continued to purchase massive amounts of Canadian exports, primarily raw materials. While that created a dependency relationship, there were few other options that could provide the standard of living to which Canadians had become accustomed. Canada, although not without some qualms, had accepted the inevitable – the North American nexus was in place.

Conclusion

The Liberals were defeated on 10 June 1957 by a resurgent Progressive Conservative party under the leadership of John George Diefenbaker. The new prime minister promised to be a vigorous and dynamic figure, in stark contrast to the rather tired leadership provided in the last years of Liberal rule by Louis St Laurent. And the changeover, completely unexpected by a population grown used to a "governing party," was made complete by the defeat of C.D. Howe in his Port Arthur seat by a young Cooperative Commonwealth Federation upstart, Douglas Fisher. The "Minister for Everything" was now consigned to the parliamentary sidelines.

In one way, it was fitting that Howe and his party lost power in 1957, for that year marked the end of an era. The reconstruction period was well and truly over and new winds were beginning to blow through the global commercial structure. Europe, including West Germany, now a valued ally in the undeclared war against Soviet communism, was again a major competitor for the world's trade. In the Far East, Asian, and more specifically Japanese, competition was heating up. By the later 1950s, Canada had concluded a number of bilateral agreements with Asian countries and dependencies, such as Japan, India, and Hong Kong, to voluntarily restrict certain exports to Canada. In a sense, the comfortable and well-understood world of the North Atlantic was being superseded by a much larger world which included the Indian and Pacific Oceans. If Canada was to maintain its position relative to other countries, new directions and policies were called for; the new government seemed much better placed to distance itself from the past and consider new solutions to old problems.

The Liberal's time in office from 1945 to 1957 has been viewed in two ways – most commonly as a period characterized by an unprecedented give-away of Canada's resource heritage to the United States and the development of a dependency relationship that far exceeded the bounds of sanity. On a domestic level, this seems to have been true: by the late 1950s American interests controlled 70 per cent of Canada's oil industry, 56 per cent of its manufacturing, and 52 per cent of its mining. Even a committed Liberal such as Walter Gordon took issue with the course of economic development as overseen by his party in those twelve years. Indeed, the 1957 *Final Report* of his Royal Commission on Canada's Economic Prospects was an indictment of Liberal economic policies.

That was not the case with respect to the development of foreign economic policy. The changed circumstances in which Canadians found themselves by 1957 were a reflection of the difficulties encountered abroad by a small trading nation attempting to develop markets where none had existed before or to keep traditional markets of long standing. Canada could not offer its own version of Marshall aid to entice potential trading partners – indeed, the country had difficulty enough in balancing its own trade books, given the division of the world into hard and soft currency areas. And one fact remained unchangeable, at least in the minds of policymakers in Ottawa: Canada was dependent on foreign trade. As the Royal Commission on Dominion-Provincial Relations had pointed out in 1940, and which was equally true during the period under investigation, "it [was] only by playing [the trading] role that Canada could maintain anything like her present standard of living."[1] Markets were paramount, but uncertain in the post-World War II world.

Developments with the British were a case in point. Separated from its major overseas export market in the postwar era because of currency difficulties, Canada nevertheless felt it necessary to extend its own slender resources to assist the British in recovering from the ravages of war. In pursuit of that objective, Canada spent billions of dollars in Britain between 1939 and 1950, some invested and some freely given, doing much more than its part to aid British recovery. The rationale for extending itself to the limit was simple: it was an article of faith among Canadian policymakers that both Britain and the United States were essential to the maintenance of Canadian prosperity. R.D. Cuff and J.L. Granatstein described that formulation as "a bilateral imbalance within a balanced North Atlantic triangle," where a trade surplus with Britain paid for Canadian deficits with the United States. Louis Rasminsky articulated that sentiment in a 1945 seminar with Harvard graduate students, noting that serious complications would arise if Canada was forced to choose between America and Britain.[2]

The $700 million loan and the billion dollar gift, given in 1941 and 1942 respectively, were the policy expressions of that belief. Beginning in 1943, Mutual Aid, the Canadian version of lend-lease, systematized and rationalized the aid-giving process to Britain and other belligerents. Finally, the $1.25 billion 1946 loan to the United Kingdom, an undertaking of staggering proportions for such a small country, was aimed at ensuring that London would not labour under a crippling postwar debt, at least to Canada. Taken together, it was an expenditure of resources on a scale that most Canadians would not have believed possible. Indeed, on a per capita basis, Canadian generosity during World War II was unparalleled, a fact that Lord Keynes, among others, clearly recognized.[3]

However, the sums were not expended in an entirely altruistic manner and national interest was a large part of the calculation in determining how much to provide. To have operated otherwise would have been irresponsible of Canadian decisionmakers. But the gap between what Canada could and the United States would provide and what Britain really needed in the transitional postwar period was too great. After a brief fling with convertibility in July–August 1947, the British settled down into a non-convertible and discriminatory régime *vis à vis* the dollar area that prevailed throughout the period under investigation. Dollar crises in 1947, 1949, and 1951, and an economic downturn in 1955–56 only buttressed London in its determination to discriminate against dollar products.

Moreover, the British adopted a very hard line against Canada, perhaps because of its refusal to be drawn into the soft currency sterling area. However much some British and Canadian policymakers might have wished for that possibility, it did not accord with Canada's economic reality. It would have been, if not impossible, too economically and politically wrenching, for Ottawa to fundamentally alter trade patterns that had been established over the nineteenth and twentieth centuries. Nor would some sort of associated status with the sterling area have served Canada's economic interests. Simply put, the area could not compete with the United States in terms of products or prices offered to Canadians. The harsh approach toward Canada demonstrated by the British and evident throughout the period under investigation also served to alienate a Canadian and officials. For example, it had turned the anglophilic Graham Towers into an anglophobic governor. Clearly London was keen to keep the sterling area together and dependent on Britain, largely, one suspects, as a replacement for a disappearing Empire. In the end, UK governments, both Labour and Conservative, paid dearly for their troubles. However wrong-headed and abstruse such a program was, it remained that Canada was excluded from the sterling area.

Nor was the situation with Europe any better; indeed, it was arguably worse, since there were no close historic ties binding Canada to the Continent. As has been noted, the Canadian government pushed the European connection because it could not envisage Canadian prosperity without European markets.[4] But supported, indeed compelled, by the Americans, the Europeans adopted a policy of discrimination and non-convertibility against the dollar area that was very similar to Britain's. Many European countries, including Belgium, France, and Holland, also had overseas empires, thus spreading discrimination against Canadian exports farther afield. As well, European institutions were developed to deal with European problems, again excluding hard currency countries. The OEEC, established in 1948, began that policy, while the EPU, which followed two years later, provided a multilateral clearing house for European, and only European, trade. Finally, the European Coal and Steel Community pointed out a likely direction for a number of interested parties. Inspired by Jean Monnet of France, and including the six states that would, in 1958, comprise the EEC, it was an attempt by Paris to place German steel under the aegis of a supranational authority.

While it was a successful experiment in European unity, its mandate was to resurrect the European coal and steel sectors and thus it discriminated against nonparticipants. Finally, the crescendo of the European movement saw the foundation of the EEC, dedicated to the achievement of a common tariff against the outside, which also discriminated against Canadian exports. Indeed, the EEC became a highly protectionist bloc – only with France and Italy did tariffs decline slightly from very high levels. With the other four members, the Benelux group and West Germany, tariffs rose because of the method of calculating the average rate across the community. By that time, however, Ottawa had largely given up on the Continent, at least in terms of trade.

Nor did those international organizations established in 1944 and later provide Canadian exporters with much solace. One in particular, the ITO, soon superseded by the GATT, was a symbol of the destruction of the multilateral and non-discriminatory impulse upon which so many hopes had been pinned. Most sobering for internationally minded businessmen and policymakers in Canada was the realization that the GATT was little more than a paper tiger whose rules and spirit were flouted with impunity by contracting parties. Nor were tariff reductions indicative of a freer trading world. Through Geneva, Annecy and Torquay, rates fell consistently, in harmony with the volume of Canadian exports to Britain and Europe. Instead of tariffs, those countries used a wide range of non-tariff barriers to trade. Quotas, quantitative restrictions, and, most of all, inconvertible currencies kept Canadian businessmen out of Europe, despite an immense effort. However, the decision in October 1950 to let the dollar float also bore some of the responsibility for this failure.[5]

The end of the above for Canada in its search for markets was that the United States represented security but, even more, it came to represent the country's only option for politicians who were mesmerized by the siren call of prosperity and the re-election that it seemed to promise. They were unwilling to consider the most obvious alternative, to be associated with the sterling area in some way. To their minds, the United States represented the future. Moreover, Canada could not accumulate sterling which could not be used – it was not that well off. To the extent of its very limited ability, Ottawa could only exhort, prod, and push potential trading partners overseas to achieve a liberalization of trade. Given the failure of those efforts, it seemed that the only option was increasing continentization. Canadian policy was multilateral and non-discriminatory by preference, but manifestly North American by default.

APPENDIX A

Canadian Exports, 1923–57, ($CAN)

	To United States	Total Exports	Percent of Total
1923	422,041,789	1,014,734,274	41
1924	412,981,614	1,058,057,898	38
1926–7*	466,419,539	1,283,939,000	36
1928–9*	500,167,599	1,388,000,000	36
1937	372,000,000	1,012,000,000	40
1949	1,524,000,000	3,022,000,000	50
1950	2,050,000,000	3,157,000,000	64
1951	2,333,000,000	3,963,000,000	58
1952	2,349,000,000	4,355,000,000	54
1953	2,463,000,000	4,172,000,000	59
1954	2,367,000,000	3,946,000,000	60
1955	2,612,000,000	4,351,000,000	60
1956	2,879,000,000	4,863,000,000	59
1957	2,941,000,000	4,934,000,000	60

	To United Kingdom	Total Exports	Percent
1923	360,819,518	1,014,734,274	35
1924	387,216,301	1,058,057,898	36
1926–7*	446,876,101	1,283,939,000	34
1928–9*	430,730,485	1,388,000,000	31
1937	403,000,000	1,012,000,000	40
1949	709,000,000	3,022,000,000	23
1950	472,000,000	3,157,000,000	14
1951	635,000,000	3,963,000,000	16
1952	751,000,000	4,355,000,000	17
1953	668,000,000	4,172,000,000	16
1954	658,000,000	3,946,000,000	16
1955	773,000,000	4,351,000,000	17
1956	818,000,000	4,863,000,000	17
1957	742,000,000	4,934,000,000	15

Source: Years 1923–1929, J. Castell Hopkins, The Canadian Annual Review of Public Affairs, (Toronto: The Canadian Annual Review Publishing Co., 1924–30). Years 1937–57, Dominion Bureau of Statistics, Review of Foreign Trade, (Ottawa: (King's) Queen's Printer, 1938–57).
* 31 March–31 March

Canadian Imports, 1923–57 ($CAN)

	From the United States	Total Imports	Percent of Total
1923	610,374,805	903,530,515	68
1924	524,611,011	808,195,573	65
1926–7*	687,746,410	1,030,892,505	67
1928–9*	868,055,897	1,388,000,000	68
1937	490,000,000	808,000,000	59
1949	1,951,000,000	2,761,000,000	71
1950	2,130,000,000	3,174,000,000	67
1951	2,812,000,000	4,084,000,000	69
1952	2,976,000,000	4,030,000,000	74
1953	3,221,000,000	4,382,000,000	74
1954	2,961,000,000	4,093,000,000	72
1955	3,452,000,000	5,705,000,000	73
1956	4,161,000,000	5,705,000,000	73
1957	3,998,000,000	5,623,000,000	71

	From United Kingdom	Total Imports	Percent of Total
1923	154,493,000	903,530,515	17
1924	148,836,000	808,195,573	18
1926–7*	163,902,361	1,030,892,505	16
1928–9*	194,020,573	1,388,000,000	15
1937	148,000,000	808,000,000	18
1949	307,000,000	2,761,000,000	11
1950	404,000,000	3,174,000,000	12
1951	420,000,000	4,084,000,000	10
1952	359,000,000	4,030,000,000	9
1953	453,000,000	4,382,000,000	10
1954	392,000,000	4,093,000,000	9
1955	400,000,000	4,712,000,000	8
1956	484,000,000	5,705,000,000	8
1957	521,000,000	5,623,000,000	9

Source: Years 1923–1929, J. Castell-Hopkins, *The Canadian Annual Review of Public Affairs*, (Toronto: The Annual Review Publishing Co., 1924–29). Years 1937–57, Dominion Bureau of Statistics, *Review of Foreign Trade*, (Ottawa: (King's) Queen's Printer, 1938, 1950–8)
* 31 March–31 March

Notes

ABBREVIATIONS

The following abbreviations or shortened references are used in the notes:

BCA	Bank of Canada Archives
CRO	Commonwealth Relations Office
DEA	Department of External Affairs
DOR	Dominion Office Records
FOR	Foreign Office Records
FRUS	*Foreign Relations of the US*
HCC	High Commission for Canada in the United Kingdom
HCUK	High Commissioner for the United Kingdom in Canada
HMG	His/Her Majesty's Government
ISCETP	Interdepartmental Sub-Committee on External Trade Policy
NA	National Archives of the United States
NAC	National Archives of Canada
ONC	Overseas Negotiating Committee
PMO	Prime Minister's Office
PREM	Premier's Records
PRO	Public Record Office
QUA	Queen's University Archives
SSCR	Secretary of State for Commonwealth Relations
SSEA	Secretary of State for External Affairs
USPGO	United States Government Printing Office
USSEA	Under-secretary of State for External Affairs

INTRODUCTION

1 R.D. Cuff and J.L. Granatstein, *Canadian-American Relations in Wartime: From the Great War to the Cold War* (Toronto: Hakkert, 1975), 74.

2 Donald Creighton, *The Forked Road: Canada, 1939–57* (Toronto: McClelland and Stewart, 1976), preface and 226. See also NA, Department of State Records, 742.00/3–1357, Embassy Ottawa to Department of State, 13 March 1957 for an interesting American analysis of these themes, developed by Creighton during a speech on 17 February 1957 at Carleton College.

3 The quotation is from James Laxer, *Canada's Economic Strategy* (Toronto: McClelland and Stewart, 1981), 10–11. See also, among others, Melissa Clark-Jones, *A Staple State: Canadian Industrial Resources in Cold War* (Toronto: University of Toronto Press, 1987); James Laxer, "Canadian Manufacturing and US Trade Policy," in Robert Laxer, ed., *Canada (Ltd.): The Political Economy of Dependency* (Toronto: McClelland and Stewart, 1973); Kari Levitt, *Silent Surrender: The Multinational Corporation in Canada* (Toronto: Macmillan, 1970).

4 Clark-Jones, *A Staple State*, 12; Creighton, *The Forked Road*, 125–6.

5 PRO, UK Treasury, Economic Policy Committee Records (T234), vol. 1974, "UK Exports to Canada," August 1948.

6 QUA Grant Dexter Papers, box 5, folder 36, "Memo of a Talk With Mr. Towers," 26 November 1949.

7 John Thompson and Allen Seager, *Canada, 1921–39* (Toronto: McClelland and Stewart, 1987), 202. For a detailed account of the 1930 and 1932 conferences, see Ian Drummond, *Imperial Economic Policy, 1917–39: Studies in Expansion and Protection* (Toronto: University of Toronto Press, 1974), 145–289. See also D.R. Annett, *British Preference in Canadian Commercial Policy* (Toronto: Ryerson Press, 1948), 149–81.

8 Ian M. Drummond, *British Economic Policy and the Empire, 1919–1939* (London: George Allen and Unwin, 1972), 69.

9 Canada, House of Commons *Debates*, 26 April 1932, 2408. See also *Documents on Canadian External Relations* (Ottawa: Canadian Government Publishing Centre, 1971) 4:227–33 for Bennett's proposal.

10 Drummond, *British Economic Policy*, 34. For a reminiscence by one of the Canadian negotiators, see Dana Wilgress, *Memoirs* (Toronto: Ryerson Press, 1967), 94–6.

11 Drummond, *British Economic Policy*, 100 for a discussion of this concept.

12 Thompson and Seager, *Canada, 1921–39*, 221.

13 Ian M. Drummond and Norman Hillmer, *Negotiating Freer Trade: The United Kingdom, the United States, Canada, and the Trade Agreements of 1938* (Waterloo, Ont.: Wilfrid Laurier University Press, 1989), 27.

14 *FRUS 1933* (Washington: USGPO, 1950) 1:476.

15 Ibid., 487.

16 A.J. Youngson, *The British Economy, 1920–1957* (Cambridge, MA: Harvard University Press, 1960), 121.

17 *FRUS 1935* (Washington: USGPO, 1952) 2:18, Canadian minister to the secretary of State, 4 January 1935. See also "Memo by the Secretary of State," 19 January 1935.

18 *FRUS 1935* 2:28, N. Armour to secretary of State, 25 October 1935.

19 J.L. Granatstein, *A Man of Influence; Norman A. Robertson and Canadian Statecraft, 1929–68* (Ottawa: Deneau, 1981), 51.

20 See Drummond and Hillmer, *Negotiating Freer Trade*, 28–34 for a discussion of this.

21 *FRUS 1936* (Washington: USGPO, 1953) 1:486, secretary of State to the ambassador in France, 11 March 1936.

22 Ibid., 783. But even Canada was not entirely clean. Hull took Herbert Marler, the Canadian minister in Washington, aside to tell him of his tremendous disappointment upon learning that Canada had signed a payments agreement with Germany which involved "the worst kind of bilateralism."

23 *Documents on Canadian External Relations* (Ottawa: Canadian Government Publishing Centre, 1971) 4:572. The Trade Agreements Act had first been passed by Congress in 1933 at the behest of the Roosevelt administration. It was the legislation that permitted the president to enter into trade agreements with foreign countries and as such was vitally important to the American program.

24 See, for example, Drummond and Hillmer, *Negotiating Freer Trade*, 68 – 70.

25 *FRUS 1936* 1:571, Memo by the assistant economic adviser, 11 May 1936.

26 Drummond and Hillmer, *Negotiating Freer Trade*, 43. The list that the Americans submitted to the British "consisted solely of goods – agricultural products and lumber – on which the Ottawa Agreements prevented Britain from granting concessions without dominion consent." And that would not be forthcoming, as the British well knew.

27 *FRUS 1936* Memo to Fowler, 17 June 1936, 1: 666–8.

28 For an account of the end result, see Drummond and Hillmer, *Negotiating Freer Trade*, 148–50.

29 Economic Cooperation Administration, *The Sterling Area: An American Analysis* (London: 1951), 21. For a thorough account of British wartime policy and practice, see L.S. Pressnell, *External Economic Policy Since the War: The Post-War Financial Settlement*, vol. 1 (London: Her Majesty's Stationery Office, 1986). For the Canadian side, see J.L. Granatstein, *Canada's War: The Politics of the Mackenzie King Government, 1939–1945* (Toronto: Oxford University Press, 1975).

30 J.C.R. Dow, *The Management of the British Economy, 1945–60* (Cambridge: Cambridge University Press, 1965), 174.

Extent of import controls, 1945–50
(percentage of imports purchased by government or subject to government restriction)

	1946	1947	1948	1949	1950
TOTAL IMPORTS					
Government imports	64	58	57	54	46
Restricted imports	32	33	34	37	27
TOTAL CONTROLLED IMPORTS	96	91	91	91	73

See also Paul Streeten, "Commercial Policy," in G.N.D. Worwick and Ph.H. Ady, eds., *The British Economy in the Nineteen-Fifties* (Oxford: Clarendon Press, 1966), 87.

31 QUA, Dexter Papers, box 2, folder 16, memorandum, 12 December 1939. On this point see also R.D. Cuff and J.L. Granatstein, "The Rise and Fall of Canadian-American Free Trade, 1947–48," *Canadian Historical Review* 58 (1977): 463.

32 J.L. Granatstein, *Canada's War: The Politics of the Mackenzie King Government, 1939–45* (Toronto: Oxford University Press, 1975), 98.

33 R.D. Cuff and J.L. Granatstein, *American Dollars-Canadian Prosperity; Canadian-American Economic Relations, 1945–50* (Toronto: Samuel-Stevens, 1978), 7.

34 Granatstein, *A Man of Influence* 114.

35 Ibid., 117. See also Robert Bothwell and John English, "Canadian Trade Policy in the Age of American Dominance and British Decline, 1943–47," *Canadian Review of American Studies* 8 (Spring 1977): 55–6.

36 *Documents on Canadian External Relations* 10 (Ottawa: Canadian Government Publishing Centre, 1987), 547.

37 BCA, Louis Rasminsky Papers, LR76–415–7, "Post-War Commercial Policy Prospects: A Proposal for Averting a Breakdown in International Trade Relations," 18 January 1945. See also J.L. Granatstein, "Settling the Accounts: Anglo-Canadian War Finance, 1943–45," *Queen's Quarterly* 83 (Summer 1976): 239.

38 Bothwell and English, "Canadian Trade Policy," 58.

CHAPTER ONE

1 NAC, W.L.M. King Papers, J-1, Howe to King, 31 August 1944, 313042. It was clear by 1944 that the UK economy would take some "re-establishing." Prime Minister Attlee pointed out in the House of

Commons in August 1945 that "the initial deficit with which we start the task of re-establishing our economy is immense." Lord Keynes of the UK Treasury called it "a financial Dunkirk." Sir Alec Cairncross, *Years of Recovery: British Economic Policy, 1945–51* (London: Methuen, 1985), 6, 10.

2 BCA, Louis Rasminsky Papers, LR76–415–7, "Post-War Commercial Policy Prospects: A Prospect for Averting a Breakdown in International Trade Relations," 18 January 1945.

3 BCA, Graham Towers Papers, memo no. 502, 22 February 1946. See L.S. Pressnell, *External Economic Policy Since the War: The Post-War Financial Settlement*, vol. 1 (London: Her Majesty's Stationery Office, 1986), 342–55 for an account of the Anglo-Canadian loan negotiations. See also Hector M. Mackenzie, "The Path to Temptation: The Negotiation of Canada's Reconstruction Loan to Britain in 1946," Canadian Historical Association *Historical Papers* (1982): 196–220.

4 Pressnell, *External Economic Policy*, 343–4.

5 Robert Bothwell and John English, "Canadian Trade Policy in the Age of American Dominance and British Decline, 1943–47" *Canadian Review of American Studies* 8 (Spring 1977): 62.

6 DEA, External Affairs Records, 154–s, Norman Robertson to Lester Pearson, 15 November 1947.

7 Hugh Dalton, *High Tide and After: Memoirs, 1945–1960* (London: Frederick Muller, 1962), 220.

8 Ibid. For a personal account of British problems in 1947, see Sir R.W.B. Clarke, *Anglo-American Economic Collaboration in War and Peace, 1942–49* (Oxford: Clarendon Press, 1982), 66–85.

9 Clarke, *Anglo-American Economic Collaboration*, 66.

10 NAC, Department of Finance Records, E2(f), vol. 3437, Clark to Bryce, February 1947.

11 R.N. Gardner, *Sterling-Dollar Diplomacy* (New York: McGraw-Hill, 1969), 315.

12 Cairncross, *Years of Recovery*, 137.

13 DEA, External Affairs Records, 154-s, Bryce to Clark, 16 September 1947. By some calculations the United Kingdom was actually better off in terms of gold and dollar reserves and hand than was Canada. A memo prepared in the Department of Finance noted that British reserves at the end of 1946 had represented nearly 40 per cent of their current account payments to all countries in that year. Canada's reserves of $800 million represented less than 30 per cent of its current account payments. Further, UK reserves were 135 per cent of her 1946 imports from dollar countries, while Canada's reserves amounted to about 50 per cent of her 1946 imports from those countries. Finally, it was forecast that in 1947 British holdings would be in excess of her

estimated dollar deficit while Canada's reserves would fall short. See BCA, Louis Rasminsky Papers, LR–76–412–5, "Memo of the Export Position and Credit to the UK," 1 May 1947.

14 Paul Wonnacott, *The Canadian Dollar, 1948–62* (Toronto: University of Toronto Press, 1965), 4.

15 PRO, DOR (DO35), vol. 3506, file 2291/36, *The New Statesman*, 21 May 1949.

16 R.D. Cuff and J.L. Granatstein, *American Dollars, Canadian Prosperity: Canadian-American Economic Relations, 1945–50* (Toronto: Samuel-Stevens, 1978), 66.

17 Ibid., 82.

18 PRO, UK Treasury, ONC Records (T236), vol. 8, B.P. (O.N.) (47) 70, "Canadian Negotiations," 2 November 1947.

19 Ibid., vol. 15, Brief for minister, "The 1948 Dollar Programme," 16 October 1947

20 Ibid., memorandum for prime minister, 7 October 1947.

21 Ibid., vol. 8, B.P. (O.N.) (47) 68, "United Kingdom Exports to Canada," 2 November 1947.

22 Sir Alec Cairncross, ed., *The Robert Hall Diaries, 1947–53* (London: Unwin Hyman, 1989), 15. Indeed, Hall noted in his diary that Sir Edwin Plowden, the chief planning officer and chairman, Economic Planning Board, that that "Ministers [were] in a panic about both the very bad situation and their own prospects." An end to bread rationing would certainly be a favourable omen. As Hall also told his diary, "Ministers are (so far) incapable of taking painful decisions."

23 ONC Records, B.P. (O.N.) (47) 66, "Scope for Negotiations with Canada," 2 November 1947. See also Clarke, *Anglo-American Economic Collaboration*, 73–4.

24 QUA, Dexter Papers, box 4, folder 31, "Long Distance Telephone Call from Max Freedman," 5 December 1947. See also ONC Records, vol. 5, B.P. (O.N.) (47) 69th Meeting, 31 December 1947.

25 I am indebted to Hector Mackenzie for this information.

26 PRO, PREM 8/978, Sir Percivale Liesching to Leslie Rowan, 10 December 1947. See also Dexter Papers, box 4, folder 31, Freedman to Dexter, 26 October 1947. For example, Deputy Minister Taggart of the Department of Agriculture told Freedman that "it would be useless to attempt a large-scale diversion of exports from the UK to the US because the farm bloc in the US [would] oppose the large-scale entry of Canadian foodstuffs ... Canada's main market is the UK. That's where we should concentrate."

27 Ibid., HCUK to SSCR, 15 December 1947. King was adamant that agreement be reached. He had just returned home from a prime ministers' meeting in London where he had been given a chilling tale of

Soviet intentions by Ernest Bevin, the United Kingdom's Foreign Secretary. Western solidarity was uppermost in his mind. I am grateful to Hector Mackenzie for this information. For a more sympathetic treatment of the British, see J.L. Granatstein, *A Man of Influence; Norman A. Robertson and Canadian Statecraft, 1929–68* (Ottawa: Deneau, 1981), 222–4.

28 Ibid., memo to Prime Minister Attlee, "Negotiations with Canada," 15 December 1947.

29 QUA, Dexter Papers, box 5, folder 31, Freedman to Dexter, 23 March 1948.

30 Alan Milward, *The Reconstruction of Western Europe, 1945–51* (London: Methuen, 1984), 267.

31 See DOR, vol. 3502, Clutterbuck to Pearson, 24 January 1948; ibid., Pearson to Clutterbuck, 6 February 1948.

32 ONC Records, vol. 210, minute sheet, A.T.K. Grant, 6 February 1948.

33 PRO, FOR (FO371), vol. 68872B, minute sheet, F.B.A. Rundall, 20 February 1948.

34 Cuff and Granatstein, *American Dollars, Canadian Prosperity,* 97. See also ONC Records, vol. 1794, A.R. Bruce to P. Harris, 9 September 1948.

35 External Affairs Records, 154-s, Robertson to Pearson, 1 March 1948.

36 Ibid., Robertson to Pearson, 16 March 1948.

37 DOR, vol. 3503, minute sheet, Sir Eric Machtig, 17 June 1948. See also Treasury Records, vol. 179, Sir James Helmore, "Note of a Discussion at the Department of Trade and Commerce with Mr. Mackenzie, Dr. Clark and Graham Towers," 25 August 1948. In the discussion, most of these points were raised, and the Canadians especially hammered the export theme with Helmore.

38 DOR, vol. 3503, minute sheet, Sir Andrew Jones to Sir John Bodinnar, 24 April 1948.

39 ONC Records, vol. 1792, UKHC to CRO, 23 August 1948.

40 Ibid., HCUK to CRO, 6 August 1948. For a summary of the Wilson-Smith meeting, see DRO, vol. 3504, "Visit to Washington and Ottawa, 28th July, 1948 to 5th August, 1948," 10 August 1948.

41 NAC, DEA Records, vol. 2084, "Memo on Informal Discussions,"12 August 1948.

42 ONC Records, vol. 1796, Clutterbuck to Machtig, 30 September 1948.

43 Oxford University, Nuffield College Library, Sir Stafford Cripps Papers, file no. 1107, Address by Chancellor of the Exchequer to Commonwealth High Commissioners, 23 February 1949. See also J.C.R. Dow, *The Management of the British Economy, 1945–60* (Cambridge: Cambridge University Press, 1965), 38.

44 See *Manchester Guardian,* 25 February 1949.

45 *Statutes-at-Large*, 80th Congress, 2nd Session, vol. 62, part 1, 137–55. According to Section 112(d) of the Economic Cooperation Act of 1948, the secretary of Agriculture was empowered to declare any agricultural commodity as surplus if an excess of any such commodity over domestic requirements existed which, it was anticipated, would be the case with wheat.

46 NAC, DEA Records, vol. 2082, file AR16/2 vol. 2, Wilgress to SSEA, 30 April 1949.

47 NAC, Department of Finance Records, vol. 4179, file 8522/U575–1 (49), UKCCC, "Report on Meetings Held at Canada House, 25–28 January 1949."

48 ONC Records, vol. 10, B.P. (O.T.N.) (47) 129, "Eastern Europe as a Source of Supply for the United Kingdom," 5 December 1947. See also Department of Finance Records, vol. 3626, ISCETP, 19 November 1948.

49 NAC, Department of Finance Records, vol. 4179, file 8522/U575–1 (40), UKCCC, "Report on Meeting."

50 *London Times*, 15 July 1949.

51 ONC Records, vol. 1800, HCUK to CRO, 5 April 1949. As Clutterbuck told London, there was "indignation aroused by what is described as our deliberate policy of trading with Russia and the satellite countries of Eastern Europe and bolstering up the economies of those who are ranged against us, simply because they will take payments in sterling, while deserting our tried friends on whom we are bound to depend again in any future emergency. On this issue emotion takes the place of reason and no amount of argument does any good." See also PRO, PREM 8/1185, Ernest Bevin to Prime Minister Attlee, 9 April 1949. Four days later, Bevin cabled Attlee from New York City that he was "disturbed about the state of the United Kingdom-Canadian commercial relationship," again highlighting the fact of UK-USSR trade in canned fish and coarse grains, while Canada had surpluses in both commodities.

52 FOR, vol. 75580, "Canadian Minister of Finance's Interview with the Secretary of State for Foreign Affairs," 12 July 1949. Abbott attributed this statement to King in 1948.

53 *Economist*, 26 March 1949, 572.

54 QUA, Dexter Papers, box 5, folder 35, Hutchison to Dexter, 8 February 1949.

55 PRO, PREM, 8/978, "Economic Relations Between the United Kingdom and Canada," 17 February 1949.

56 NAC, Department of Finance Records, vol. 4179, file 8522/U575–1 (49), "Record of a Meeting Held in Commonweath Relations Office," 29 April 1949

57 DOR, vol. 3508, Sir Alexander Clutterbuck, "Note of a Private and

Confidential Conversation with Governor and Deputy-Governor of the Bank of Canada," 14 April 1949.

58 ONC Records, vol. 1801, E.P.C. (49) 40, memo by chancellor of the exchequer, 22 April 1949.

59 BCA, Bank of Canada Records, 5D-200, Cripps to Abbott, 27 June 1949.

60 PRO, PREM 8/978, Clutterbuck to CRO, 6 July 1949.

61 NAC, DEA Records, vol. 2085, file AR16/31 vol.1, Robertson to Heeney, 22 June 1949. See also ONC Records, vol. 1867, Sir Stephen Holmes to Sir Roger Makins, 23 June 1949.

62 See Granatstein, *A Man of Influence*, 262.

63 *FRUS 1949* (Washington: USGPO, 1975) 4:781; "Concern of the United States over the British Financial Crisis," 9 June 1949.

64 BCA, Bank of Canada Records, 5D-200, Abbott to St Laurent, 9 July 1949.

65 FOR, vol. 75580, Makins to SSFA, 9 July 1949.

66 *Economist*, 12 July 1949.

67 *FRUS 1949*: 789, ambassador in the UK to the secretary of State, 22 June 1949.

68 Dean Acheson, *Present at the Creation; My Years in the State Department* (New York: W.W. Norton, 1969), 322.

69 Harry S. Truman Presidential Library, John Snyder Papers, box 33, file: Trip file – Europe, 2–24 July 1949, Summary and Conclusions, "Memo for the President," July 1949. See also NA, Department of State Records, file 841.51/6–1649, Lewis Douglas to Undersecretary Webb, 16 June 1949. In the telegram, Douglas pointed out that the British were contemplating the establishment of a rigid soft currency bloc that would discriminate against hard currency countries. He wrote that "I am informed from wholly authentic sources that HMG has developed a program which, if necessary to adopt, will insulate the UK from strong American pressure to devalue sterling and which the US will not like."

70 NAC, DEA Records, vol. 2085, file AR16/31 vol. 1, "Discussion under the Aegis of the UKCCC," 11 July 1949.

71 At the same time that the British were making this demand, Canada, the United Kingdom, and other countries were engaged in a tariff-cutting exercise at Annecy, France, under the auspices of the GATT. Such a policy, if enacted, were have surely compromised Ottawa's position there, as well as drawn the ire of the United States, a very important consideration in the development of any Canadian policy. See chapter 2.

72 NAC, Department of Finance Records, vol. 772, file 304SB-1, meeting of Commonwealth finance ministers, "Long-Term Programme," 14 July 1949.

73 Ibid., vol. 769, "Short-Term Measures," 15 July 1949.

74 *FRUS* 4: 789, ambassador in the UK to the Secretary of State, 22 June 1949.

75 *Economist*, 23 July 1949, 164.

76 NAC, DEA Records, vol. 2085, file AR16/31, vol. 2, SSEA to HCC, 9 August 1949. See also Foreign Office Records, vol. 75583, Washington to FO, 5 August 1949. It should also be noted that Cairncross, *Years of Recovery*, 165–211 tells a story different to Ritchie's with respect to British preparedness. I am indebted to Ian Drummond for bringing this to my attention.

77 NAC, DEA Records, vol. 2085, file AR16/31, vol. 2, Canadian ambassador in Washington to SSEA, 1 September 1949.

78 Alec Cairncross, ed., *The Robert Hall Diaries, 1947–53* (London: Unwin Hyman, 1989), 6.

79 Harry S. Truman Presidential Library, Dean Acheson Papers, box no. 64, memoranda of conversation, August-September 1949, Douglas to Acheson, August 1949. Relations between the two had been deteriorating over a wide front for a number of months. With respect to the OEEC, Alan Milward writes that Averall Harriman, the US ambassador to the ERP, was suspected of launching an anti-British press campaign which became so vitriolic that the Foreign Office hoped for President Truman's defeat in 1948 in order to have Harriman replaced. Alan S. Milward, *The Reconstruction of Western Europe, 1945–51* (London: Methuen, 1984), 184–5.

80 NA, Department of State Records, file 841.51/8–449, Julian Harrington to William Snow, 4 August 1949.

81 *Economist*, 17 September 1949, 593.

82 NAC, Department of Finance Records, vol. 772, file 304SB-1–1, HCC to SSEA, 22 September 1949. See also PRO, PREM 8/973, Oliver Franks to Edward Bridges and William Strang, 20 September 1949. Franks went further in his telegram, claiming that as a result of the Tripartite Talks, there was "a real conviction that the three countries ... have it in their power to remake the economic and trade pattern of the Western world if they can agree together, and a conviction that as a result of the week's work, such agreement will be progressively possible."

83 PRO, PREM 8/973, Franks to Edward Bridges and William Strang, 20 September 1949.

84 *Economist*, 24 September 1949, 683.

85 NA, Department of State Records, box 5898, file 842.50/1–147–12–3147, 48–9, consul-general in Montreal to Department of State, November, 1949. See also PRO, PREM 8/1185, "Exports to the United States," 11 January 1950. Although writing of the United States, the same applied to Canada. As Hall noted, "my own impression is that businessmen in England do not really believe that the Government is serious

enough in its desire for dollar exports to do anything that discrimi-
nates openly in favour of dollar earners and against non-dollar earners." See also Cairncross, *Years of Recovery*, 74: "Over the distribution
of exports between markets, the government had little or no influence
... a circumstance creating some tension between the Treasury, with
its list of desirable and undesirable markets, and the Board of Trade,
more concerned to keep up the momentum behind exports, irrespec-
tive of destination."

86 NA, Department of State Records, box 5898, file 842.50/1–147–12–3147,
48–49.

87 See, for example, FOR, file 75595, HCUK to CRO, 2 November 1949. See
also ibid., minute sheet, Sir Roger Makins, "Financial and Economic
Relations with Canada," 7 November 1949.

88 NAC, DEA Records, vol. 2082, file AR16/3/1, "General Considerations
on the Overall UK Import Programme," 26 September 1949.

89 QUA, John Deutsch Papers, box 67, folder 471, "The UK Import Programme," October 1949. See also FOR, file 75596, "Financial and Economic Relations with Canada," October, 1949.

90 NAC, DEA Records, vol. 2082, file AR16/3/1, "General Considerations ...."

91 QUA, Dexter Papers, box 5, folder 37, memo, 31 January 1950. See also
FOR, vol. 75595, minute sheet, Sir Roger Makins, "Financial and Economic Relations with Canada," 7 November 1949.

92 NAC, DEA Records, vol. 2082, file AR16/3/1, "Text of a Personal Communication Addressed to the Chancellor of the Exchequer by the Canadian Minister of Finance," 16 November 1949.

93 DOR, vol. 3509, E.P.C. (49) 123, "Financial and Economic Relations
with Canada," 7 November 1949.

94 NAC, DEA Records, vol. 2082, file AR16/3/1, HCC to SSEA, November
1949.

95 QUA, Deutsch Papers, box 67, folder 472, "Memo for Mr. Abbott,"
11 November 1949.

96 NAC, DEA Records, vol. 2082, file AR16/3/1, "Text of a Personal Communication Addressed to the Chancellor of the Exchequer by the Canadian Minister of Finance," 16 November 1949. See also Dominons
Office Records, vol. 3509, Sir Roger Makins, "Canada," 17 November
1949. Makins wrote of this issue that "the trouble is that the Chancellor's extremely logical and inflexible attitude on the arithmetic of our
programme with Canada, and the state of our reserves is not matched
when it comes to the point in our negotiations about drawings from
the blocked balances of other sterling area countries. If the reserves
are so sacrosanct that we cannot add a few dollars to our purchases
from Canada, how is it that whenever India or Pakistan ... come to us
to negotiate releases, we always start by saying that X is the maxi-

mum we can let them spend, but they go away with X plus a great deal more. This equally runs down the reserves. Canada's generosity to us suggests that some mild flexibility should apply all round."

97 QUA, Dexter Papers, box 5, folder 36, "Memo of a Talk with Mr. Towers," 26 November 1949. As Towers told Dexter, "There was a large and influential body of financial and industrial opinion, supported by powerful political groups both on the right ... and left ... The purpose was to loosen our economic ties with the US and pull us toward the sterling area ... My understanding is that he was saying that these groups in the UK desired to use Canada to drain strength from us to help them." Later, Towers was "very sour on the British. He says they always wanted us in the sterling cage and expected to have us by this time," ibid., folder 37, 30 January 1950.

98 NAC, DEA Records, vol. 2082, file AR16/3/1, "Text of a Personal Communication Addressed to the Chancellor of the Exchequer by the Canadian Minister of Finance," 16 November 1949.

99 FOR, vol. 75595, Clutterbuck to CRO, 2 November 1949.

100 Ibid., HCUK to CRO, 4 November 1949.

101 Ibid., vol. 75596, Roger Makins, 15 November 1949.

102 *Economist*, 14 January 1950, 86.

103 *Economist*, 28 January 1950, 188.

104 BCA, Bank of Canada Records, RD5D-450, "Comments by C.D. Howe on Mr. Pearson's Memorandum entitled 'A Review of Measures to Promote Canadian Exports to Soft Currency Countries,'" 21 April 1950.

105 R. Bothwell and W. Kilbourn, *C.D. Howe* (Toronto: McClelland and Stewart, 1979), 235.

106 BCA, Bank of Canada Records, RD5D-450, "Comments by C.D. Howe."

107 Dale C. Thomson, *Louis St. Laurent: Canadian* (Toronto: Macmillan of Canada, 1967), 283–6.

108 Bank of Nova Scotia *Monthly Review*, August 1949.

109 NAC, Department of Finance Records, vol. 3987, file P-2–9, C.C.E.P., doc. no. 25

CHAPTER TWO

1 John English and Robert Bothwell, "Canadian Trade Policy in the Age of British Decline and American Predominance," *Canadian Review of American Studies* 8 (Spring 1977):57

2 Robert Solomon, *The International Monetary System, 1941–1976* (New York: Harper and Row, 1977), 11. For a comprehensive account of the IMF, see J, Keith Horsefield, ed., *The International Monetary Fund, 1945–65* (Washington, D.C.: International Monetary Fund, 1969).

3 Government of Canada, *White Paper on Employment and Income* (Ottawa: 1945), 7.

4 R.N. McCormick, *Journal of Public Affairs* 13 (Spring 1950). The quotation is attributed to the then undersecretary of State, Sumner Welles, in May 1942.

5 Joyce and Gabriel Kolko, *The Limits of Power: The World and United States Foreign Policy, 1945–54* (New York: Harper and Row, 1972), 84.

6 NAC, Department of Finance Records, vol. 559, file 152–17, "Address of Hon. L.D. Wilgress ... At Final Plenary Meeting of ITO Preparatory Committee," 22 August 1947.

7 Ibid., vol. 567, file 152–17, Wilgress to Pearson, 30 September 1947. Wilgress wrote that "this status has enabled us to play a leading role in all the discussions leading up to the formulation of the Draft Charter. We [have] participated on an equal footing with the United Kingdom and the United States ... This is an indication not only of the ability of of the members of the delegations, but also of our status as a commercially great power."

8 See the *Final Act Adopted at the Conclusion of the Second Session of the Preparatory Committee of the United Nations Conference on Trade and Employment* (Geneva: Interim Commission for the International trade Organization, 1947).

9 Robert E. Hudec, *The GATT Legal System and World Trade Diplomacy,* (New York: Praeger, 1975), 45–6

10 *FRUS 1949* (Washington, D.C.: USGPO, 1976), 1:725. See n. 72 for a discussion of the Trade Agreements Act.

11 NAC, Department of Finance Records, E3(k)2, vol. 3610, file ITO-26, "United States Concessions to Canada," 26 September 1947.

12 Ibid., vol. 2117, file 429/3/5, SSEA to HCC, 25 September 1947.

13 Ibid., King to Atlee, 3 September 1947

14 Ibid., vol. 3608, file ITO-18, "Exchange of Notes," 30 October 1947.

15 Ibid., vol. 3610, file ITO-26, Wilgress to SSEA, 26 August 1947. See Joyce and Gabriel Kolko, *The Limits of Power,* 366. As Wilcox wrote to Clayton, "what we must have is a front-page headline that says 'Empire Preference System Broken at Geneva.' With this, the success of this whole series of negotiations is assured, Without it, there is grave danger that the whole program will end in defeat."

16 NAC, Department of Finance Records, E3(k)2, vol. 3610, file ITO-26, "Statement Made By Mr. Clair Wilcox to Representatives of the British Commonwealth," 15 September 1947.

17 Ibid., Wilgress to SSEA, 23 September 1947.

18 Ibid.

19 Ibid., "Minute of a Meeting with Rt. Hon. Mr. St. Laurent on Crisis in United Kingdom-United States Negotiations at Geneva," 30 September 1947

20 Ibid., Canadian Trade Delegation, Geneva to SSEA, 2 October 1947.

21 See "Memorandum by the Minister-Counsellor for Economic Affairs at London and by Mr. Winthrop G. Brown, 24 September 1947", FRUS 1947 (Washington, D.C.: USGPO, 1973) 1:996–8. Even given the perceived lack of movement by Britain, the United States had no intention of completely breaking off negotiations. See also Ibid., 1015, "Memorandum by the Chairman of the Committee on Trade Agreements to President Truman," 17 October 1947. The Anglo-Canadian exchange of notes greatly eased the US-UK situation by releasing the other from the contractual obligation to maintain existing margins of preference assumed at Ottawa in 1932. This meant that in all future US-Canada and US-UK tariff negotiations, either of those two countries could negotiate with the Americans "with respect to their most-favoured-nation rates free of any contractual obligation to the other to maintain preferential margins. It amounts to the abrogation of the most important part of the Ottawa Agreements and can fairly be considered to be substantial action with respect to preferences."

22 See R.D. Cuff and J.L. Granatstein, *American Dollars, Canadian Prosperity; Canadian-American Economic Relations, 1945–50* (Toronto: Samuel-Stevens, 1978), 64–82.

23 *London Times*, 31 October 1947, 4.

24 NAC, William Lyon Mackenzie King Diaries, 20 October 1947, 999.

25 Canada, House of Commons *Debates*, 9 December 1947, 99.

26 Robert Spencer, *Canada in World Affairs, 1946–49* (Toronto: Oxford University Press, 1957), 215. For example, the underdeveloped countries at Havana demanded that a committee on economic development be established to protect their interests. This was opposed by the developed bloc, which favoured a tariff committee that would have administered the GATT with quasi-autonomous powers. The underdeveloped group viewed the tariff committee as an instrument through which industrialized nations would try to maintain economic dominance. Accordingly, the former played up the economic development committee as their protector. As a result, both committees disappeared. The Canadian delegation felt, however, the concessions made to the underdeveloped bloc went further than were warranted. See NAC, DEA Records, vol. 2117, file AR429/3/6, circular document no. A. 131, 4 June 1948.

27 PRO, UK Treasury, ONC Records (T236), vol. 3806, Bank of England, "Memorandum," 29 March 1951. See also ibid., minute sheet, A.C. Sparks to Sir Herbert Brittain, 12 April 1951. See also Paul Streeten, "Commercial Policy" in G.D.N. Worswick and P.H. Ady, eds., *The British Economy in the 1950s* (Oxford: Clarendon Press, 1962), 97.

28 QUA, Dexter Papers, box 5, folder 32, Max Freedman to Dexter, 18 March 1948. See also BCA, Bank of Canada Records, 5A-250, file: GATT 1947–1948, Canadian Trade Delegation Havana to SSEA, 28 Feb-

ruary 1948. The American interpretation was that the British had counted all along on Havana failing. When the United States had pulled the CPs through, "the United Kingdom Government [was] alarmed and [was] therefore making a last desperate effort to prevent a formalization [of the] Charter." However, even prior to the British return, the American delegation had not been unduly concerned: London would accept the charter – it had no choice.

29 *Winnipeg Free Press*, 24 November 1947, 15.

30 *Economist*, 27 March 1948, 361.

31 Michael Heilperin, "Notes on the Havana Charter," *Canadian Banker* 55: 57.

32 QUA, Dexter Papers, box 5, folder 36, "Memo on Johnny," n.d.

33 *The Attack on Trade Barriers*, (Geneva: Interim Commission for the ITO, August 1949).

34 QUA, Dexter Papers, box 5, folder 32, Max Freedman to Dexter, 18 March 1948.

35 Cuff and Granatstein, *American Dollars, Canadian Prosperity*, 52.

36 Kolko and Kolko, *The Limits of Power*, 454.

37 NA, Department of State Records, file 560AL/9–2049, memorandum of conversation, "Annecy Conference," 20 September 1949. That was entirely understandable, given the political and economic weight the United States carried. As the graph indicates, in per capita terms, Western Europe *combined* had less than 33 per cent of the US gross national product, while the British had about 50 per cent.

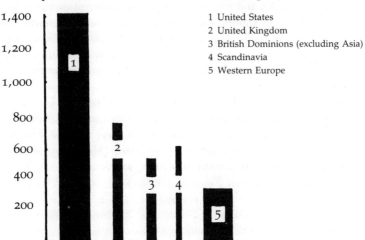

Note [a]The height of the pillars is proportional to national income per head, the width to population. The area of the pillars is therefore proportional to aggregate national income.

Figure 2
National income, United States, United Kingdom, British Dominions, Scandinavia, and Western Europe (dollars per head)[a]

38 Article II read in part, "They will seek to eliminate conflict in their international economic policies and will encourage economic collaboration between any or all of them." See Escott Reid, *Time of Fear and Hope: The Making of the North Atlantic Treaty, 1947–49* (Toronto: McClelland and Stewart, 1977), 167–84 for an account of the genesis of Article II. It was not worth the paper it was written on because, as the powerful US secretary of State, Dean Acheson, later wrote, "the plain fact [was] ... that NATO was a military alliance." See R.D. Cuff and J.L. Granatstein, *Canadian-American Relations in Wartime: From the Great War to the Cold War*, (Toronto: Hakkert, 1975), 127.

39 QUA, Deutsch Papers, box 47, folder 328, Perry to Deutsch, 7 September 1949.

40 *Economist*, 9 July 1949, 84.

41 NAC, Department of Finance Records, vol. 578, "Discussions with Mr. Raymond Vernon," 23 January 1950. See also Department of State Records, file 560AL/12–1349, "Confidential Report of Woodbury Willoughby, Chairman of the United States Delegation to the Third Session of the Contracting Parties to the GATT, Supplementary Official Report of the Chairman," n.d. In that regard, both Canada and the United States were incensed by the blatant attempt on the part of the United Kingdom and Western Europe to keep South Africa on side in the dollar versus sterling debate. If Pretoria did not discriminate against hard currency countries and buy from soft currency sources, then the British and West Europeans would drastically slash imports from South Africa and curtail the flow of investment capital. According to Willoughby, this represented "a callous disregard for the multilateral, non-discriminatory trade objectives of the General Agreement, as well as a disregard of the interests of South Africa, Canada, the United States, and even of their own long-term interests."

42 QUA, Deutsch Papers, box 47, folder 328, G.N. Perry to Deutsch, 7 September 1949. The consultation as required under Article XII, para. 4(b) of the GATT took place in March, 1950. For the British line on this question, see ONC Records, vol. 2396, "Memo," 25 July 1949.

43 *FRUS 1949* (Washington: USGPO, 1976) 1:712.

44 NA, Department of State Records, file 560AL/6–149, Carl Corse to Woodbury Willoughby, 1 June 1949.

45 Canada, House of Commons *Debates,* 21 October 1949, 1026.

46 Toronto *Globe and Mail*, 10 October 1949, 1.

47 *Economist*, 27 August 1949, 446.

48 Toronto *Globe and Mail*, 18 August 1949, 6. Wilgress's prognostications seemed to be coming true several months later. In a letter sent by Raymond Vernon to Winthrop Brown, chief, Division of Commercial

Policy, Department of State, in March 1950 during a mid-session meeting of the GATT, he pointed out that "the CPs came to this meeting, most of them, determined to let as little happen as they possibly could." The reasons for that varied, but among OEEC countries "Paris [was] the real show," while the sterling area was "huddled together in a common crisis front." As a result, "the typical committee session [was] a dialogue between the US and the UK ... with the Canadians chirping prettily from the sidelines." NA, Department of State Records, file 394.31/3–250, Vernon to Brown, 11 March 1950.

49 *Economist*, 9 July 1949, 84.
50 NA, Department of State Records, file 394.31/3–3151, Beale to Corse, 31 March 1951.
51 DEA, External Affairs Records, 50092-C-40, ICETP-82, 17 April 1951.
52 ONC Records, vol. 3806, Sir Stephen Holmes, "Meeting of UK and US Representatives at Torquay," 5 November 1950.
53 Harry S. Truman Library, Harry Truman Papers, White House Central Files, Confidential File, box 50, file: negotiations folder 17. Emphasis in original.
54 Ibid. See also PRO, FOR (FO371), vol. 91903, Foreign Office to Washington, 23 March 1951.
55 *FRUS 1951* (Washington, D.C.: USGPO, 1979) 1:1254, "Results of the Torquay Negotiations," 9 April 1951. See also FOR, vol. 91903, "Record of a Meeting Between Sir Stephen Holmes and Mr. Carl Corse," 23 March 1951.
56 FOR, Roger Makins, "Anglo-American Tariff Negotiations," 27 March 1951. See also Department of State Records, 394.31/5–951, US Embassy Ottawa to Department of State, 9 May 1951. Some Canadian and American officials later claimed that Anglo-American negotiations failed because Harold Wilson, the president of the Board of Trade, assumed direct responsibility for the discussions. As was pointed out to Washington, "he was [very] anti-American ... and ... intractable in negotiations." See also PRO, Board of Trade, Commercial Relations and Exports Division Records (BT241), vol. 2, "GATT Tariff Negotiations with the US at Torquay," May, 1954.
57 NAC, Department of Finance Records, vol. 3012, file GATT-3 vol. 2, ISCETP, 10 November 1950.
58 Ibid., vol. 566, file 152–17 vol. 6, Abbott to McKinnon, 22 February 1951.
59 QUA, Deutsch Papers, box 47, folder 328, Reisman to Deutsch, 15 January 1951.
60 Ibid., 5 January 1951.
61 Ibid., 15 March 1951.
62 Ibid.

63 NA, Department of State Records, file 394.31/3–1751, Corse to Beale, 17 March 1951.
64 NAC, Department of Finance Records, vol. 566, file 152–17, vol. 6, "Notes on Torquay for Mr. Howe," 8 May 1951.
65 See *International Financial News Survey* 3 (13 April 1951): 309.
66 Ibid., (27 April 1951): 325.
67 *Economist*, 21 April 1951, 901.
68 QUA, Dexter Papers, box 6, folder 40, Bruce Hutchison, "Talk with Johnny," 4 May 1951.
69 NA, Department of State Records, 394.31/5–951, Ottawa to Department of State, 9 May 1951.
70 NAC, Department of Finance Records, vol. 567, file 152–17, vol. 6, GATT Fourth Session of the Contracting Parties, "Problems Facing Low Tariff Countries," 8 March 1950. See also Department of State Records, 394.31/10–250, "Memorandum of Conversation with Benelux Delegation," 28 September – 2 October 1950.
71 NAC, Department of Finance Records, vol. 567, file 152–17, vol. 6, GATT Fourth Session of the Contracting Parties, "Problems Facing Low Tariff Countries," 8 March 1950.
72 Ibid., vol. 578, HCC to SSEA, 9 March 1951. See also John Deutsch, "Recent American Influence in Canada with Particular Reference to Economic Factors and Canadian Reaction" in H.G. Aitken et al, *The American Economic Impact on Canada* (Durham, N.C.: Duke University Press, 1959), 47–8.
73 Ibid.
74 DEA External Affairs Records, 50092-C-40, ICETP-85, 25 June 1951. Both the renewal of the Trade Agreements Act, first passed in 1934 and renewed every three years thereafter, and the repudiation of the Customs Simplification Bill by the Congress represented sharp setbacks for the Truman administration. The Trade Agreements Act was the authority by which the president entered into various trade agreements with foreign countries, such as the GATT negotiations at Geneva in 1947. After some political infighting, the act, which had expired in June 1949, was renewed on 16 June 1951, but in an unusual way. Congress had endowed the president with the necessary authority to bind or reduce tariffs but, having given such authority, the restrictions inserted into the new legislation by Congress to limit the presidential exercise of this power was confusing.
   In the case of the Customs Simplification Act, it appeared to be a case of Congress not wanting to make US tariff legislation more comprehensible. This was a Department of the Treasury-sponsored bill that had the strong support of the secretary of State, Dean Acheson.

He wrote that it was "the cardinal objective of the foreign economic policy of the US to reduce unnecessary trade barriers. One important aspect of this problem [related] to the simplification of customs procedures." Had it been passed, it would have been a significant statement of *intent*. See *FRUS 1950* (Washington, D.C.: USGPO, 1977) 1:787.

The furor surrounding the Customs Simplification Bill affected the Canadian government. An aide-memoire was despatched to Washington, pointing out that provisions dealing with customs administration had been among the most important undertakings of the GATT. US customs practices had come to be regarded as an obstacle to the expansion of US imports and world trade no less formidable than the tariff itself. As of the end of the Torquay round, the United States had still not taken action to bring customs procedures into line with the GATT. That was a subject of serious complaint for Canada and others. NAC, C.D. Howe Papers, vol. 4, file S-4, "United States Customs Administration," 16 February 1950.

75 DEA, External Affairs Records, 50092-C-40, ICETP-85, 25 June 1951.

76 Ibid.

77 QUA, Dexter Papers, box 6, folder 40, "Talk with Johnny," 4 May 1951.

78 NAC, Department of Finance Records, vol. 566, file 152–17, vol. 6, Louis Couillard to C.M. Isbister, 4 April 1951.

79 W.S. Woytinsky and E.S. Woytinsky, *World Commerce and Governments* (New York: The Twentieth Century Fund, 1955), 222.

80 A.F.W. Plumptre, *Three Decades of Decision: Canada and the World Monetary System, 1944–75* (Toronto: McClelland and Stewart, 1977), 123.

81 W.A. Macintosh, "Canadian Economic Policy from 1945 to 1957 – Origins and Influences" in H.G. Aitken et al, *The American Economic Impact on Canada* (Durham, N.C.: Duke University Press, 1959), 62. See also Alan Milward, *The Reconstruction of Western Europe, 1945–51* (London: Methuen, 1984), 219.

82 *Economist*, 9 July 1949, 84.

83 Hudec, *The GATT Legal System*, 51.

84 Woytinsky and Woytinsky, *World Commerce and Governments* 261, 266. As they point out, "the extent of [that danger to the exporter] depends on the interpretation of the escape clause provision by the Administration ... By December 1, 1952, the Tariff Commission had completed investigations on 15 applications." However trivial or minor some of these cases were, the provisions were interpreted by many prospective exporters as significant in terms of US protectionism. See also *FRUS 1952–54* (Washington D.C.: USGPO, 1983) 1(prt 1): 163, acting chairman of the US delegation to the Eighth Session of the

GATT to the director of Foreign Operations in the United Kingdom, 20 October 1953.

85 *Economist*, 30 June 1951, 1544

CHAPTER THREE

1 NAC, Lester B. Pearson Papers, N1, vol. 21, file: Commonwealth Economic Conference 1952, Wilgress to Pearson, "Statement of Canadian Views," 6 September 1952.

2 See President's Materials Policy Commission, *Resources for Freedom* 1 (Washington, D.C.: USGPO, 1952).

3 United Kingdom, House of Commons *Debates*, 28 October 1950, col. 479.

4 BCA, Bank of Canada Records, 3B-178, W.C. Clark, Marcel Boyer and Alex Skelton, "Memorandum to Cabinet Committee on Economic Policy," 13 October 1949.

5 *Economist*, 28 January 1950, 188. By contrast, the United States was taking ever-larger amounts of Canadian newsprint:
    1947–3,685,000 tons
    1948–3,881,000 tons
    1949–4,056,000 tons
    1950–4,302,000 tons
See Canada, House of Commons *Debates*, 14 June 1951, 4103.

6 BCA, 3B-634, R.M. Fowler, "Canada's Trade in Pulp and Paper," 23 August 1949.

7 Ibid.

8 *Economist*, 22 July 1950, 161. See also PRO, DOR (DO35), vol. 3512, Harold Wilson to P. Gordon-Walker, 25 November 1950.

9 See PRO, Cabinet Records, 129/41, C.P. (50) 173, memorandum by president of the Board of Trade, "Supplies of Newsprint," 18 July 1950.

10 NAC, Department of Trade and Commerce Records, vol. 756, file 23–2–78, "An Analysis of Foreign Demand for Canadian Agricultural Products for the Period 1949/50–1952/53," 15 July 1949, 6.

11 NAC, Department of Finance Records, vol. 789, file 501–0–116–2, Canadian ambassador Washington to SSEA, 17 March 1950.

12 DEA, External Affairs Records, 50012–40, UKCCC (50), 2nd Meeting, 19 June 1950. For the British side, see DOR, vol. 3512, "Anglo-Canadian Relations," 23 November 1950.

13 John Holmes, *The Shaping of Peace: Canada and the Search for World Order, 1943–57*, vol. 2, (Toronto: University of Toronto Press, 1982), 234.

14 NAC, Department of Finance Records, vol. 569, file 152–17, "The Overall Balance of Payments of the United Kingdom," 18 September 1950.

15 Ibid. See also DOR, vol. 3501, report by the chancellor of the Exchequer, "Financial Discussions with Commonwealth Ministers," September, 1950.

16 NAC, Department of Finance Records, vol. 569, file 152–17. Acting
HCC to SSEA, 21 September 1950.

17 PRO, PMO Records 8/1147, EPC (50) 25th Meeting, Minute 3, 31 October 1950.

18 NAC, Department of Finance Records, vol. 569, file 152–17, Towers to
Abbott, "Remarks by G.F. Towers at a Meeting of Commonwealth Finance Ministers," 28 September 1950.

19 NAC, Department of Finance Records, vol. 766, file 304-SB vol. 3, Abbott to Gaitskell, 27 April 1950.

20 See Bank of Nova Scotia *Monthly Review* (June 1950).

21 DEA, External Affairs Records, 50012–40, Abbott to Clutterbuck, 9 February 1951.

22 G.D.N. Worwick and P.H. Ady, eds., *The British Economy in the 1950s*
(Oxford: Clarendon Press, 1962), 8.

23 NAC, Department of Finance Records, vol. 4179, file 8522/475–1 (51),
UKCCC, May 1951, 1st Meeting, 21 May 1951.

24 Ibid., 2nd Meeting, 21 May 1951.

25 NA, Department of States Records, decimal file 1950–54, 641.42/3–
2151, Ottawa to Department of State, 21 March 1951. The issue at
stake then had been the "have regard to" clause of the agreement and
Westminister's refusal to compensate Western Canadian farmers for
the low prices paid over the term of the agreement.

26 Ibid., 742.00(W)/1–2552, Ottawa to Department of State, 25 January
1952.

27 Bank of Nova Scotia *Monthly Review* "The Revolution in Canada's
Trade," (July-August 1951).

28 QUA, Dexter Papers, box 6, folder 40, 11 June 1951.

29 NAC, Department of Finance Records, vol. 4179, file 8522/475–1 (51),
UKCCC, May, 1951, 2nd Meeting, 21 May 1951.

30 Ibid., vol. 4231, file 8810/U57–1, Bower to Newman, 6 April 1951.

31 Canada, House of Commons *Debates*, 3 June 1952, 2855. Howe went
on, "there is a large domestic market and I suppose the other markets
served were the traditional markets of the United Kingdom, such as
Australia, New Zealand and other countries which ordinarily purchase machine tools in the United Kingdom ... We find a lack of
availability, or if availability is there, the delivery date is too far in advance to be practical. We also find that orders placed in the United
Kingdom with a reasonable delivery date have to be cancelled because
the delivery date is pushed back and it is necessary for us to replace
the goods in other markets ... I am not blaming the United Kingdom
manufacturers ... I am merely explaining why the tremendous market

which is available in Canada is not being filled by the United Kingdom."

32 NAC, Department of Finance Records, vol. 772, file 304-SB-3, "Review
of Canada's External Trade and Financial Policies," September 1952,
10.

33 *Economist*, 22 November 1952, 588.

34 NAC, Department of Finance Records 3(k)2, vol. 3616, "Review of Balance of Payments and International Financial Position of the United
Kingdom and the Sterling Area," September, 1948.

35 Ibid., vol. 3617, "Long Term Problems," 2 September 1948.

36 J.C.R. Dow, *The Management of the British Economy, 1945–60* (Cambridge: Cambridge University Press, 1965), 71.

37 Lord Butler, *The Art of the Possible* (London: Hamish Hamilton, 1971),
157.

38 DEA, External Affairs Records, 50012–40, Gaitskell to Abbott, 7 November 1951. See also PRO, UK Treasury, ONC Records (T236),
vol. 3290, R.W.B. Clarke to M.T. Flett, 25 October 1951. As Butler
notes in his memoirs, he followed the £350 million cut up with £150
million in January 1952 and another £100 million in March. Butler, *The
Art of the Possible*, 157. See also Dow, *The Management of the British
Economy* 58–65.

39 BCA, Bank of Canada Records, 4D-100, G.E. Freeman, "The New
Chancellor's Speech on the UK Economic Situation," 7 November
1951.

40 Butler, *The Art of the Possible*, 159.

41 *Economist*, 13 February 1954, 440.

42 BCA, Graham Towers Papers, memorandum no. 665, November
1951.

43 BCA, Bank of Canada Records, 4D-100, Freeman. See also PRO, UK
Treasury, ONC Records (T236), M.T. Flett to R.W.B. Clarke, "Commonwealth Conference," 26 November 1951

44 QUA, Dexter Papers, box 6, folder 40, 6 January 1952.

45 PRO, Cabinet Records, 133/123, F.M.(M) (52) 1st Meeting, "Meeting of
Commonwealth Finance Ministers," 16 January 1952.

46 Dow, *The Management of the British Economy*, 72.

47 DOR, vol. 6502, "Brief on the Paper on Convertibility," 29 August
1952. See also Dow, *The Management of the British Economy*, 70.

48 QUA, Dexter Papers, box 6, folder 41, Hutchison to Sifton, 9 February
1952. See also Dow, *The Management of the British Economy*, 72. They
did tighten their belts, although not as Britain had anticipated. Australia, which took about 10 per cent of the United Kingdom's exports,
imposed restrictions against British exports in the aftermath of the
conference. As was pointed out, the conference communiqué had not

been couched in terms of non-sterling imports, but rather "that each sterling country should seek to live within its means."

49 BCA, Bank of Canada Records, 4A-955 "Convertibility and Non-Discrimination," 7 April 1952. See also ONC Records, vol. 3089, Hugh Ellis-Rees to Sir Herbert Brittain, 19 September 1952. Ellis-Rees agreed, writing to Brittain that "the Americans and Europeans would see very little advantage in convertibility which did not automatically carry with it a return to non-discrimination."

50 DEA, External Affairs Records, 50012–40, Bower to Isbister, 15 February 1952

51 ONC Records, vol. 3089, R.W.B. Clarke, "Convertibility, Multilateralism, Etc.," 17 July 1952. In his memoirs, Butler lays the blame for maintaining inconvertibility at the feet of "Lord Cherwell and the cautious conservatism of the elder statesmen" of the Conservative Party. Butler, *The Art of the Possible,* 160.

52 BCA, Bank of Canada Records, 4A-955, "Convertibility and Non-Discrimination."

53 *Economist,* 9 August 1952, 344.

54 BCA, Bank of Canada Records, 4A-955, "Convertibility and Non-Discrimination." Indeed, there had been strong rumours throughout the Spring and summer of 1952 that the pound was to be made convertible.

55 Ibid.

56 ONC Records, vol. 3345, "Publicity in Canada – General," 26 February 1953.

57 NAC, Pearson Papers, vol. 21, file: Commonwealth Economic Conference, Robertson to Pearson, 22 August 1952.

58 Ibid., 24 August 1952.

59 NAC, Department of Finance Records, vol. 772, file 304-SB, vol. 3, Canadian delegation to the preparatory meeting of the Commonwealth Economic Conference to SSEA, 24 September 1952.

60 Ibid.

61 Pearson Papers, vol. 21, file: Commonwealth Economic Conference, Wilgress to Pearson, "Statement of Canadian Views," 6 September 1952.

62 BCA, Towers Papers, memorandum no. 698, 27 September 1952.

63 NAC, Department of Finance Records, vol. 772, file 304-SB-3, vol. 1, "Report to Ministers at a Meeting in the Privy Council Chamber on Friday, October 31st, 1952, by Officials who were present in London at the Preparatory Meeting of the Commonwealth Economic Conference." See also ONC Records, vol. 3368, Ellis-Rees to Brittain, 19 September 1952. As before, Ellis-Rees agreed with this interpretation: "I cannot see how the Americans could be persuaded to put up a large

support fund with the certainty that there would be continued discrimination against dollar goods."

64 NAC, Pearson Papers, vol. 21, file: Commonwealth Economic Conference, Wilgress to Pearson, "Statement of Canadian Views," 6 September 1952.

65 Ibid., Canadian delegation to the preparatory meeting of the Commonwealth Economic Conference to SSEA, 2 October 1952.

66 DEA, External Affairs Records, 50012–40, Canadian chargé (Washington) to SSEA, 4 August 1952.

67 NAC, C.D. Howe Papers, vol. 4, file S-4 External Affairs, Mutual Aid (12), 1949–57, Pearson to Howe, 8 October 1952.

68 BCA, Towers Papers, memorandum no. 699, "Some Reflections on Discussions in London to Date – Commonwealth Economic Conference," 4 October 1952.

69 Harry S. Truman Presidential Library, John Snyder Papers, box 3, file: Trip – NATO Meeting, Paris, France, December 12–19, 1952, "Commonwealth Economic Conference Communiqué," December, 1952. See also DOR, vol. 6504, Memorandum by Chancellor of the Exchequer, P.E.C. (52) 46, 29 October 1952.

70 ONC Records, vol. 3094, Commonwealth Economic Conference, C.E.C. (FT) (52) 1st Meeting, 28 November 1952.

71 QUA, Dexter Papers, box 6, folder 43, January, 1953.

72 See United Kingdom, House of Commons *Debates,* 6 April 1954, col. 195–227.

73 *Economist,* 5 June 1954, 821, as quoted in Dow, *The Management of the British Economy,* 77, n.5.

74 PRO, Cabinet Records 129/59, C(53) 70, "Commerical Policy in Europe," 19 February 1953. See also ONC Records, vol. 3817, "Note for Record," 8 January 1953, and "Note of an Informal Meeting between M. Marjolin, Secretary-General of OEEC, and United Kingdom officials ....," 16 January 1953 for a specific discussion of the EPU aspect. See chapter 4 for a description of the EPU.

75 Butler, *The Art of the Possible,* 167.

76 NAC, DEA Records, vol. 2286 file 5–37–1, P.M.M. (53) 5th Meeting, 9 June 1953.

77 BCA, 4A-955 – Collective Approach, Plumptre to Rasminsky, 18 May 1954.

78 ONC Records, vol. 3695, "Note of a Conversation Between Mr. Burgess and Sir Robert Hall," 27 January 1954. For a stark account of the US budget story see Sherman Adams, *Firsthand Report: The Story of the Eisenhower Administration* (New York: Harper and Row, 1961), 153–6.

79 PRO, FOR (FO371), vol. 105115, "Discussions Between Chancellor of

the Exchequer and Secretary to the United States Treasury," 22 December 1953, Minute–Sir Pierson Dixon, 22 December 1953.

80 Ibid., vol. 103526, "Mr. St. Laurent's Visit with President Eisenhower," 8 May 1953. In the interview, Eisenhower reaffirmed that his administration was "solidly opposed" to restrictive trade policies and "readily assented to Mr. St. Laurent's plea that if for the moment they could not move forward on liberalization, at least there should be no backsliding." To that, a British official had minuted, "If only [the Americans] would give some proof of this."

81 BCA, Bank of Canada Records, 5D-232, Rasminsky to Towers, 12 January 1954.

82 Ibid. See also Treasury Records, vol. 3580, Sir Archibald Nye to J.J. Garner, 4 March 1954.

83 NAC, Department of Finance Records, vol. 4182, file 8522/U575–1, ICETP, 10 February 1954.

84 Economist, 13 February 1954, 471.

85 Economist, 12 June 1954, 869.

86 BCA, Bank of Canada Records, 4A-955, "Collective Approach and Trade Policy," 13 May 1954.

87 Ibid., "Collective Approach," 2 September 1954.

88 Ibid., 5A-200, file IMF memos, 1954–57, "Report on the 9th Annual Meeting of the Boards of Governors of the IMF and the International Bank for Reconstruction and Development," 24–29 September 1954. For an account of Butler's impressions of the upcoming meeting, see ONC Records, vol. 3595, Minute – W.Armstrong, "Commonwealth Finance Ministers' Meeting – Washington, September 1954," 17 February 1954. See also ONC Records, vol. 3089, R.W.B. Clarke to Sir Leslie Rowan, 26 November 1954. In this letter, Clarke echoes both Canadian opinion and Rooth's sentiments. As he noted, "I profoundly believe that the convertibility operation is in our own essential interests and that if we lose another opportunity of doing it, it many be postponed for a very long time – possibly even sine die. The world does not stand still while we sit and contemplate the position of sterling ... It is not as if we had a satisfactory alternative to convertibility; we have not."

89 BCA, Bank of Canada Records, 5A-200, file IMF memos, 1954–57, "Report on the 9th Annual Meeting."

90 London Financial Times, 16 October 1954. See also Cabinet Records 128/27, C.C. (54) 59th Conclusions, 8 September 1954. Prior to the September meetings, Butler decided to make it clear that the US government record with respect to good creditor policies "fell far short of what he hoped."

91 BCA, Bank of Canada Records, 5D-234, file: Commonwealth Finance Ministers' Meeting, Washington, September, 1954, Canadian Ambassador Washington to SSEA, 4 October 1954.

92 Ibid.

93 Ibid., 4A-955, G.F. Towers, "Memorandum," 7 October 1954.

94 NAC, A.D.P. Heeney Papers, vol. 1, Heeney to Robertson, 2 October 1954. On this point see also Arnold Heeney, *The Things That Are Caesars: Memoirs of a Canadian Public Servant* (Toronto: University of Toronto Press, 1972), 132–3.

95 BCA, Bank of Canada Records, 5D-240, file: Commonwealth Finance Ministers' Meeting, January-February, 1955, "Economic Questions," 20 January 1955.

96 Ibid., 4A-955, Rasminsky to Plumptre, 14 April 1955.

97 Ibid., 5D-242, file: Commonwealth Finance Ministers' Meeting, September, 1955, HCC to SSEA, 19 September 1955. See also DOR, vol. 5633, F.M. (1) (55) 2nd meeting, "Meeting of Commonwealth Finance Ministers," 17 September 1955.

98 DOR, vol. 5633, "Talks with Canadian Delegation," 14 September 1955.

99 NAC, Department of Finance Records, vol. 4231, file 8810/U57–1, Bower to Bull, 12 August 1955.

100 Ibid., vol. 4180, file 8522/U575–1 (55), UKCCC (55), R.2, 8 December 1955.

101 Ibid.

102 London *Financial Times*, 5 July 1955.

103 NAC, Department of Finance Records, vol. 4180, file 8522/U575–1 (55), UKCCC (55), R.2, 8 December 1955.

104 Ibid., Bower to Isbister, 23 September 1955.

105 Ibid., UKCCC (55) R.3, 8 December 1955.

106 Ibid., vol. 4231, file 8800/U57–1, R.P. Bower, "Statement to the Conservative Committee on Anglo-Canadian Trade," 2 November 1955.

107 Harold Macmillan, *Riding the Storm, 1956–59* (London:Macmillan, 1971), 137.

108 FOR, vol. 120816, Sir H. Caccia to Foreign Office, 23 November 1956.

109 NA, Department of State Records, 1955–59, decimal file, 842.00/5–1057, Ottawa to Department of State, 10 May 1957.

110 NAC, Department of Finance Records, vol. 4180, file 8522/U575–1 (58), UKCCC (58), R.2, 20 June 1958.

111 *Economist*, 9 August 1952, 344.

112 Although Diefenbaker wished to forget the whole affair, or so the British felt, it had become "a source of embarrassement if not grief, to Mr. Diefenbaker." See also J.L. Granatstein, *Canada, 1957–67: The Years of Uncertainty and Innovation* (Toronto: McClelland and Stewart, 1986), 43–5.

113 A.F.W. Plumptre, *Three Decades of Decision: Canada and the World Monetary System, 1944–75* (Toronto: McClelland and Stewart, 1977), 141

CHAPTER FOUR

1 *Economist*, 29 October 1949, 932. For an American perspective on European integration, see FRUS 1951, (Washington, D.C.: USGPO, 1985) 4:1–138. The American demand for economic integration was not taken altogether seriously in Western Europe and, by late 1949, the ERP Administrator, Paul Hoffman, felt compelled to threaten "to terminate dollar support unless the OEEC moved on toward a single European market." Sidney Dell, *Trade Blocs and Common Market* (London: Constable, 1963), 43.

2 Alan Milward, *The Reconstruction of Western Europe, 1945–51* (London: Methuen and Co., 1984), 476. For a more radical analysis of American policy, see Joyce and Gabriel Kolko, *The Limits of Power: The World and United States Foreign Policy, 1945–54* (New York: Harper and Row, 1972).

3 R.D. Cuff and J.L. Granatstein, *American Dollars, Canadian Prosperity* (Toronto: Samuel Stevens, 1978), 258.

4 Bank of Nova Scotia, *Monthly Review*, December 1948. See also John Holmes, *The Shaping of Peace: Canada and the Search for World Order, 1943–57* (Toronto: University of Toronto Press, 1982), 2:113.

5 As Alan Milward writes, "the gross dimensions of aid allocations to each country were determined by its dollar balance of payments deficits. European countries were required in the OEEC to draw up in one comprehensive programme a statement of their annual requirements in dollar imports and it was against this programme that aid was awarded to cover costs. The bigger the dollar deficit on foreign trade, the larger the share of Marshall Aid." Alan Milward, *The Reconstruction of Western Europe, 1945–51* (London: Methuen and Co., 1984), 95.

6 NAC, DEA Records, vol. 2079, file AR12/1 vol.7,? to S.D. Pierce, 31 July 1948.

7 Cuff and Granatstein, *American Dollars, Canadian Prosperity*, 118.

8 Bank of Nova Scotia, *Monthly Review*, December 1948.

9 Cuff and Granatstein, *American Dollars, Canadian Prosperity*, 118. See also Milward, *The Reconstruction of Western Europe*, 184. For example, ERP Ambassador Harriman threatened the French that unless Paris voted in favour of the US choice for OEEC director-general, then Congress "would not next time round vote any aid for France." That attitude spilled over into trade affairs.

10 NAC, DEA Records, vol. 2079, file AR12/1 vol. 8, Ritchie to Robertson, "Memo," 31 August 1948.

11 PRO, PREM 8/971, memo by the president of the Board of Trade, "European Import Relaxations and Non-Discrimination," 22 July 1949.

12 NAC, Department of Finance Records, vol. 578, ICETP, 15 February 1950. For a variation of this theme, see PRO, FOR (FO371), vol. 91942, Geneva to Foreign Office, 7 October 1951. As was then noted with respect to tariff disparities, which had an indirect effect on European cooperation, the UK delegation in Geneva pointed out that "on the assumption that the French plan is really intended to be a general application, *or at least not exclusively European*, Canada would be prepared to play her part." (emphasis added). That reflected the Canadian mindset. See also PRO, UK Treasury, ONC Records (T236), vol. 2552, United Kingdom high commissioner in Canada to Commonwealth Relations Office, 25 February 1950.

13 Milward, *The Reconstruction of Western Europe,* 168–211.

14 NAC, Department of Finance Records, vol. 567, file 152–17, HCC to SSEA, 30 June 1947.

15 DEA, External Affairs Records, 500-B-40, ISCETP document no. 51–38, May 1951.

16 F.A. Knox, "The March of Events," *Canadian Banker* 56 (1951): 31.

17 ONC Records, vol. 2552, memo to cabinet by president of the Board of Trade, "Extension of OEEC Liberalization to Sterling Commonwealth Countries," 20 February 1950.

18 OEEC, *12th Annual Economic Review* (September 1961): 185–6, as quoted in Robert Solomon, *The International Monetary System, 1945–1976* (New York: Harper and Row, 1977).

19 Brian Tew, *The Evolution of the International System, 1945–77* (New York: John Wiley and Sons, 1977), 46.

20 Ibid.

21 ONC Records, vol. 3369, "The Commonwealth Conference and the OEEC," n.d.

22 DEA, External Affairs Records, 4901-F-40, undersecretary of State for External Affairs to permanent delegation to NATO/OEEC, 21 September 1953.

23 NA, Department of State Records, 394.31/11–651, Ottawa to Department of State, "Notes on Canadian Impressions on Geneva GATT Conference," 6 November 1951.

24 ONC Records, vol. 3818, "Record of a discussion with M. Marjolin and Mr. Cahan at the Jr. Carleton Club," 25 February 1953.

25 NAC, Department of Finance Records, vol. 4195, file 8628–06–3, Canadian delegation to NATO/OEEC to USSEA, 5 October 1953.

26 Ibid.

27 PRO, DOR (DO35), vol. 6493, OEEC-UK delegation, "UK Record of Statements on OEEC Mission to Washington," 4 May 1953.

28 NAC, Department of Finance Records, vol. 4195, file 8628–06–3, Canadian delegation to NATO/OEEC to USSEA, 5 October 1953.

29 D.D. Eisenhower Presidential Library, Records as president of the United States, White House Central Files (Confidential File), 1953–61, subject series box 84, "Extent of Progress by OEEC Countries in Dollar Liberalization," n.d.

30 NAC, Department of Finance Records, vol. 4195, file 8628–06–3, Canadian delegation to North Atlantic Council and OEEC to USSEA, 10 March 1954.

31 Ibid.

32 Ibid., 16 April 1954.

33 NAC, Department of Finance Records, vol. 4195, file 8628–06–3, Permanent Representative of Canada to North Atlantic Council and OEEC to SSEA, 26 April 1954.

34 Ibid., 26 April 1954.

35 Ibid., "Statement Delivered by the Canadian Permanent Representative to the OEEC, Mr. L.D. Wilgress," 6 May 1954.

36 DEA, External Affairs Records, 4901-F-40, Canadian delegation to USSEA, 4 June 1954.

37 Ibid., USSEA to permanent delegation, 4 June 1954.

38 ONC Records, vol. 3808, "Note of a meeting with Canadian officials at the Board of Trade," 23 June 1954. See also ibid., vol. 3821, "Washington Briefs on the Collective Approach," 9 September 1954.

39 NAC, Department of Finance Records, vol. 4195, file 8628–06–3, SSEA to permanent representative, 20 August 1954.

40 Ibid., Plumptre to P.A. Bridle, 25 August 1954.

41 Ibid., Isbister to Bridle, 26 August 1954.

42 DEA, External Affairs Records, 4901-F-40, permanent delegation to USSEA, 16 September 1954.

43 Ibid., 16 September 1954.

44 Ibid.

45 Ibid., Canadian delegation to OEEC to SSEA, 4 December 1954. Not surprisingly, the Americans emphatically agreed with the Canadian insistence that the speed of dollar liberalization in Europe should not be linked to US commercial policies.

46 Ibid., SSEA to Canadian delegation to NATO/OEEC, 9 December 1954.

47 Ibid., Canadian embassy Washington to SSEA, 9 December 1954.

48 Ibid., 17 December 1954. The Americans would vote for the OEEC resolution, then press for an agreed interpretation with the OEEC. However, many State Department officials responsible for commercial policy favoured the harder line taken by Canada.

49 NAC, Department of Finance Records, vol. 4195, file 8628–06–3, Canadian Embassy Washington to SSEA, 17 December 1954.

50 Ibid., "Statement by Canadian Representative at the OEEC Ministerial Council, 14–15-January 1955."

51 Ibid., Canadian delegation to OEEC to SSEA, 19 May 1955.

52 Ibid., vol. 768, file 304SB-1C-1 pt. 2, Canadian delegation to USSEA, 24 June 1955.

53 Ibid.

54 Ibid., "Canadian Ministerial Statement," OEEC ministerial council, 10 July 1955.

55 Ibid., vol. 4195, file 8628–06–3, USSEA to Canadian delegation to OEEC, 7 September 1955.

56 DEA, External Affairs Records, 4901–F–40, USSEA to Canadian Delegation to OEEC, 7 September 1955.

57 Ibid., Canadian Delegation to USSEA, 3 October 1955.

58 Ibid., Canadian delegation to USSEA, 3 October 1955. For an explanation of the French attitude, see PRO, Board of Trade, Commercial Relations and Export Division Records (BT241), vol. 220, UK permanent delegation Paris to Foreign Office, 14 September 1955.

59 Commercial Relations and Export Division Records, vol. 219, UK delegation to OEEC, "Annual Review for 1954," 15 March 1955. On this subject, the Belgian foreign minister, Paul-Henri Spaak, remarked to the British chancellor of the exchequer, Harold Macmillan, that even in the OEEC the French "did not keep the rules regarding export subsidies and import taxes." As chairman of the council of the OEEC, Macmillan entered a protest with Paul Ramadier, the French minister of Finance. In return, he received "very smooth words ... but I doubt if we shall get much action." Harold Macmillan, *Riding the Storm, 1956–1959* (London: Macmillan, 1971), 75.

60 DEA, External Affair Records, 4901–F40, Canadian Delegation to USSEA, 3 October 1955.

61 NAC, Department of Finance Records, vol. 768, file 304SB-1C-1 pt. 2, SSEA to OEEC Delegation, 13 December 1955.

62 DEA, External Affairs Records, 4901-E-40 vol. 12, Bulletin on the OEEC, "Meeting of Ministers in Paris," 12–14 January 1956.

63 Ibid., Canadian delegation to USSEA, 17 October 1955.

64 NAC, Department of Finance Records, vol. 4195, file 8628–06–3 pt. 2, Isbister to Ritchie, 22 December 1955: Ibid., Rasminsky to Ritchie, 14 December 1955. See also DEA, External Affairs Records, 4901-F-40, Canadian delegation to USSEA, 23 January 1956.

65 See PRO, Commercial Relations and Export Division Records, vol. 219, UK delegation to OEEC, "annual review for 1954," 15 March 1955. See also ibid., statement by president of the Board of Trade, "Report by the Steering Board on Further Liberalization," 6 January 1955.

66 NAC, Department of Finance Records, vol. 4195, file 8628–06–3 pt. 2, Isbister to Ritchie, 22 December 1955.

67 "Statement Made by the Canadian Representative at the OEEC Ministerial Council," 10 February 1956.
68 DEA, External Affairs Records, 4901-F-4–40, Plumptre – memorandum to Ritchie, Isbister, and Rasminsky, 17 December 1956.
69 NAC, Department of Finance Records, vol. 4195, file 8628–06–3 pt. 3, NATOParis to External, 25 March 1957.
70 DEA, External Affairs Records, 4901-F-4–40, External to NATOParis, 4 March 1957.
71 NAC, Department of Finance Records, vol. 4207, file 8718–03–15, Washington D.C. to External, 21 December 1959.

CHAPTER FIVE

1 Robert E. Hudec, *The GATT Legal System and World Trade Diplomacy* (New York: Praeger, 1975), 53–5.
2 NA, Department of State Records, 394.31/11–651, "Notes on Canadian Impressions of Geneva GATT Conference," 6 November 1951.
3 PRO, DOR (DO35), vol. 6905, "Notes on Pre-GATT Discussions with Canadian Delegation," 23–25 September 1952.
4 NA, Department of State Records, 394.31/11–2351, Department of State to American Embassy Ottawa, 23 November 1951.
5 PRO, UK Treasury, ONC Records (T236), vol. 3248, "Future External Commercial Policy," 23 March 1952.
6 NA, Department of State Records, 394.31/7–2753, memo for undersecretary, "British Proposal to Modify GATT Obligations Affecting Preferences," 27 July 1953.
7 PRO, FOR (FO371), vol. 105086, "United Kingdom Proposal Regarding the Application of Article 1," 2 September 1953.
8 PRO, DOR, vol. 6899, "Address by the Right Honourable C.D. Howe … at the Eighth Session of the Contracting Parties to the General Agreement on Tariffs and Trade, 1953." See also PRO, UK Treasury, ONC Records (T236), vol. 3577, F.G. Lee to Sir Leslie Rowan, 10 November 1953.
9 NA, Department of State Records, 394.31/2753, memo for undersecretary, 27 July 1953.
10 PRO, DOR, vol. 6899, Gordon Bowen to E.A. Cohen, 5 August 1953. See also NAC, Department of Finance Records, vol. 567, file 152–17 pt. 10, High Commissioner for Canada in the UK to SSEA, 11 July 1953.
11 PRO, FOR, vol. 105089, Geneva to Foreign Office, 25 October 1953.
12 Ibid., vol. 105087, Peter Wakefield to Dennis Wright, 24 September 1953.
13 Section 22, first enacted into law as a provision of the Agricultural Adjustments Act of 1935, authorized the president to raise tariffs or

establish quotas on certain imported commodities where low prices tended to undermine domestic agricultural programs. The Trade Agreements Extension Act of 1951 further stipulated that no international agreement could be administered in a manner inconsistent with the requirements of Section 22.

14 Hudec, *The GATT Legal System*, 175.

15 *FRUS 1952–54*, 1, pt. 1, (Washington, D.C.: USGPO, 1985), 199, memo by the deputy assistant secretary of State for Economic Affairs to the secretary of State, 27 May 1954.

16 D.D. Eisenhower Presidential Library, White House central files, 1953–61, Sub-series box 84, file: Trade Agreements and Tariff Matters (1953) 7, "Statement Delivered to the Randall Commission by Mr. L.D. Wilgress," 11 November 1953. See also Department of State Records, 394.31/2–1954, memo of conversation, "UK Convertibility," 19 February 1954.

17 NAC, Department of Finance Records, vol. 4182, file 8522/4585–1, Canadian ambassador Washington to SSEA, 24 February 1954.

18 Ibid.

19 D.D. Eisenhower Presendential Library White House central files (confidential file) 1953–61, subject series box 69, file: State, Department of, "Meeting of US-Canadian Committee on Trade and Economic Affairs," 16 March 1954.

20 PRO, Board of Trade, Commercial Relations and Export Division Records (BT241), vol. 248, "Note of a Meeting with Canadian Officials on the GATT," 24 June 1954.

21 NAC, Department of Trade and Commerce Records, vol. 993, file 1–7–336 pt. 2, R.G.C. Smith to C.M. Isbister, 27 January 1954. See also Bank of Nova Scotia, *Monthly Review*, April 1954. "To many outsiders, including Canadians, the Randall Report is a rather discouraging document severely limiting the scope of possible tariff reductions and placing emphasis on broad hopes and aspirations without making concrete proposals which would contribute toward their realization."

22 Ibid., file 7–11–87, vol. 3, Canadian delegation to North Atlantic Council and OEEC to USSEA, 21 April 1954.

23 DEA, External Affairs Records, 50093-B-40 "The General Agreement on Tariffs and Trade," 19 February 1954.

24 NAC, Department of Finance Records, vol. 4182, file 8522/4585–1, Canadian ambassador Washington to SSEA, 24 February 1954.

25 DEA, External Affairs Records, 9100-A0-40, Wyndham-White to Isbister, 15 April 1954.

26 Ibid.

27 Ibid., Canadian ambassador Washington to SSEA, 20 May 1954.

28 PRO, Commercial Relations and Export Division Records, vol. 2, "Note of a meeting with US officials," 9 June 1954.

29 John H. Jackson, *The World Trading System: Law and Policy of International Economic Relations* (Cambridge, Mass.: MIT, 1989), 44.

30 DEA, External Affairs Records, 50093-B-40, "The General Agreement on Tariffs and Trade," 24 February 1954.

31 BCA, Bank of Canada Records, 5C-150, file US-Canada ministerial meeting 1954, "Meeting of 16 March 1954."

32 NAC, Department of Finance Records, vol. 4182, file 8522/U585-1, "Notes for Mr. Howe to Open Joint Meeting," 10 March 1954.

33 DOR, vol. 5629, "Note on Pre-GATT Meeting of Canadian Delegations," 24 October 1954. Further, when Canadian and American officials met a number of months later, largely at the behest of Benson, it was clear that *none* of the many US agencies concerned with disposals knew what policy the others were following.

34 BCA, Bank of Canada Records, 4A-955, "Note on Commercial Policy Discussions with United States Officials," 26–27 May 1954.

35 Ibid.

36 PRO, DOR, vol. 6900, The Review of the GATT, "Summary of a Discussion in Ottawa," 20 September 1954.

37 DEA, External Affairs Records, 9100-AO-40, "Collective Approach and Trade Policy," 13 May 1954.

38 Ibid., The GATT Review, "International Trade Policy," 13 May 1954.

39 Ibid.

40 PRO, Commercial Relations and Export Division Records, vol. 248, Geoffrey Parker to Cyril Sanders, 15 September 1954.

41 See G.E. Britnell, "Implications of United States Policy for the Canadian Wheat Economy," *Canadian Journal of Economics and Political Science* 22 (1956): 10.

42 *FRUS, 1955–57,* vol. 9, (Washington: USGPO, 1987) 9: 155, telegram from the embassy in Canada to the Department of State, 12 October 1955

43 PRO, CAB133/118, CRG (54) 4th Meeting, "Commonwealth Meeting on the Review of the GATT," 6 October 1954.

44 Ibid.

45 PRO, CAB 129/74, note by president of the Board of Trade to cabinet, "A Review of GATT," 28 March 1954.

46 DEA, External Affairs Records, 9100-AO-40, Barrow to A.E. Ritchie, "Notes on Informal Discussions Between Canadian and United Kingdom Officials ... to Discuss the Review of GATT," 7 July 1954. See also CAB133/118, CRG (54) 5th Meeting, "Commonwealth Meeting on the Review of the General Agreement on Tariffs and Trade," 7 October 1954.

47 Interview with Dr C.M. Isbister.

48 A.G. Kenwood and A.L. Loughheed, *The Growth of the International Economy, 1820–1980* (London: George Allen and Unwin, 1984), 259.

49 DEA, External Affairs Records, 50092–40, ICETP doc. no. 168, 16 September 1954.

50 Ibid.

51 Ibid., 9100-AO-40, SSEA to permanent Canadian Representative to North Atlantic Council and OEEC, 18 September 1954.

52 Ibid.

53 BCA, Bank of Canada Records, 4A-955, notes for the Hon. W.E. Harris, "Informal Meeting of Commonwealth Finance Ministers – General Commercial Policy and the GATT," 30 September 1954.

54 PRO, Commercial Relations and Export Division Records, vol. 249, "Speech by Rt. Hon. C.D. Howe ... delivered in Plenary Session on 6 December 1954."

55 ONC Records, vol. 4032, D.A.V. Allen, "Report from Geneva-3," n.d.

56 Ibid., D.A.V. Allen, "Report from Geneva-6(a) – A Canadian Attitude," 8 November 1954.

57 NAC, Lester B. Pearson Papers, vol. 23, file: Commonwealth prime ministers' Conference, 1955, "Commonwealth Prime Ministers' Conference, London, January–February 1955," 3 February 1955.

58 DEA, External Affairs Records, 50092-B-40, ICETP-132, 29 December 1954.

59 NAC, C.D. Howe Papers, vol. 54, file S-14–9, Howe to George Bateman, 3 January 1955. See also ONC Records, vol. 4032, Allen, "Report from Geneva-11," n.d. On this point, Allen suggested that US "unreasonableness" was because the Americans were "so obsessed with the idea of making the GATT presentable to Congress that they wish to remove from the existing text any passages which Congress may find it difficult to accept or to understand." See also Department of State Records, 394.31/12–3054, memo of conversation, "Canadian Pessimism on GATT," 30 December 1954.

60 DEA, External Affairs Records, 50092-B-40, ICETP-132, 29 December 1954.

61 Canada, House of Commons Debates, 14 January 1955.

62 Economist, 22 January 1955, 281.

63 BCA, Bank of Canada Records, 5C-150, file: US-Canada Ministerial Meeting, GATT-Proposed Waiver of United States Agricultural Obligation, 6 January 1955.

64 Ibid.

65 FRUS 1955–57 9, 74.

66 Bank of Canada Records, 5C-150, file: US-Canada ministerial meeting, GATT – Proposed Waiver of United States Agricultural Obligation, 6 January 1955.

67 Ibid., SSEA to Canadian delegation to the GATT, 20 January 1955.

68 ONC Records, vol. 4032, D.A.V. Allen, "Report from Geneva-9 –

OEEC-GATT Problems," 9 December 1954. With respect to the French, the acting chairman of the US delegation to the 9th Session of the GATT accused them of deplorable behaviour. "Throughout the meeting, they did their best to disrupt and sabotage the efforts of those who wished to strengthen the GATT ... They would not, however, for prestige reasons, leave the GATT." *FRUS 1955–57* 9, 100, "Draft Report by the Acting Chairman of the Delegation to the Ninth Session of the General Agreement on Tariffs and Trade," 9 March 1955

69 NAC, Department of Finance Records, vol. 4203, file 8710–01, "Note for Mr. Howe on Position of United Kingdom at this Session," 7 December 1954.

70 *Canadian Banker* 62 (1955) 10.

71 NAC, Department of Finance Records, vol. 4184, file 8522/4585–8, "Statement by the Canadian Delegation to the Ninth Session of the Contracting Parties to the GATT," n.d. See also Department of State Records, 842.00/5–1955, Amembassy [sic] Ottawa to Department of State, 19 May 1955. Even the establishment of the Royal commission on Canada's Economic Prospects was, according to the Canadian ambassador the United States, A.D.P. Heeney, part of a policy of moving away from a traditional free trade position. The Department of State saw this threat as "merely another shot in the campaign which Mr. Heeney has been waging to convince the US that Canada might adopt a policy of retaliation if restrictive measures are taken by the US which would seriously affect Canadian trade."

72 NAC, Department of Finance Records, vol. 4184, file 8522/4585–8 Canadian Delegation to GATT to SSEA, 13 February 1955.

73 Ibid., ICETP-134, 22 February 1955.

74 BCA, Bank of Canada Records, 5A-260, file: GATT memos-1957, ICETP doc. no. 177, July 1955.

75 Ibid., 5C-200, US-Canada Joint Committee on Trade and Economic Affairs, September 1955, "Trade and Commercial Policy," 26 September 1955.

76 Ibid.

77 Ibid.

78 NAC, Department of Finance Records, vol. 4208, file 8720/T186–4, A.F.W. Plumptre, "Memo to Harris," 10 January 1956.

79 BCA, Bank of Canada Records, 5A-260, GATT memos-1957, ICETP doc. no. 177, July 1955.

80 NA, Bureau of Foreign and Domestic Commerce, Special Trade and Economic Program File, 1947–63, RG 151, Office of International Regional Economics, European Division/Canada Section, RSC box 5018, Trade Agreements Committee, "Requests on Canada," 17 October 1955.

81 BCA, Bank of Canada Records, 5A-260, file: GATT Memos-1957, ICETP document no. 177, July 1955.
82 Ibid.
83 PRO, Commercial Relations and Export Division Records, vol. 18, S.H. Levine, "Memo," December 1955. As the British now recognized, at least among Commonwealth countries, "preferences [were] ... no longer a really live issue." See CAB129/71, "The Commonwealth Discussion on the Review of the G.A.T.T.," 4–11 October 1954.
84 Canada, House of Commons *Debates*, 8 March 1956, 1809–10.
85 Toronto *Globe and Mail*, 6 March 1955, 5.
86 BCA, Bank of Canada Records, 5A-260, GATT memos – 1957, ICETP doc. no. 177, July 1955.
87 *FRUS 1955–57* 9: 196–203, letter from the executive secretary of the GATT to John M. Leddy, 18 July 1956
88 Canada, Royal Commission on Canada's Economic Prospects, *Final Report* (Ottawa: Queen's Printer, 1957)
89 Ibid., 65. See also NA, US Treasury, Special Trade and Economic Program File, 1947–63, "Renegotiation of Certain Tariff Concessions by Austria, Canada, Ceylon, Greece and the Union of South Africa," 16 September 1957. As a press release pointed out, those countries "have expressed a desire to avail themselves of the opportunity, on January 1, 1958, to modify or withdraw concessions in their schedules to the General Agreement." Canadian items included steel pipe, zinc products, electrical instrument parts, and some fruits and vegetables.

CHAPTER SIX

1 NAC, Department of Finance Records, vol. 768, file 304SB-1, statement by Mr Pearson, "European Economic Cooperation," n.d.
2 Ibid., vol. 4191, file 8625–01 pt. 2, A.E. Ritchie to A.F.W. Plumptre, "European Common Market," 31 January 1956.
3 Final Act Adopted at the Conclusion of the Second Session of the Preparatory Committee of the United Nations Conference on Trade and Employment (Geneva: Interim Commission for the International Trade Organization, 1947).
4 Ibid., vol. 768, file 304SB-1, statement by Mr Pearson, "European Economic Cooperation."
5 Harold Macmillan, *Riding the Storm, 1956–1959* (London: Macmillan, 1971), 67, 69.
6 NAC, Department of Finance Records, vol. 4181, file 8522/U575–1 (56), "Messina Common Market Proposals," May 1956.
7 Ibid., vol. 4191, file 8625–01 pt. 2, Brussels to External, 22 September 1956.

8 Ibid.

9 See, for example, Ibid., vol. 4181, file 8522/U575–1 (56), "General Implications for Canadian Exports to the Benelux Countries Participating in the Customs Union Associated with the Free Trade Area," 5 October 1956.

10 Ibid., "The Messina Common Market Proposals," n.d.

11 Ibid., "Messina Common Market Proposals, n.d.

12 Ibid., "General Implications for Canadian Exports of Italy's Participation in the Customs Union Associated with the European Free Trade Area," 3 October 1956.

13 Ibid., SSEA to Canac Paris, 23 February 1956. See also PRO, CAB128/30, CM(56), 68th conclusions, 3 October 1956.

14 PRO, DOR (DO35), vol. 5637, meeting of Commonwealth Finance Ministers, F.M.(W)(56) 2nd meeting, 29 September 1956.

15 NAC, Department of Finance Records, vol. 4180, file 8522/U575–1 (55), UKCCC (55) R.1, 8 December 1955. See also BCA, Bank of Canada Records, 5D-244, file Commonwealth Finance Ministers' Meeting, September 1956, chancellor of the Exchequer to minister of Finance, September 1956. See also PRO, CAB129/82, Harold Macmillan and Peter Thorneycroft, "United Kingdom Commercial Policy," 28 July 1956.

16 NAC, Department of Finance Records, vol. 4190, file 8625–01 pt. 1, Léger to deputy governor Bank of Canada, deputy minister of Finance, deputy minister of Trade and Commerce, secretary to the cabinet, 30 December 1955.

17 Ibid., Robertson to External, 30 December 1955.

18 Macmillan, *Riding the Storm*, 74.

19 Victoria Curzon, "European Integration and Atlantic Partnership" in *The European Free Trade Area and the Crisis of European Integration* (Geneva: Michael Joseph, 1968), 26.

20 BCA, Bank of Canada Records, 5D-244, file: Commonwealth Finance Ministers Meeting, September 1956, chancellor of the Exchequer to minister of Finance, September 1956.

21 PRO, DOR, vol. 5637, meeting of Commonwealth finance ministers, F.M. (W) (56) 2nd Meeting, 29 September 1956.

22 DEA, External Affairs Records, 50092–4–40, ICETP-141, 4 October 1956

23 Ibid.

24 Ibid.

25 Ibid., vol. 4181, file 8522/U575–1 (56), A.F.W. Plumptre, "Canadian Commercial Policy and European Integration," 27 December 1956.

26 Ibid.

27 Ibid.

28 Ibid., file 8522/U575–1 (57), "Memorandum for Prime Minister on Common Market," 26 February 1957.

29 Sidney Dell, *Trade Blocs and Common Markets* (London: Constable, 1963), 86.

30 DEA, External Affairs Records, 50092–4–40, "Quantitative Restrictions and Extracts from Relevant Dispatches To and From Our Missions Abroad," n.d. See also DEA, External Affairs Records, 4901-F-4–40, SSEA to Canac Paris, 23 February 1956.

31 Robert E. Hudec, *The GATT Legal System and World Trade Diplomacy* (New York: Praeger, 1975) 243.

32 DEA, External Affairs Records, 500–92–40, Annex "A" to ICETP-144, 18 January 1957.

33 DEA, External Affairs Records, 500–92–40, ICETP-144, 18 January 1957.

34 Ibid., Annex "A" to ICETP-144.

35 NAC, Department of Finance Records, vol. 4181, file 8522/U575–1 (57), "Memorandum for Prime Minister on the Common Market," 26 February 1957.

36 Ibid., UKCCC (57) R.3, 7 May 1957.

37 BCA, Bank of Canada Records, 5A-312, file: Background to European Integration and Reorganization, "Canadian Interest in European Trade Arrangements," 28 December 1959.

38 Ibid.

39 Ibid. 5D-248, file: Commonwealth Finance Ministers Meeting, Mont Tremblant, September 1957, F.M. (c), 2nd Meeting, 28 September 1957. See also Ibid., 5D-400, file: Meeting of St. Laurent-Macmillan, March 1957, External to London, 1 April 1957.

40 Bank of Montreal, *Business Review*, 26 January 1960.

CONCLUSION

1 Robert Bothwell, Ian Drummond, John English, *Canada Since 1945: Power, Politics and Provincialism* (Toronto: University of Toronto Press, 1981), 78.

2 BCA, Bank of Canada Records, JD-27, "Anglo-American Trade Prospects: A Canadian View," 18 March 1945.

3 *Documents on Canadian External Relations* 10 (Ottawa: Canadian Government Publishing Centre, 1987), 547.

4 Bank of Nova Scotia, *Monthly Review* (December 1948).

5 For an account of this see Bothwell, Drummond, English, *Canada Since 1945*, 184–7. In October 1950, the Canadian government allowed the dollar to float, in violation of its IMF commitments. The floating dollar did have an impact on export and import trade through its value, determined by "market forces." In September 1950, in terms of the US dollar, it was 90.5 cents, in November 1950, it was 95 cents, in the third quarter of 1952, it rose to $1.04, and dropped to par in 1956.

Index

Burgess, Randolph 97, 123
Butler, R.A. 88, 90–2, 96–7, 100–2, 118, 148
butter. *See* agricultural products

Cabinet Committee on Economic Policy 46, 78
Cairncross, Sir Alec 20
Canadian, Banker, The 156
Canadian/UK trade agreement 1932 6–7
Ceylon 44, 82, 151
CFEP. *See* Commission on Foreign Economic Policy
cheese. *See* agricultural products
chemical products 104, 128, 160
Chicago 25
china. *See* pottery products
Churchill, Winston 14, 76, 88, 94
Clark, Clifford 12, 19, 37, 40, 43, 54–5
Clark-Jones, Melissa 3, 4
Clarke, R.W.B. 85, 91
Clayton, William 53–4
Clutterbuck, Sir Alexander 24, 26, 28–9, 33, 43, 67
coffee. *See* agricultural products
Cohen, Edgar 151
Cold War 24, 27, 37, 64, 111
Commission on Foreign Economic Policy 138, 140–1
Commonwealth 5–7, 9–10, 13, 20, 26–7, 34–5, 44–5, 47, 49–53, 55, 63, 65–7, 69, 86, 89, 95, 137, 152, 167; 1949 Commonwealth meeting 34–5, 37, 40, 44; 1950 Commonwealth meeting 44; Commonwealth Relations Office

90. *See also* sterling area, and the Commonwealth
Communism 27, 37, 64, 111–12, 115, 166
Congress, U.S. 27
Conservative governments 6, 163.
Conservative Party (Canada) 91, 106, 153
Conservative party (Britain) 100; government of 76, 88–9, 90, 94, 98, 135–6
continentalism 3–4, 8–9, 70, 77, 106, 131, 143, 154, 162, 174
convertibility. *See* inconvertibility
copper. *See* mining products
Corse, Carl 68–9
Couillard, Louis 73, 152
Creighton, Donald 3, 4
Cripps, Sir Stafford 25–6, 28–9, 31, 34, 36–9, 42–3, 53, 77–8
Cuba 48–50, 53, 56
Cuff, R.D. 3, 12, 22
Cunliffe-Lister, Philip, Lord Swinton 88–9
currency: devaluations 48, 61; dollar crises 18–29, 29–46, 56, 63–7, 88–96, 111; dollar restrictions/liberalization 115–34, 139; European currencies 20; gold 84, 88, 96, 105–6, 108, 114; hard currency markets 32, 36, 51, 144, 172, 179; pound sterling 11–12, 20, 37, 40, 41, 43, 53, 70, 84, 89; soft currency markets 30–3, 41, 103, 114, 128, 179. *See also* inconvertibility
Customs Simplification Bill 72
Czechoslovakia 27

Dalton, Hugh 18, 20

Dell, Sydney 171
Denmark 30–1, 61, 71, 160, 175
depression years 5–11, 163
Deutsch, John 32–3, 43, 54–5, 58, 65, 70, 72, 86, 89–90, 98
Dexter, Grant 12
Diefenbaker, John 106–7, 153, 163
Dixon, Sir Pierson 97
dollar area 29
dollar crisis 5; 1947 18–29; 1949 29–46
dollar, the. *See* currencies.
Dominican Republic 160
Douglas, Lewis 37–9
Drummond, Ian 6, 7
Dulles, John Foster 125, 138–9, 144, 153, 158

ECA. *See* European Cooperation Administration
economic nationalism 8. *See also* tariffs barriers
Economist, The 8, 32, 36, 38, 44, 57, 63–4, 69, 74–5, 79, 87, 89, 91, 98, 153
Eden, Anthony 136
ECC. *See* European Economic Community
EFTA. *See* European Free Trade Area
eggs. *See* agricultural products
Eisenhower, Dwight 97, 138, 141–2, 144, 146, 151
Ellis-Rees, Sir Hugh 124
empire 89. *See also* Britain; commonwealth; imperialism; imperial preference.
employment; *See* unemployment
England. *See* Britain
English, John 47
EPA. *See* European Payments Area
EPU. *See* European Payments Union